Werner Herzog: Interviews

Conversations with Filmmakers Series
Gerald Peary, General Editor

Werner Herzog
INTERVIEWS

Edited by Eric Ames

University Press of Mississippi / Jackson

www.upress.state.ms.us

The University Press of Mississippi is a member
of the Association of American University Presses.

Copyright © 2014 by University Press of Mississippi

Manufactured in the United States of America

First printing 2014

∞

Library of Congress Cataloging-in-Publication Data

Herzog, Werner, 1942–
Werner Herzog : interviews / edited by Eric Ames.
pages cm — (Conversations with filmmakers series)
Includes bibliographical references and index.
Includes filmography.
ISBN 978-1-61703-968-3 (cloth : alk. paper) — ISBN 978-1-61703-969-0 (ebook)
1. Motion picture producers and directors—Germany—Interviews. I. Ames, Eric, 1969–
editor of compilation. II. Title.
PN1998.3.H477A3 2014
791.4302'33092—dc23   2013046019

British Library Cataloging-in-Publication Data available

A train of letters even near
Spell real the unexpected dream.

Subvention by
Figure Foundation

Contents

Introduction

"Far from the hazards of a South American jungle or the wilderness of Alaska, I met up with Werner Herzog in the suburban wilds of L.A., which he currently calls home. We wanted to get a quick exterior shot of Herzog in his native habitat, when things took an unexpected turn." The television camera shows Herzog talking with British journalist Mark Kermode. Suddenly, we hear what sounds like the hiss of a bullet; we see the director wince, his body slightly bending at the middle. Somebody shot Werner Herzog.

After moving to a safe location, they resume the interview. The journalist almost gleefully pops the question: "Have you got a wound? Let's see!" Without hesitation, Herzog literally takes down his pants, mumbles an apology for doing so on camera, and reveals a bleeding wound on his abdomen. Zipping up, he comments with a German accent, "It is not a significant bullet."

The BBC sniper interview, as it's called on YouTube, tells us something vital about Herzog and about how he gives interviews—or, at least, what makes them so memorable. That is, in one way or another, they involve the filmmaker taking down his pants and showing his scars in public. Interviews become the occasion for a performance by the filmmaker that is revealing, embarrassing, and head-shaking all at once. Who is this guy? What is he saying? And why on earth is somebody shooting at him?

Aside from his many films, and closely related to them, the interview has always been Herzog's best genre. For one thing, he is a storyteller with considerable linguistic skills and truly extraordinary experiences. For another, audiences relate to him as a storyteller. When the director is present at screenings, people in the audience inevitably ask him not just to talk about his latest film, but also—more importantly, perhaps—to recount the very stories that people have already heard at least once if not many times before. "Could you tell us about the cactus leap that you made after *Even Dwarfs Started Small*?" This, after a 1999 screening of work in progress (what would later be called *My Best Fiend*) at the Walker Arts Center in Minneapolis. Clearly, people remember Herzog's stories and respond to them almost as strongly as they respond to his films. Over time, the sheer number of stories has itself become extraordinary. In this respect, interviews have played a central role. To date, Herzog has given around eight hundred interviews in various languages and through a broad range of media, spanning print, radio, film, television, and the Internet. Why? What is the point of giving so many interviews?

Like other directors, Herzog uses interviews in various ways: to promote new films, to recommend certain terms for their reception, to manage his public image, to set the record straight, and so on. And yet, there is one use that deserves more attention, because it is both singular and exemplary: that is, interviews serve Herzog as a key form of autobiography. The tendency began in the late 1960s and early 1970s, with the interviews conducted in West Germany, France, and Peru (several of which appear in this volume). It expanded to filmed and videotaped conversations such as *I Am My Films: A Portrait of Werner Herzog* (Christian Weisenborn and Erwin Keusch, 1977) and *Burden of Dreams* (Les Blank, 1982). And it culminated with *Herzog on Herzog*, a book-length retrospective interview conducted by Paul Cronin in 2002—a book that has since been revised and greatly expanded for a new edition. There is doubtless more to come.

Interviews have provided Herzog a platform for establishing his own identity as a filmmaker. Read as autobiography (complete with its issues of ethics, truth, authenticity, and individuality), the interview becomes a creative process of narrating a life through a series of vibrant and memorable stories. It also highlights the relational side of that process, how the filmmaker's life unfolds in terms of other people—the most famous example being the actor Klaus Kinski, with whom Herzog made five films—sometimes even in relation to interviewers. Alan Greenberg offers a case in point. His book, called *Heart of Glass*, a report on the film's production interspersed with scenarios from the screenplay, was first published by Herzog's own press (Skellig Edition, 1976), then revised and reprinted as *Every Night the Trees Disappear* (Chicago Review Press, 2012). Throughout the original narrative, Greenberg refers to himself in the third person as "the witness." Indeed, the interviewer literally attests to the filmmaker's life and work, as if Herzog were a living saint. In this extreme case, their relationship can only be described as devotional.

For decades now, interviews have shaped our understanding of Herzog's life as it informs and blends with his films. How else would we know that, at age fourteen, he converted to Catholicism and traveled on foot around the border of Albania? That he later worked as a bull rider in a Mexican rodeo? That he once tried to hypnotize movie spectators? Or that he plotted to burn down Kinski's house with him in it? Like his films, however, the interviews too are fraught. Most viewers notice how Herzog's films blur the lines between fiction and documentary. Less obvious and equally important is that the interviews extend this dynamic. However much has been written of the filmmaker's life, little is known for certain. Biographical information is not just vague and difficult to verify; it's almost impossible to separate from all the rumors, legends, and fabrications that have come to define this material.

This brings us to the problem of repetition. It's not a problem within this book (I made sure of that in selecting and editing materials). And I don't mean the fact that interviewers tend to ask the same questions again and again, which is unfortunate but understandable, especially considering Herzog's role as a storyteller. I mean rather a problem that cuts deep into the interviews and much of the way across them. Reading through these hundreds of interviews, you cannot help but notice how Herzog repeats himself, sometimes at great length and almost verbatim, over a period spanning years, even decades. Repetition of this kind is so remarkable that it gradually becomes a point of reflection. What are we to make of it?

There are many possible answers, and not just one. Repetition could be understood psychologically as revealing the director's inner character, whether imagined in terms of conviction or obsession. Rather than speculate on psychology, however, it is more useful to see repetition as a long-term strategy for Herzog to manage his public image and to frame his films to be seen and discussed by others. Even though it wasn't designed for this purpose, the present collection could be read as a compendium of Herzog's preferred terms, signature expressions, and fossilized forms—ways of speaking that have virtually become fixed over time. Thus he speaks of the mythic, the ecstatic, the mysterious, the visionary, and the primordial—terms that may make scholars uncomfortable, but that also clearly resonate with large numbers of people. To some extent, the enduring fascination of Herzog's films relies on their continued success in visualizing such ideas.

But what happens when entire passages repeat from one interview to the next? The key example comes from *Heart of Glass*. The longest, most detailed discussion of its production appears in Greenberg's book from 1976. In one chapter, the witness recalls a hypnosis session, a private experiment held in the back room of a Munich restaurant. When the witness enters the room, Martje Herzog (the filmmaker's wife at the time) hands him "some typed pages" containing Herzog's explanation for hypnotizing the film's cast, a document the witness dutifully quotes at great length (see 14–19). But then several paragraphs of this explanation reappear in another interview published that same year in the German scholarly journal *Medium* (cf. Wiedemann in this collection). Flash forward to 2002. These and other passages from the original explanation return in slightly altered form as part of *Herzog on Herzog* (cf. 126–30). Then, in the 2012 edition of Greenberg's book, *Every Night the Trees Disappear*, the "typed pages" disappear and the entire scene is restaged as an intimate conversation between the filmmaker and his American confidant, who transcribes it all by hand (cf. 11–14). "Are you getting all this?" Herzog asks. "Good. We are within a historical context here. You, too, will be held accountable" (13). And yet, to verify the accuracy of this account (assuming the conversation really took place this way, and I suspect it didn't) would be to miss the larger point. Only by tracking Herzog's comments as they move from source to source do we start to see a pattern. What begins as a report on a mysterious document evolves into a lively scenario, one which then repeats in various forms and locations. In other words, we discover the dynamics of performance—scripting, rehearsal, staging, citation, fabrication, transformation, and improvisation—that we usually associate with Herzog's method of filmmaking. Only here we find them in an unexpected place, throughout the collected interviews.

As dynamic performances the stories also change over time. Indeed, many of them become even more vivid and change their meaning from earlier interviews. The differences allow us to see how Herzog as a filmmaker and especially his public persona have adapted and evolved, in ways that any one interview is simply unable to capture.

Werner Herzog: Interviews is an unauthorized collection—a "rogue" volume, no less. Rather than claim to be definitive or comprehensive, it features a mix of voices, moments, and perspectives, and offers them for comparison and for enjoyment. Most of the selected interviews were conducted around the premiere of a new film. As a result, each has its own sense of urgency, a sense of events as they are unfolding in the present. Three of these interviews were previously unpublished: one on the American reception of Herzog's films, another on staging his first opera, plus a rare interview on *Lessons of Darkness*. More than half of the interviews have been translated for this volume, where they appear in English for the very first time. Together, they convey a sense of the many wonderful interviews that Herzog has given throughout his career, and how they change and intersect over time. They are offered not to reinforce the reader's already existing impression of Herzog, but in the hope that they will add to it, question it, and maybe even contradict it.

The chronology and filmography were compiled from various sources in print, online, and on DVD. I am particularly indebted to Chris Wahl for sharing information compiled for his study *Lektionen in Herzog* (2011), a key resource in German. All translations are my own, unless otherwise indicated.

I am grateful to the many authors, journals, and publishers who allowed me to reprint their interviews. For their help and support in preparing this book, I want to thank Olivia Albiero, Jane Brown, Paul Cronin, Tobias Grünthal, Japhet Johnstone, Verena Kick, Jasmin Krakenberg, Laura McKee, Brad Prager, Chris Wahl, Stephanie Welch, the interlibrary loan staff at the University of Washington, Werner Sudendorf and Anke Vetter of the Deutsche Kinemathek, Lucki Stipetić of Werner Herzog Filmproduktion, Leila Salisbury and most especially her assistant Valerie Jones at the University Press of Mississippi, and series editor Gerald Peary. Finally, and for everything else, I thank Veronika Zantop. This book is for Isaac and Max because they give me moments of clarity, a disclosure which may astonish those who know me, but one which is really not so surprising. As Herzog says in one of the following interviews, "A situation always becomes clear with monkeys."

EA
Seattle
November 2012

Chronology

1942   Born September 5 in Munich, Germany. After the bombing of Munich, evacuated with his mother and older brother to the remote mountain village of Sachrang.

1947   Father returns from war. Parents divorce the next year.

1948–51   Primary school in Sachrang.

1951–53   Attends Theodor-Heuss Gymnasium (high school) in Heilbronn.

1953   Family moves to a boarding house in Munich, where the young Klaus Kinski would also spend three months. Sees his first films at age eleven.

1953–61   Attends Maximiliansgymnasium in Munich. During high school, works part-time as a parking-lot attendant, as a spot welder in a steel factory, etc.

1956   Travels on foot along the Albanian-Yugoslavian border, and then to Greece. Converts to Catholicism (later quits the church) and decides to make films.

1957–64   Travels to Egypt, Sudan, England, Scotland, and multiple times to Greece.

1959   Proposes (unrealized) documentary film on penal reform in West Germany.

1961–65   Studies literature, history, and theater at the Ludwig-Maximilians-Universität in Munich. Chairman of Student Film Club, 1962–63.

1962   Self-taught, makes his first short film, *Herakles* (reedited in 1965).

1963   Creates his own production company, Werner Herzog Filmproduktion, joined by his younger brother, Lucki Stipetić, as principal production assistant and business manager.

1964   *Game in the Sand* (unreleased). Publishes articles in the German journal *Filmstudio*, including a review of films by Stan Brakhage, Kenneth Anger, and other notables of the American avant-garde. "Feuerzeichen" ("fire signals"), written

	under a pseudonym, wins Carl Mayer Prize for best German screenplay; later realized as *Signs of Life*.
1965	Goes to Duquesne University in Pittsburgh on a Fulbright Fellowship, only to return the scholarship and drop out after a few days. Drives to Mexico, where he earns money smuggling goods across the border and working part-time as a rodeo bull rider.
1966	Returns to Germany. Steals a camera from the German Institute for Film and Television in Munich, and uses it to make *The Unprecedented Defence of the Fortress Deutschkreutz* and the next ten films.
1967	*Last Words* is screened at the West German Short Film Festival in Oberhausen. Using various pseudonyms, wins three prizes in a literary competition sponsored by Bavarian Radio. Marries Martje Grohmann (who later plays Mina in *Nosferatu*).
1968	*Signs of Life* wins the German Film Prize as well as the Silver Bear for best debut film at the Berlin International Film Festival. Organizes "free" alternative to the festival, at the "Rollkrug" cinema, in the working-class district of Neukölln. Begins shooting *Fata Morgana* at various locations in Africa and the Canary Islands. Mistaken for mercenaries, he and his crew are jailed and abused in Cameroon.
1969	*The Flying Doctors of East Africa* and *Precautions against Fanatics*. Completes *Fata Morgana*, but the film is shelved until 1971, when Lotte Eisner and Henri Langlois "borrow" a copy and show it at Cannes.
1970	Releases *Even Dwarfs Started Small*.
1971	*Handicapped Future* and *Land of Silence and Darkness*. Appears in an episode of *Geschichten vom Kübelkind* by Edgar Reitz and Ula Stöckl.
1972	*Aguirre, the Wrath of God*, starring Klaus Kinski. Thomas Mauch's short film, *Der Welt zeigen, dass man noch da ist*, is the first personal portrait of Herzog.
1973	Birth of son Rudolph Amos Achmed. *The Great Ecstasy of Woodcarver Steiner* premieres on West German television.
1974	Travels on foot from Munich to Paris, in an effort to forestall the death of his mentor, film historian Lotte Eisner. Appears in György Polnauer's film, *Anderthalb Tage Fußweg*.

Aguirre begins its twenty-month run at an art-house cinema in Paris.

1975   *The Enigma of Kaspar Hauser,* starring Bruno S. [Schleinstein], wins Grand Prize at the Cannes Film Festival.

1976   *Heart of Glass, How Much Wood Would a Woodchuck Chuck, No One Will Play with Me,* and *La Soufrière,* filmed on an explosive Caribbean volcano. Featured with Wim Wenders in Hans-Christoph Blumenberg's television documentary, *Neues Deutsches Kino.*

1977   *Stroszek,* starring Bruno S., is released. Publishes two volumes of screenplays.

1978   *Nosferatu—The Vampyre.* Publishes *Of Walking in Ice,* a poetic account of his pilgrimage to Eisner. Subject of documentary, *Was ich bin, sind meine Filme (I Am My Films,* dir. Christian Weisenborn and Erwin Keusch).

1979   *Woyzeck.* Publishes another volume of screenplays. Begins pre-production on *Fitzcarraldo,* which is almost immediately followed by protests; production troubles make international headline news. The film would take more than three years to complete.

1980   *Huie's Sermon* and *God's Angry Man.* A documentary short by Les Blank, *Werner Herzog Eats His Shoe,* shows the German director making good on a promise to Errol Morris for completing his first film, *Gates of Heaven.* Daughter Hanna Mattes, born to German actress Eva Mattes (who plays Eva in *Stroszek* and Marie in *Woyzeck,* and appears in *My Best Fiend*).

1982   *Fitzcarraldo* released, alongside *Burden of Dreams,* a documentary by Les Blank on the making of Herzog's film. Wins Best Director for *Fitzcarraldo* at the Cannes Film Festival. Appears in Wim Wenders's film, *Room 666,* and in Nina Gladitz's *Land der Bitterkeit und des Stolzes,* a polemic against Herzog and the making of *Fitzcarraldo.* Walks along the German border more than one thousand miles before falling ill—a symbolic act of unification recounted in his 1984 speech "Über das eigene Land."

1983   Plays silent role of The Father in Paul Cox's film, *Man of Flowers.*

1984   *Ballad of the Little Soldier, The Dark Glow of the Mountains,* and *Where the Green Ants Dream.*

1985   Stages his first opera, Ferruccio Busoni's *Doktor Faust*, in Bologna. Appears in Wim Wenders's *Tokyo-Ga*.

1986   *Portrait Werner Herzog.*

1987   *Cobra Verde*. Stages Richard Wagner's *Lohengrin* at Bayreuth. Subject of Steff Gruber's film, *Herzog in Afrika*. Voices part of Oliver Herbrich's film, *Bikini—Mon amour*. Divorces Grohmann. Marries Christine Ebenberger (sound technician on *Ballad of the Little Soldier*, *The Dark Glow of the Mountains*, and *Portrait Werner Herzog*).

1989   *Wodaabe*. Stages *Giovanna d'Arco* (Giuseppe Verdi) in Bologna. Subject of Peter Buchka's made-for-television portrait, *Bis ans Ende . . . und dann noch weiter: Die ekstatische Welt des Filmmemachers Werner Herzog*. Plays the role of Mita in Peter Fleischmann's film, *Es ist nicht leicht, ein Gott zu sein*, and the role of Businger in Urs Odermatt's film, *Gekauftes Glück* (*Bride of the Orient*). Birth of Simon, his son with Ebenberger.

1990   *Echoes from a Sombre Empire.*

1991   *Jag Mandir*, *Scream of Stone*, and *Film Lesson*, an eight-part series made for Austrian TV, when Herzog was director of the Vienna Film Festival. Stages Mozart's *Die Zauberflöte* in Catania. Along with Leonard Cohen, Dennis Hopper, Alexander Kluge, Timothy Leary, Sean Penn, and Wim Wenders, appears in *SchneeweissRosenrot* by Christa Ritter and Rainer Langhans. Kinski dies of a heart attack.

1992   *Lessons of Darkness*. Stages *La donna del lago* (Gioacchino Rossini), in Milan. Directs *Floresta Amazonica* (*A Midsummer Night's Dream*) at the Teatro Joao Caetano in Rio de Janeiro.

1993   *Bells from the Deep*. Stages Richard Wagner's *Der fliegende Holländer* in Paris. Directs *Spezialitäten* at the Etablissement Ronacher theater in Vienna and *Variété* at the Hebbel Theater in Berlin.

1994   *The Transformation of the World into Music*, a back-stage view of the Richard Wagner Festival in Bayreuth. Stages *Il Guarany* (Antonio Carlos Gomes) in Bonn and *Norma* (Vincenzo Bellini) in Verona. Appears in an episode of the BBC miniseries *Tales from the Opera*, and in Edgar Reitz's documentary, *Die Nacht der Regisseure*. Divorces Ebenberger.

1995   *Death for Five Voices*. Moves to the United States, lives in San Francisco, later in Los Angeles.

1996   Stages *Il Guarany* (Antonio Carlos Gomes) in Washington,

D.C. Plays the role of Joris Ivens in Peter Patzak's *Brennendes Herz* (*Burning Heart*).

1997   *Little Dieter Needs to Fly*. Stages *Chusingura* (Shigeaki Saegusa) in Tokyo and Wagner's *Tannhäuser* in Seville and in Liège.

1998   Stages Wagner's *Tannhäuser* in Naples and Palermo. Plays the role of Face in Vincent Ward's *What Dreams May Come*.

1999   *God and the Burdened, Wings of Hope*, and *My Best Fiend*. Delivers "The Minnesota Declaration" at the Walker Arts Center in Minneapolis. Stages Wagner's *Tannhäuser* in Madrid, Mozart's *Die Zauberflöte* in Catania, and Beethoven's *Fidelio* in Milan. Appears in Jan Sebening and Daniel Sponsel's *Der letzte Dokumentarfilm* and plays the role of Father in Harmony Korine's *Julien Donkey-Boy*. Marries Lena Pisetski, now Lena Herzog.

2000   Stages Wagner's *Tannhäuser* in Baltimore. Appears in Christian Weisenborn and Rudolph Herzog's *Der Ball ist ein Sauhund* (*The Ball Is a Scumbag*).

2001   *Invincible*. Collaborates with composer John Tavener to make *Pilgrimage* for the BBC series "Sound on Film." Stages Verdi's *Giovanna d'Arco* in Genoa, Wagner's *Tannhäuser* in Rio de Janeiro and in Houston, and Mozart's *Die Zauberflöte* in Baltimore.

2002   *Ten Thousand Years Older*. Stages Wagner's *Der fliegende Holländer* in Erfurt.

2004   *Wheel of Time* and *The White Diamond*. Plays himself in Zak Penn's mock-documentary, *Incident at Loch Ness*. Publishes *Conquest of the Useless: Reflections from the Making of "Fitzcarraldo"* (in English, 2010).

2005   *Grizzly Man* and *The Wild Blue Yonder*.

2006   *Rescue Dawn*. Pulls actor Joaquin Phoenix from a car wreck on a canyon road in Los Angeles.

2007   *Encounters at the End of the World*. Appears in Regina Schilling's documentary *Bierbichler*, and plays the role of Father Umbrillo in Harmony Korine's *Mister Lonely*.

2008   *Encounters at the End of the World* is nominated for an Academy Award, a first for Herzog. Stages Wagner's *Parsifal* in Valencia. Appears in Dominik Wessely's documentary, *Gegenschuss: Aufbruch der Filmmemacher*, and plays The German in Zak Penn's comedy, *The Grand*.

2009   *Bad Lieutenant—Port of Call: New Orleans*, the "opera short"
        La Bohème, and *My Son, My Son, What Have Ye Done*. Lends
        his voice to Ramin Bahrani's short film and internet sen-
        sation, *Plastic Bag*. Donates his production archive to the
        Deutsche Kinemathek in Berlin. Named by *Time* magazine
        on its annual list of "The 100 Most Influential People."

2010   Filmed in digital 3D, *Cave of Forgotten Dreams* becomes the
        year's top-grossing documentary. Opens his Rogue Film
        School, a private seminar taught by Herzog. Serves as Jury
        president of the Berlin International Film Festival. Subject
        of Christian Weisenborn's documentary, *Was ich bin, sind
        meine Filme—Teil 2—Nach 30 Jahren*. Produces and narrates
        Happy People: A Year in the Taiga, by Dmitry Vasyukov. Voices
        the role of a German reporter in Chicago covering the 2008
        election of Barack Obama in *The Boondocks* episode, "It's a
        Black President, Huey Freeman." Voices the role of drug rep
        Walter Hotenhoffer (formerly Augustus Gloop) in *The Simp-
        sons* episode, "The Scorpion's Tale."

2011   *Into the Abyss*.

2012   *On Death Row*, four-part television series airs on cable televi-
        sion. Exhibits *Hearsay of the Soul*, a five-channel video in-
        stallation projecting landscapes by Hercules Segers, at the
        Whitney Museum of American Art, New York City; later
        purchased by the Getty Museum, Los Angeles. Lends his
        voice to *American Dad!* episode, "Ricky Spanish." Narrates
        the computer-animated film *Dinotasia*. Directs live webcast
        of performance by The Killers and short webvideo about the
        band. Plays the villain, opposite Tom Cruise, in *Jack Reacher*.
        Credited as executive producer of Joshua Oppenheimer's
        documentary, *The Act of Killing*.

2013   *From One Second to the Next*, documentary short on the dan-
        gers of texting and driving; the webvideo went viral. Plays
        Alexander von Humboldt in Edgar Reitz's *Die andere Heimat*.
        Completes *On Death Row—Season Two*, to appear on cable
        television.

Filmography

HERAKLES (1962)
Director: **Werner Herzog**
Screenplay: **Werner Herzog**
Producer: **Werner Herzog**
Production Company: Cineropa Film
Camera: Jaime Pacheco
Editing: **Werner Herzog**
Sound: **Werner Herzog**
Music: Uwe Brandner
Featuring: Mr. Germany 1962
10 minutes

SPIEL IM SAND / GAME IN THE SAND (1964)
Director: **Werner Herzog**
Screenplay: **Werner Herzog**
Producer: **Werner Herzog**
Production Company: Werner Herzog Filmproduktion
Camera: Jaime Pacheco
Editing: **Werner Herzog**
Sound: **Werner Herzog**
Music: Uwe Brandner
14 minutes (unreleased)

DIE BEISPIELLOSE VERTEIDIGUNG DER FESTUNG DEUTSCHKREUTZ
/ THE UNPRECEDENTED DEFENCE OF THE FORTRESS DEUTSCH-
KREUTZ (1966)
Director: **Werner Herzog**
Screenplay: **Werner Herzog**
Producer: **Werner Herzog**
Production Companies: Werner Herzog Filmproduktion and Arpa-Film
Bruno Zöckler
Camera: Jaime Pacheco

Editing: **Werner Herzog**
Sound: Uwe Brandner
Cast: Peter H. Brumm, Georg Eska, Karl-Heinz Steffel, Wolfgang von
    Ungern-Sternberg, **Werner Herzog**, Bruno Zöckler
15 minutes

LETZTE WORTE / LAST WORDS (1967)
Director: **Werner Herzog**
Screenplay: **Werner Herzog**
Producer: **Werner Herzog**
Production Company: Werner Herzog Filmproduktion
Camera: Thomas Mauch
Editing: Beate Mainka
Sound: Herbert Prasch
Music: folk music of Crete
13 minutes

LEBENSZEICHEN / SIGNS OF LIFE (1968)
Director: **Werner Herzog**
Screenplay: **Werner Herzog**
Producer: **Werner Herzog**
Production Company: Werner Herzog Filmproduktion
Camera: Thomas Mauch
Editing: Beate Mainka, Maximiliane Mainka
Sound: Herbert Prasch
Music: Stavros Xarchakos
Cast: Peter Brogle (Stroszek), Wolfgang Reichmann (Meinhard), Athina
    Zacharopoulou (Nora), Wolfgang von Ungern-Sternberg (Becker),
    Wolfgang Stumpf (captain), Henry van Lyck (lieutenant), Julio Pin-
    heiro (gypsy), Florian Fricke (pianist), Heinz Usener (doctor), **Wer-
    ner Herzog** (soldier), Achmed Hafiz (Achmed)
87 minutes

FATA MORGANA (1969)
Director: **Werner Herzog**
Screenplay: **Werner Herzog**
Producer: **Werner Herzog**
Production Company: Werner Herzog Filmproduktion
Camera: Jörg Schmidt-Reitwein
Editing: Beate Mainka-Jellinghaus

Sound: Hans von Mallinckrodt

Music: Blind Faith, Leonard Cohen, François Couperin, Georg Friedrich
Händel, Wolfgang Amadeus Mozart, Third Ear Band

Cast: Wolfgang von Ungern-Sternberg, James William Gledhill, Eugen
des Montagnes

Narrators: Lotte H. Eisner, Wolfgang Bächler, Manfred Eigendorf

74 minutes

DIE FLIEGENDEN ÄRZTE VON OSTAFRIKA / THE FLYING DOCTORS
OF EAST AFRICA (1969)

Director: **Werner Herzog**

Screenplay: **Werner Herzog**

Producer: **Werner Herzog**

Production Company: Werner Herzog Filmproduktion for the African
Medical and Research Foundation (AMREF)

Camera: Thomas Mauch

Editing: Beate Mainka-Jellinghaus

Sound: **Werner Herzog**

Narrator: Wilfried Klaus

44 minutes

MASSNAHMEN GEGEN FANATIKER / PRECAUTIONS AGAINST
FANATICS (1969)

Director: **Werner Herzog**

Screenplay: **Werner Herzog**

Producer: **Werner Herzog**

Production Company: Werner Herzog Filmproduktion

Camera: Dieter Lohmann, Jörg Schmidt-Reitwein

Editing: Beate Mainka-Jellinghaus

Sound: **Werner Herzog**

Cast: Petar Radenkovic, Mario Adorf, Hans Tiedemann, Herbert Hisel,
Peter Schamoni

12 minutes

AUCH ZWERGE HABEN KLEIN ANGEFANGEN / EVEN DWARFS
STARTED SMALL (1970)

Director: **Werner Herzog**

Screenplay: **Werner Herzog**

Producer: **Werner Herzog**

Production Company: Werner Herzog Filmproduktion

Camera: Thomas Mauch
Editing: Beate Mainka-Jellinghaus
Sound: Herbert Prasch
Music: Florian Fricke (Popol Vuh), folk songs of the Ivory Coast, West
    Africa, and the Canary Islands, Spain
Cast: Helmut Döring (Hombre), Paul Glauer (teacher), Gisela Hertwig
    (Pobrecita), Hertel Minkner (Chicklets), Gertraud Piccini (Pic-
    cini), Marianne Saar (Theresa), Brigitte Saar (Cochina), Gerd Gickel
    (Pepe), Erna Gschwendtner (Azúcar), Gerhard März (Territory),
    Alfredo Piccini (Anselmo), Erna Smolarz (Schweppes), Lajos Zsar-
    noczay (Chaparro)
96 minutes

BEHINDERTE ZUKUNFT / HANDICAPPED FUTURE (1971)
Director: **Werner Herzog**
Screenplay: **Werner Herzog**
Producer: **Werner Herzog**
Production Company: Werner Herzog Filmproduktion for the West
    German state of North Rhine-Westphalia
Camera: Jörg Schmidt-Reitwein
Editing: Beate Mainka-Jellinghaus
Sound: **Werner Herzog**
Narrator: Rolf Illig
43 minutes

LAND DES SCHWEIGENS UND DER DUNKELHEIT / LAND OF
    SILENCE AND DARKNESS (1971)
Director: **Werner Herzog**
Screenplay: **Werner Herzog**
Producer: **Werner Herzog**
Production Company: Werner Herzog Filmproduktion
Camera: Jörg Schmidt-Reitwein
Editing: Beate Mainka-Jellinghaus
Sound: **Werner Herzog**
Music: Johann Sebastian Bach, Antonio Vivaldi
Narrator: Rolf Illig
Featuring: Fini Straubinger, Else Fährer, Heinrich Fleischmann, Vladi-
    mir Kokol, M. Baaske, Resi Mittermeier, Joseph Riedmeier, Ursula
    Riedmeier
82 minutes

AGUIRRE, DER ZORN GOTTES / AGUIRRE, THE WRATH OF GOD
    (1972)
Director: **Werner Herzog**
Screenplay: **Werner Herzog**
Producer: **Werner Herzog**
Production Company: Werner Herzog Filmproduktion
Camera: Thomas Mauch
Editing: Beate Mainka-Jellinghaus
Sound: Herbert Prasch
Music: Florian Fricke (Popol Vuh)
Cast: Klaus Kinski (Aguirre), Helena Rojo (Inez), Del Negro (Carvajal),
    Ruy Guerra (Ursúa), Peter Berling (Guzman), Cecilia Rivera (Flores),
    Daniel Ades (Perucho), Edward Roland (Okello), Armando Polanah
    (Armando)
93 minutes

DIE GROSSE EKSTASE DES BILDSCHNITZERS STEINER / THE GREAT
    ECSTASY OF WOODCARVER STEINER (1973)
Director: **Werner Herzog**
Screenplay: **Werner Herzog**
Producer: **Werner Herzog**
Production Companies: Werner Herzog Filmproduktion and Süddeut-
    scher Rundfunk
Camera: Jörg Schmidt-Reitwein
Editing: Beate Mainka-Jellinghaus
Sound: Benedikt Kuby
Music: Florian Fricke (Popol Vuh)
Featuring: Walter Steiner, **Werner Herzog**
Narrator: **Werner Herzog**
44 minutes

JEDER FÜR SICH UND GOTT GEGEN ALLE / THE ENIGMA OF KASPAR
    HAUSER (1974)
Director: **Werner Herzog**
Screenplay: **Werner Herzog**
Producer: **Werner Herzog**
Production Companies: Werner Herzog Filmproduktion and Zweites
    Deutsches Fernsehen
Camera: Jörg Schmidt-Reitwein
Editing: Beate Mainka-Jellinghaus

Set Design: Henning von Gierke
Sound: Haymo Henry Heyder
Music: Florian Fricke (Popol Vuh), Johann Pachelbel, Orlando di Lasso,
    Tommaso Albinoni, Wolfgang Amadeus Mozart
Cast: Bruno Schleinstein (Kaspar), Walter Ladengast (Prof. Daumer),
    Brigitte Mira (Käthe), Hans Musäus (an unknown), Willy Semmel-
    rogge (circus director), Michael Kroecher (Lord Stanhope), Henry
    van Lyck (cavalry captain), Enno Patalas (Pastor Fuhrmann), Elis
    Pilgrim (second pastor), Volker Prechtel (Hiltel), Gloria Doer (Mrs.
    Hiltel), Helmut Döring (The Little King), Kidlat Tahimik (Hombre-
    cito), Andi Gottwald (Young Mozart), Herbert Achternbusch (coun-
    try lad), Wolfgang Bauer (country lad), Walter Steiner (country lad),
    Clemens Scheitz (scribe), Florian Fricke (Florian)
109 minutes

HERZ AUS GLAS / HEART OF GLASS (1976)
Director: **Werner Herzog**
Screenplay: **Werner Herzog** (adapted from the screenplay by Herbert
    Achternbusch)
Producer: **Werner Herzog**
Production Companies: Werner Herzog Filmproduktion and Zweites
    Deutsches Fernsehen
Camera: Jörg Schmidt-Reitwein
Editing: Beate Mainka-Jellinghaus
Set Design: Henning von Gierke
Sound: Haymo Henry Heyder
Music: Florian Fricke (Popol Vuh), Studio der Frühen Musik
Cast: Josef Bierbichler (Hias), Stefan Güttler (factory owner), Clemens
    Scheitz (Adalbert), Volker Prechtel (Wudy), Sonja Skiba (Ludmilla),
    Brunhilde Klöckner (Paulin), Wolf Albrecht (Sam), Thomas Binkley
    (lute player), Janos Fischer (Ägide), **Werner Herzog** and Herbert
    Achternbusch (glass carriers)
95 minutes

HOW MUCH WOOD WOULD A WOODCHUCK CHUCK (1976)
Director: **Werner Herzog**
Screenplay: **Werner Herzog**
Producer: **Werner Herzog**
Production Companies: Werner Herzog Filmproduktion and Süddeut-
    scher Rundfunk

Camera: Thomas Mauch
Editing: Beate Mainka-Jellinghaus
Sound: Walter Saxer
Music: Shorty Eager and the Eager Beavers
Featuring: Steve Liptay, Ralph Wade, Alan Ball, Abe Diffenbach, **Werner Herzog**, Scott McKain
Narrator: **Werner Herzog**
45 minutes

MIT MIR WILL NIEMAND SPIELEN / NO ONE WILL PLAY WITH ME (1976)
Director: **Werner Herzog**
Screenplay: **Werner Herzog**
Producer: **Werner Herzog**
Production Company: Werner Herzog Filmproduktion for the Institut für Film und Bild in Wissenschaft und Unterricht (Munich)
Camera: Jörg Schmidt-Reitwein
Editing: Beate Mainka-Jellinghaus
Sound: Haymo Henry Heyder
14 minutes

LA SOUFRIÈRE (1976)
Director: **Werner Herzog**
Screenplay: **Werner Herzog**
Producer: **Werner Herzog**
Production Companies: Werner Herzog Filmproduktion and Süddeutscher Rundfunk
Camera: Jörg Schmidt-Reitwein, Ed Lachman
Editing: Beate Mainka-Jellinghaus
Sound: **Werner Herzog**
Music: Sergei Rachmaninoff, Felix Mendelssohn-Bartholdy, Johannes Brahms, Richard Wagner
Narrator: **Werner Herzog**
30 minutes

STROSZEK (1977)
Director: **Werner Herzog**
Screenplay: **Werner Herzog**
Producer: **Werner Herzog**

Production Companies: Werner Herzog Filmproduktion and Zweites
   Deutsches Fernsehen
Camera: Thomas Mauch
Editing: Beate Mainka-Jellinghaus
Set Design: Henning von Gierke
Sound: Haymo Henry Heyder
Music: Ludwig van Beethoven, Chet Atkins, Tom Paxton, Sonny Terry
Cast: Bruno Schleinstein (Stroszek), Eva Mattes (Eva), Clemens Scheitz
   (Scheitz), Norbert Grupe (pimp), Burkhard Driest (pimp), Pitt
   Bedewitz (pimp), Clayton Szlapinski (mechanic), Ely Rodriguez
   (mechanic's assistant), Scott McKain (bank employee), Ralph Wade
   (auctioneer), Michael Gahr (prisoner Hoss), Vaclav Vojta (doctor),
   Yüksel Topçugürler (Turkish prisoner), Alfred Edel (prison director)
108 minutes

NOSFERATU—PHANTOM DER NACHT / NOSFERATU—THE VAMPYRE
   (1978)
Director: **Werner Herzog**
Screenplay: **Werner Herzog**
Producer: **Werner Herzog**
Production Companies: Werner Herzog Filmproduktion, Zweites
   Deutsches Fernsehen, Gaumont International
Camera: Jörg Schmidt-Reitwein
Editing: Beate Mainka-Jellinghaus
Set Design: Henning von Gierke
Sound: Harald Maury
Music: Florian Fricke (Popol Vuh), Gordela Vocal Ensemble, Richard
   Wagner, Charles Gounod
Cast: Klaus Kinski (Count Dracula), Isabelle Adjani (Lucy Harker),
   Bruno Ganz (Jonathan Harker), Roland Topor (Renfield), Walter
   Ladengast (Dr. Van Helsing), Dan van Husen (warden), Carsten
   Bodinus (Schrader), Martje Grohmann (Mina), Ryk de Gooyer
   (official), Clemens Scheitz (town employee), Lo van Hensbergen
   (inspector), John Leddy (coachman), Margiet van Hartingsveld
   (maid), Tim Beekman (coffin bearer), Jacques Dufilho (captain)
107 minutes

WOYZECK (1979)
Director: **Werner Herzog**

Screenplay: **Werner Herzog** (from the dramatic fragment by Georg Büchner)
Producer: **Werner Herzog**
Production Companies: Werner Herzog Filmproduktion and Zweites Deutsches Fernsehen
Camera: Jörg Schmidt-Reitwein
Editing: Beate Mainka-Jellinghaus
Set Design: Henning von Gierke
Sound: Harald Maury
Music: Fidelquartett Telč, Rudolf Obruca, Benedetto Marcello, Antonio Vivaldi
Cast: Klaus Kinski (Woyzeck), Eva Mattes (Marie), Wolfgang Reichmann (captain), Willy Semmelrogge (doctor), Josef Bierbichler (drum major), Paul Burian (Andres), Volker Prechtel (journeyman), Dieter Augustin (market crier), Irm Hermann (Margret), Wolfgang Bächler (Jew), Rosemarie Heinikel (Käthe), Herbert Fux (subaltern), Thomas Mettke (innkeeper), Maria Mettke (innkeeper's wife)
81 minutes

GLAUBE UND WÄHRUNG / GOD'S ANGRY MAN (1980)
Director: **Werner Herzog**
Screenplay: **Werner Herzog**
Producer: **Werner Herzog**
Production Companies: Werner Herzog Filmproduktion and Süddeutscher Rundfunk
Camera: Thomas Mauch
Editing: Beate Mainka-Jellinghaus
Sound: Walter Saxer
Featuring: Dr. Gene Scott
Narrator: **Werner Herzog**
44 minutes

HUIES PREDIGT / HUIE'S SERMON (1980)
Director: **Werner Herzog**
Screenplay: **Werner Herzog**
Producer: **Werner Herzog**
Production Companies: Werner Herzog Filmproduktion and Süddeutscher Rundfunk
Camera: Thomas Mauch
Editing: Beate Mainka-Jellinghaus

Sound: Walter Saxer
Featuring: Bishop Huie L. Rogers
42 minutes

FITZCARRALDO (1982)
Director: **Werner Herzog**
Screenplay: **Werner Herzog**
Producers: **Werner Herzog,** Lucki Stipetić
Production Companies: Werner Herzog Filmproduktion, Zweites
    Deutsches Fernsehen, Pro-ject Filmproduktion im Filmverlag der
    Autoren
Camera: Thomas Mauch
Editing: Beate Mainka-Jellinghaus
Set Design: Henning von Gierke
Sound: Dagoberto Juarez
Music: Florian Fricke (Popol Vuh), Richard Strauss, Giuseppe Verdi,
    Ruggero Leoncavallo, Giacomo Meyerbeer, Giacomo Puccini, Mi-
    chel Vuylsteke, Jules Massenet, Vincenzo Bellini
Cast: Klaus Kinski (Fitzcarraldo), Claudia Cardinale (Molly), José
    Lewgoy (Don Aquilino), Miguel Angel Fuentes (Cholo), Paul Hitt-
    scher (captain), Huerequeque Enrique Bohórquez (Huerequeque),
    Grande Otelo (station master), Peter Berling (opera director), David
    Pérez Espinosa (Campa chief), Milton Nascimento (opera door-
    man), Rui Polanah (Don Araujo), Salvador Godinez (old mission-
    ary), Dieter Milz (young missionary), Bill Rose (lawyer), Leoncio
    Bueno (prison guard)
157 minutes

BALLADE VOM KLEINEN SOLDATEN / BALLAD OF THE LITTLE
    SOLDIER (1984)
Director: **Werner Herzog**
Screenplay: **Werner Herzog**
Producer: Lucki Stipetić
Production Companies: Werner Herzog Filmproduktion and Südde-
    utscher Rundfunk
Camera: Jorge Vignati
Editing: Maximiliane Mainka
Sound: Christine Ebenberger
Music: folksongs sung by Isidoro Reyes and Paladino Taylor

Featuring: Miskito Indians of Nicaragua, **Werner Herzog**, Denis
Reichle
Narrator: **Werner Herzog**
45 minutes

GASHERBRUM—DER LEUCHTENDE BERG / THE DARK GLOW OF THE
MOUNTAINS (1984)
Director: **Werner Herzog**
Screenplay: **Werner Herzog**
Producer: Lucki Stipetić
Production Companies: Werner Herzog Filmproduktion and Süddeut-
scher Rundfunk
Camera: Rainer Klausmann
Editing: Maximiliane Mainka
Sound: Christine Ebenberger
Music: Florian Fricke (Popol Vuh), Renate Knaup, Daniel Fichelscher
Featuring: Reinhold Messner, Hans Kammerlander
Narrator: **Werner Herzog**
45 minutes

WO DIE GRÜNEN AMEISEN TRÄUMEN / WHERE THE GREEN ANTS
DREAM (1984)
Director: **Werner Herzog**
Screenplay: **Werner Herzog**
Producer: Lucki Stipetić
Production Companies: Werner Herzog Filmproduktion and Zweites
Deutsches Fernsehen, Pro-ject Filmproduktion im Filmverlag der
Autoren
Camera: Jörg Schmidt-Reitwein
Editing: Beate Mainka-Jellinghaus
Set Design: Ulrich Bergfelder
Sound: Claus Langer
Music: Gabriel Fauré, Ernest Bloch, Richard Wagner, Klaus-Jochen
Wiese, Wandjuk Marika
Cast: Bruce Spence (Hackett), Wandjuk Marika (Miliritbi), Roy Marika
(Dayipu), Ray Barrett (Cole), Norman Kaye (Ferguson), Colleen Clif-
ford (Miss Strehlow), Ralph Cotterill (Fletcher), Nicolas Lathouris
(Arnold), Basil Clarke (Judge Blackburn), Ray Marshall (Coulthard),
Gary Williams (Watson), Tony Llewellyn-Jones (Fitzsimmons), Paul

Cox (photographer), Marraru Wunungmurra (Daisy Barunga), Robert Brissenden (Professor Stanner)
107 minutes

WERNER HERZOG—FILMMEMACHER / PORTRAIT WERNER HERZOG
   (1986)
Director: **Werner Herzog**
Screenplay: **Werner Herzog**
Producer: Lucki Stipetić
Production Company: Werner Herzog Filmproduktion for Transtel
Camera: Jörg Schmidt-Reitwein
Editing: Maximiliane Mainka
Sound: Christine Ebenberger
Featuring: **Werner Herzog**
Narrator: **Werner Herzog**
29 minutes

COBRA VERDE (1987)
Director: **Werner Herzog**
Screenplay: **Werner Herzog** (from the novel *The Viceroy of Ouidah* by
   Bruce Chatwin)
Producers: Lucki Stipetić, **Werner Herzog**
Production Companies: Werner Herzog Filmproduktion and Zweites
   Deutsches Fernsehen
Camera: Viktor Ružička
Editing: Maximiliane Mainka
Set Design: Ulrich Bergfelder
Sound: Haymo Henry Heyder
Music: Florian Fricke (Popol Vuh)
Cast: Klaus Kinski (Francisco Manoel da Silva), King Ampaw (Taparica),
   José Lewgoy (Don Octavio Coutinho), Salvatore Basile (Captain
   Fraternidade), Peter Berling (Bernabo), Guillermo Coronel (Eu-
   clides), Nana Agyefi Kwame II of Nsein (Bossa Ahadee), Yolanda
   Garcia (Dona Epiphania), Nana Fedu Abodo (Yovogan), Kofi Yeren-
   kyi (Bakoko), Kwesi Fase (Kankpé), Benito Stefanelli (Captain Pedro
   Vicente), Kofi Bryan (messenger), Carlos Mayolo (governor), Zigi
   Cultural Troupe of Ziavi (singing girls)
111 minutes

LES FRANÇAIS VU PAR . . . / THE FRENCH AS SEEN BY . . . ; Episode 1:
Les gauloises (1988)
Director: **Werner Herzog**
Screenplay: **Werner Herzog**
Production Company: Erato Films
Camera: Jörg Schmidt-Reitwein
Editing: Rainer Standke
Sound: Bernard Aubouy
12 minutes

WODAABE—DIE HIRTEN DER SONNE / WODAABE—HERDSMEN OF
THE SUN (1989)
Director: **Werner Herzog**
Screenplay: **Werner Herzog**
Producer: Patrick Sandrin
Production Companies: Werner Herzog Filmproduktion and Factory 2
(Berlin) for Antenne 2 (Paris) and for Süddeutscher Rundfunk
Camera: Jörg Schmidt-Reitwein
Editing: Maximiliane Mainka
Sound: Walter Saxer
Music: Charles Gounod, Wolfgang Amadeus Mozart, Georg Friedrich
Händel, Giuseppe Verdi
Narrator: **Werner Herzog**
49 minutes

ECHOS AUS EINEM DÜSTEREN REICH / ECHOES FROM A SOMBRE
EMPIRE (1990)
Director: **Werner Herzog**
Screenplay: **Werner Herzog**
Producers: **Werner Herzog**, Galeshka Moravioff
Production Companies: SERA Filmproduktion, Les films sans frontières,
Werner Herzog Filmproduktion
Camera: Jörg Schmidt-Reitwein
Editing: Rainer Standke
Sound: Harald Maury
Music: Michael Kreihsl, Béla Bartók, Sergei Prokofiev, Witold
Lutosławski, Franz Schubert, Dmitri Shostakovich, Johann Sebas-
tian Bach, Esther Lamandier
Featuring: Michael Goldsmith, **Werner Herzog,** François Gibault,

Augustine Assemat, Francis Szpiner, David Dacko, Marie-Reine Has-
sen, Jean-Bédel Bokassa (from archival footage)
87 minutes

FILMSTUNDE / FILM LESSON (1991)
Director: **Werner Herzog**
Producer: Gerda Weissenberger
Production Company: Österreichischer Rundfunk
Camera: Michael Ferk, Karl Kofler
Editing: Albert Skalak
Sound: Gerhard Sandler
Featuring: **Werner Herzog**, Philippe Petit, Volker Schlöndorff,
    Michael Kreihsl, Peter Turrini, Kamal Saiful Islam, Ryszard
    Kapuściński, Jeff Sheridan
240 minutes; 8 parts

JAG MANDIR—DAS EXZENTRISCHE PRIVATTHEATER DES MAHARA-
DJAH VON UDAIPUR / JAG MANDIR—THE ECCENTRIC PRIVATE
THEATRE OF THE MAHARAJAH OF UDAIPUR (1991)
Director: **Werner Herzog**
Screenplay: **Werner Herzog**
Producer: **Werner Herzog**
Production Companies: Neue Studio Film, Österreichischer Rundfunk,
    Zweites Deutsches Fernsehen
Camera: Rainer Klausmann
Editing: Michou Hutter
Staging: André Heller
Sound: Rainer Wiehr
Narrator: **Werner Herzog**
83 minutes

SCHREI AUS STEIN / SCREAM OF STONE (1991)
Director: **Werner Herzog**
Screenplay: Hans-Ulrich Klenner, Walter Saxer
Producer: Walter Saxer
Production Companies: SERA Filmproduktion, Les Stock Films Interna-
    tional, Zweites Deutsches Fernsehen, Molécule Films
Camera: Rainer Klausmann
Editing: Suzanne Baron

Set Design: Juan Santiago, Cornelius Siegel, Wolfgang Siegel, Kristine
    Steinhilber
Sound: Chris Price
Music: Heinrich Schütz, Richard Wagner, Ingram Marshall, Sarah Hop-
    kins, Alan Lamb, Atahualpa Yupanqui
Cast: Vittorio Mezzogiorno (Roccia), Mathilda May (Katharina), Stefan
    Glowacz (Martin), Donald Sutherland (Ivan), Brad Dourif (Finger-
    less), Al Waxman (Stephen), Gunilla Karlzen (Carla), Chavela Var-
    gas (Indian woman), Georg Marischka (advertising agent), Volker
    Prechtl (Himalayan climber), Hans Kammerlander (mountain
    climber), Lautaro Murúa (Estancerio), Amelie Fried (TV anchor),
    Werner Herzog (TV director)
103 minutes

LEKTIONEN IN FINSTERNIS / LESSONS OF DARKNESS (1992)
Director: **Werner Herzog**
Screenplay: **Werner Herzog**
Producers: Paul Berriff, **Werner Herzog**, Lucki Stipetić
Production Companies: Werner Herzog Filmproduktion and Premiere
    Medien
Camera: Paul Berriff
Editing: Rainer Standke
Sound: John G. Pearson
Music: Richard Wagner, Edvard Grieg, Sergei Prokofiev, Arvo Pärt,
    Giuseppe Verdi, Franz Schubert, Gustav Mahler
Narrator: **Werner Herzog**
54 minutes

GLOCKEN AUS DER TIEFE / BELLS FROM THE DEEP (1993)
Director: **Werner Herzog**
Screenplay: **Werner Herzog**
Producers: Lucki Stipetić, Ira Barmak
Production Company: Werner Herzog Filmproduktion for Momentous
    Events
Camera: Jörg Schmidt-Reitwein
Editing: Rainer Standke
Sound: Vyacheslav Belozerov
Music: Choir of the Spiritual Academy in St. Petersburg, Choir of the
    Zagorsk Monastery, Oorzak Chunashtaar-ool, Mongusch Mergen,
    Ondar Mönghün-ool

Narrator: **Werner Herzog**
60 minutes

DIE VERWANDLUNG DER WELT IN MUSIK / THE TRANSFORMATION
    OF THE WORLD INTO MUSIC (1994)
Director: **Werner Herzog**
Screenplay: **Werner Herzog**
Producer: Lucki Stipetić
Production Company: Werner Herzog Filmproduktion for Zweites
    Deutsches Fernsehen and for ARTE
Camera: Jörg Schmidt-Reitwein
Editing: Rainer Standke
Sound: Ekkehart Baumung
Music: Richard Wagner
Featuring: Sven Friedrich, **Werner Herzog**, Wolfgang Wagner, Dieter
    Dorn, Plácido Domingo, Henning von Gierke, Yohji Yamamoto,
    Heiner Müller, Daniel Barenboim, James Levine, Deborah Polasky,
    Eva Johansson, Norbert Balatsch, Peter Schneider, Paul Frey, Wer-
    ner Junold, Siegfried Jerusalem, Waltraud Meier
90 minutes

GESUALDO—TOD FÜR FÜNF STIMMEN / DEATH FOR FIVE VOICES
    (1995)
Director: **Werner Herzog**
Screenplay: **Werner Herzog**
Producer: Lucki Stipetić
Production Company: Werner Herzog Filmproduktion for Zweites
    Deutsches Fernsehen
Camera: Peter Zeitlinger
Editing: Rainer Standke
Sound: Ekkehart Baumung
Music: Carlo Gesualdo, Richard Wagner, Francesco d'Avalos
Featuring: Alan Curtis, Gerald Place, Milva, Pasquale D'Onofrio, Salva-
    tore Catorano, Angelo Carrabs, Angelo Michele Torriello, Raffaele
    Virocolo, Vincenzo Giusto, Giovanni Iudica, Walter Beloch, An-
    tonio Massa, Gennaro Miccio, Silvano Milli, Marisa Milli, Alberto
    Lanini
Narrator: **Werner Herzog**
60 minutes

FLUCHT AUS LAOS / LITTLE DIETER NEEDS TO FLY (1997)
Director: **Werner Herzog**
Screenplay: **Werner Herzog**
Producer: Lucki Stipetić
Production Company: Werner Herzog Filmproduktion for Zweites
    Deutsches Fernsehen
Camera: Peter Zeitlinger
Editing: Rainer Standke
Sound: Ekkehart Baumung
Music: Béla Bartók, Carlos Gardel, Glenn Miller, Kongar-ol Ondar, Rich-
    ard Wagner, Antonin Dvořák, Johann Sebastian Bach
Featuring: Dieter Dengler
Narrator: **Werner Herzog**
78 minutes (52 minutes for German television)

GOTT UND DIE BELADENEN / GOD AND THE BURDENED, A.K.A.
    CHRIST AND DEMONS IN NEW SPAIN (1999)
Director: **Werner Herzog**
Screenplay: **Werner Herzog**
Producers: Martin Choroba, Joachim Puls, Lucki Stipetić
Production Company: Tellux Film
Camera: Jorge Vignati
Editing: Joe Bini
Sound: Francisco Adrianzén
Music: Charles Gounod, Orlando di Lasso
Narrator: **Werner Herzog**
43 minutes

JULIANES STURZ IN DEN DSCHUNGEL / WINGS OF HOPE (1999)
Director: **Werner Herzog**
Screenplay: **Werner Herzog**
Producers: Lucki Stipetić, Peter Firstbrook
Production Company: Werner Herzog Filmproduktion for Zweites
    Deutsches Fernsehen
Camera: Peter Zeitlinger
Editing: Joe Bini
Sound: Eric Spitzer
Music: Richard Wagner, Igor Stravinsky
Featuring: Juliane Köpcke (Diller), **Werner Herzog**, Moisés Rengito

Chavez, Juan Limer Ribera Soto, Richard Silva Manujama, Ricardo Oroche Rengite, El Moro, Simon Herzog
Narrator: **Werner Herzog**
66 minutes

MEIN LIEBSTER FEIND / MY BEST FIEND (1999)
Director: **Werner Herzog**
Screenplay: **Werner Herzog**
Producer: Lucki Stipetić
Production Companies: Werner Herzog Filmproduktion, Cafe Productions, Zephir Film
Camera: Peter Zeitlinger
Editing: Joe Bini
Sound: Eric Spitzer
Music: Florian Fricke (Popol Vuh)
Featuring: Klaus Kinski (from archival footage), **Werner Herzog**, Eva Mattes, Claudia Cardinale, Beat Presser, Justo Gonzales, Baron and Baroness von der Recke
Narrator: **Werner Herzog**
99 minutes

INVINCIBLE (2001)
Director: **Werner Herzog**
Screenplay: **Werner Herzog**
Producers: Gary Bart, **Werner Herzog**, James Mitchell, Christine Ruppert, Lucki Stipetić
Production Companies: Werner Herzog Filmproduktion and Tatfilm Produktion
Camera: Peter Zeitlinger
Editing: Joe Bini
Set Design: Ulrich Bergfelder
Sound: Simon Willis
Music: Hans Zimmer, Klaus Badelt
Cast: Tim Roth (Hanussen), Jouko Ahola (Zische Breitbart), Anna Gourari (Marta Farra), Jacob Wein (Benjamin), Max Raabe (master of ceremonies), Gustav-Peter Wöhler (Landwehr), Udo Kier (Count Helldorf), Herbert Golder (Rabbi Edelmann), Gary Bart (Yitzak Breitbart), Renate Krößner (Mother Breitbart), Ben-Tzion Hershberg (Gershon), Rebecca Wein (Rebecca), Raphael Wein (Raphael), Daniel Wein (Daniel), Chana Wein (Chana)
133 minutes

PILGRIMAGE (2001)
Director: **Werner Herzog**
Screenplay: **Werner Herzog**
Producers: Rodney Wilson, Christian Seidel, Lucki Stipetić
Production Companies: Werner Herzog Filmproduktion, British Broadcasting Corporation, Pipeline Films
Camera: Jorge Pacheco, Erik Söllner, Jörg Schmidt-Reitwein
Editing: Joe Bini
Sound: Neil Pemperton
Music: John Tavener
18 minutes

TEN THOUSAND YEARS OLDER (2002)
Director: **Werner Herzog**
Screenplay: **Werner Herzog**
Producer: Lucki Stipetić
Production Companies: Werner Herzog Filmproduktion and Ten Minutes Older
Camera: Vicente Ríos
Editing: Joe Bini
Sound: Walter Saxer
Music: Paul Englishby
Narrator: **Werner Herzog**
10 minutes

WHEEL OF TIME (2003)
Director: **Werner Herzog**
Screenplay: **Werner Herzog**
Producer: Lucki Stipetić
Production Companies: Werner Herzog Filmproduktion and Cafe Productions
Camera: Peter Zeitlinger, **Werner Herzog**
Editing: Joe Bini
Sound: Eric Spitzer
Music: Prem Rana Autari, Surendra Shrestha, Bihaya Vaidya, Florian Fricke (Popol Vuh), Lhamo Dolma
Featuring: The Dalai Lama, Lama Lhundup Woeser, Takna Jigme Sangpo, Matthieu Ricard, Madhureeta Anand, Tenzin Dhargye, Ven. Geshe, Manfred Klell, Chungdak D. Koren, Thupten Tsering Mukhimsar

Narrator: **Werner Herzog**
80 minutes

THE WHITE DIAMOND (2004)
Director: **Werner Herzog**
Screenplay: **Werner Herzog**
Producers: Annette Scheurich, Lucki Stipetić, **Werner Herzog**
Production Company: Marco Polo Film
Camera: Henning Brümmer, Klaus Scheurich
Editing: Joe Bini
Sound: Eric Spitzer, Simon Normanton
Music: Ernst Reijseger, Eric Spitzer
Featuring: Graham Dorrington, Mark Anthony Yhap, Dieter Plage
    (from archival footage), **Werner Herzog**, Anthony Melville, Mi-
    chael Wilk, Jan-Peter Meewes, Jason Gibson
Narrator: **Werner Herzog**
88 minutes

GRIZZLY MAN (2005)
Director: **Werner Herzog**
Screenplay: **Werner Herzog**
Producer: Erik Nelson
Production Company: Real Big Productions for Lions Gate Films and for
    Discovery Docs
Camera: Peter Zeitlinger, Timothy Treadwell
Editing: Joe Bini
Sound: Ken King, Spencer Palermo
Music: Richard Thomson
Featuring: Timothy Treadwell (from archival footage), Franc G. Fallico,
    Jewel Palovak, **Werner Herzog**, Willy Fulton, Amie Huguenard
    (from archival footage), Warren Queeny, Larry Van Daele, Kathleen
    Parker, Val Dexter, Carol Dexter, Sam Egli, Marc Gaede, Marnie
    Gaede, Sven Haakanson Jr.
Narrator: **Werner Herzog**
104 minutes

THE WILD BLUE YONDER (2005)
Director: **Werner Herzog**
Screenplay: **Werner Herzog**
Producer: André Singer

Production Companies: Werner Herzog Filmproduktion, West Park Pictures, and Tetra Media, for British Broadcasting Corporation (BBC) and France 2

Camera: Tanja Koop, Henry Kaiser, the astronauts of Space Shuttle STS-34, Klaus Scheurich

Editing: Christophe Nadeau, Joe Bini

Sound: Joe Crabb

Music: Ernst Reijseger

Cast: Brad Dourif (Alien), Capt. Donald Williams (commander), Dr. Ellen Baker (physician), Franklin Chang-Diaz (plasma physician), Shannon Lucid (biochemist), Michael McCulley (pilot), Roger Diehl, Ted Sweetser, and Martin Lo (mathematicians)

78 minutes

RESCUE DAWN (2006)

Director: **Werner Herzog**

Screenplay: **Werner Herzog**

Producers: Elton Brand, Steve Marlton, Harry Knapp

Production Company: Top Gun Productions for Gibraltar Entertainment & Production

Camera: Peter Zeitlinger

Editing: Joe Bini

Set Design: Arin Pinijvararak

Sound: Paul Paragon, Tammy Douglas

Music: Klaus Badelt

Cast: Christian Bale (Dieter Dengler), Steve Zahn (Duane), Jeremy Davies (Gene), Galen Yuen (Y.C.), Abhijati Jusakul (Phisit), Chaiyan Chunsuttiwat (Procet), Zach Grenier (squad leader), Toby Huss (Spook), Pat Healy (Norman), Evan Jones (Lessard), Marshall Bell (admiral), François Chau (province governor)

126 minutes

ENCOUNTERS AT THE END OF THE WORLD (2007)

Director: **Werner Herzog**

Screenplay: **Werner Herzog**

Producer: Henry Kaiser

Production Company: Discovery Channel

Camera: Peter Zeitlinger

Editing: Joe Bini

Sound: **Werner Herzog**

Music: Henry Kaiser, David Lindley
Featuring: Scott Rowland, Stefan Pashov, Doug MacAyeal, Ryan An-
    drew Evans, Kevin Emery, Olav T. Oftedal, Regina Eisert, David R.
    Pacheco Jr., Samuel S. Bowser, Jan Pawlowski, William Jirsa, Karen
    Joyce, Libor Zicha, Ashrita Furman, David Ainley, William McIn-
    tosh, Clive Oppenheimer, Peter Gorham
Narrator: **Werner Herzog**
101 minutes

BAD LIEUTENANT—PORT OF CALL: NEW ORLEANS (2009)
Director: **Werner Herzog**
Screenplay: William M. Finkelstein
Producers: Edward R. Pressman, Nicholas Cage
Production Companies: Edward R. Pressman Film and Nu Image Films
Camera: Peter Zeitlinger
Editing: Joe Bini
Set Design: Tony Corbett
Sound: Jay Meagher
Music: Mark Isham
Cast: Nicholas Cage (Terence McDonagh), Eva Mendes (Frankie Don-
    nenfeld), Val Kilmer (Steve Pruit), Alvin "Xzibit" Joiner (Big Fate),
    Fairuza Balk (Heidi), Shawn Hatosy (Armand Benoit), Jennifer
    Coolidge (Geneviève), Tom Bower (Pat McDonagh), Vondie Curtis-
    Hall (Captain James Brasser), Brad Dourif (Ned Schoenholtz), Den-
    zel Whitaker (Daryl), Irma P. Hall (Binnie Rogers), Shea Whigham
    (Justin), Michael Shannon (Mundt)
122 minutes

LA BOHÈME (2009)
Director: **Werner Herzog**
Screenplay: **Werner Herzog**
Producer: André Singer
Production Company: West Park Pictures for Sky Arts and National Eng-
    lish Opera
Camera: Richard Blanshard
Editing: Joe Bini
Music: Giacomo Puccini
4 minutes

MY SON, MY SON, WHAT HAVE YE DONE (2009)
Director: **Werner Herzog**
Screenplay: Herbert Golder, **Werner Herzog**
Producer: Eric Bassett
Production Companies: Defilm, Paper Street Films, Industrial
    Entertainment
Camera: Peter Zeitlinger
Editing: Joe Bini, Omar Daher
Sound: Ronald Eng
Music: Ernst Reijseger
Cast: Michael Shannon (Brad McCullum), Willem Dafoe (Detective Ha-
    venhurst), Chloë Sevigny (Ingrid), Michael Peña (Detective Vargas),
    Udo Kier (Lee Myers), Grace Zabriskie (Mrs. McCullum), Loretta
    Devine (Miss Roberts), Irma P. Hall (Mrs. Roberts), Brad Dourif
    (Uncle Ted), James C. Burns (Swat commander Brown)
92 minutes

CAVE OF FORGOTTEN DREAMS (2010)
Director: **Werner Herzog**
Screenplay: **Werner Herzog**
Producers: Erik Nelson, Adrienne Ciuffo
Production Companies: Creative Differences Productions and History
    Films
Camera: Peter Zeitlinger
Editing: Joe Bini, Maya Hawke
Sound: Eric Spitzer
Music: Ernst Reijseger
Featuring: Jean Clottes, Dominique Baffier, Jean-Michel Geneste, Nich-
    olas Conard, Wulf Hein, Julien Monney, Gilles Tosello, Carole Fritz,
    Werner Herzog, Maurice Maurin, Michel Philippe, Maria Malina,
    Valérie Feruglio
Narrator: **Werner Herzog**
90 minutes

HAPPY PEOPLE: A YEAR IN THE TAIGA (2010)
Directors: Dmitry Vasyukov, **Werner Herzog**
Screenplay: **Werner Herzog**, Dmitry Vasyukov, Rudolph Herzog
Executive Producers: **Werner Herzog**, Yanko Damboulev, Timur Bek-
    mambetov, Klaus Badelt
Production Company: Studio Babelsberg

Camera: Alexey Matveev, Gleb Stepanov, Arthur Sibirski, Michael
  Tarkovsky
Editing: Joe Bini
Music: Klaus Badelt
Narrator: **Werner Herzog**
94 minutes

INTO THE ABYSS (2011)
Director: **Werner Herzog**
Screenplay: **Werner Herzog**
Producer: Erik Nelson
Production Companies: Creative Differences and Werner Herzog
  Filmproduktion
Camera: Peter Zeitlinger
Editing: Joe Bini
Sound: Eric Spitzer, Steve Osmon
Music: Mark De Gli Antoni
Featuring: Michael Perry, Jason Burkett, Fred Allen, Richard Lopez, Del-
  bert Burkett, Melyssa Burkett
Narrator: **Werner Herzog**
105 minutes

ON DEATH ROW (2012)
Director: **Werner Herzog**
Screenplay: **Werner Herzog**
Producer: Erik Nelson
Production Companies: Creative Differences, Spring Films, Werner Her-
  zog Filmproduktion, Discovery Communications
Camera: Peter Zeitlinger
Editing: Joe Bini
Sound: Eric Spitzer, Steve Osmon
Music: Mark De Gli Antoni
Featuring: James Barnes, Joseph Garcia, George Rivas, Linda Carty,
  Hank Skinner
Narrator: **Werner Herzog**
188 minutes; four episodes

FROM ONE SECOND TO THE NEXT (2013)
Director: **Werner Herzog**
Screenplay: **Werner Herzog**

Production Company: AT&T
Camera: Peter Zeitlinger
Editing: Joe Bini, RockPaperScissors
Music: Mark De Gli Antoni
35 minutes

ON DEATH ROW—SEASON TWO (2013)
Director: **Werner Herzog**
Screenplay: **Werner Herzog**
Producer: Erik Nelson
Production Companies: Creative Differences and Skellig Rock Produc-
    tions for Investigation Discovery
Camera: Dave Roberson
Editing: Marco Capalbo
Sound: Steve Osmon
Music: Mark De Gli Antoni
Featuring: Robert Fratta, Darlie Routier, Blaine Milam, Douglas Feldman
Narrator: **Werner Herzog**
223 minutes; four episodes

Werner Herzog: Interviews

Platform for the Young German Film: Werner Herzog

Frieda Grafe, Enno Patalas, and Florian Fricke / 1968

From "Tribüne des Jungen Deutschen Films: Werner Herzog," *Filmkritik* 3 (March 1968): 176–79. Reprinted by permission.

Question: When you were making *Signs of Life*, did you have a certain audience in mind?

Werner Herzog: I can't actually say who my audience is, though I can say with some certainty who it is not: I did not make the film for tree frogs, because so far I haven't seen any tree frogs at the box-office, nor have I ever seen a squirrel behind a camera. That much seems clear, but hardly anything does beyond it. I don't have a precise sense of my audience. At most, I could say that I've sent out signals and I hope they reach a few people. But I think my film is entirely comprehensible. I believe in an audience that will provide an understanding for the film. Above all, I believe in the film's staying power. One shouldn't be too stingy and imagine people watching it for the next four years, but rather forty or forty thousand years. When I say forty thousand, I don't mean a million years, because by then there may be dinosaurs back on the planet. And I didn't make the film for dinosaurs either. I know my limits.

Q: It almost seems that you underestimate how comprehensible your film is. In some places you give easily recognizable clues, for example, the closing voice-over.

WH: You mean the final sentence, where it is said that Stroszek, the main character, undertook something titanic in the scale of his rebellion, and that he therefore failed as miserably as all others of his kind. For me, that's not so much a concluding interpretation as the possibility of the film's continuation. If Stroszek were to die, after having been overpowered by his own men, then he could just die a wretched death, and

3

that to me is the nature of the titanic. In six weeks, he'd die of a gunshot wound to the abdomen, unshaven, coughing, a scarf around his neck, in moldy bedclothes. If I were to continue the film, I would have Stroszek just cough into the camera for a good quarter of an hour. Admittedly, the army doctor's comments have a certain associative quality, because as a physician, when asked about what initially seems to be a pathological case, he refers to a totally different, non-medical possibility. As I see it, after barricading himself in, fighting against friends and enemies, singlehandedly laying siege to the town, and trying to set it ablaze with fireworks, Stroszek is not at all insane. He merely articulates himself in an unexpected way: through signs which, in principle, correspond to his previous endeavor. Surrounded, as it were, by a symbolic world that is becoming increasingly dense, all of a sudden he takes hold of these signs and makes them his own language. He counters violence with violence, lunacy with lunacy, and light with light. Only his exertion of energy is disproportionate.

Q: Your project originates from a story by Achim von Arnim, doesn't it?
WH: From "The Mad Invalid of Fort Ratonneau"? No, that would be misleading. The underlying story is based on a newspaper report about an actual incident from the Seven Years' War, which I stumbled upon in the [eighteenth-century] journal *Der Freymüthige*. This report was also probably the source for Arnim's novella, but unfortunately there's no direct evidence of that. So it's not an adaptation of the novella. The most important parts of the film were in any case conceived before the story fell into my hands.

Q: Which ones?
WH: Almost all the episodes up to the point where Stroszek drives his two comrades and his wife out of the fort and barricades himself in. For example, the episode with the little walnut-owl, whose eyes and ears seem to move on their own. Later we learn there were flies living inside of it. Or the encounters with the pianist and with the shepherd, and certainly the story of the half-dead rooster that the children have buried up to its neck in the sand. You know that I once filmed this episode by itself and under totally different circumstances, only then [in *Game in the Sand*] I was interested in how violence emerges from a playful situation. In *Signs of Life*, the rooster, whose head and neck are barely sticking out of the ground, only interests me as landscape, as a quality of landscape. That's why the events leading up to it are left obscure.

Q: Can you tell us something about your method? Were the shots and the dialogue all fixed in advance?

WH: There was a script, but we rarely followed it. Almost all the dialogue was changed according to the shooting situation and the personal speaking situation of the actors. We used sync sound for almost the entire film, and that automatically makes the technical apparatus more cumbersome. On another level, however, it also increases the film's immediacy. An entire series of scenes first emerged in the process of shooting. Mostly, and especially with the lay actors, I tried to confront them with obstacles while we were filming, so that, in reacting to the obstacle, they were thrown back on themselves. You can see that with the actor who plays Becker, who's physically awkward to an unusual degree. If he were to play such a person, he couldn't do it. Working with the professional actors was also peculiar in many ways. I almost never spoke with them about conceptual questions around the characters. Rather, for example, I drove them in a car to the other end of the island, to a place that is so intensely and indescribably strange that they immediately understood the project. During the shoot we had to work in a very concentrated manner, and the team functioned very precisely. On the set the team almost never raised their voices, they mostly just whispered. In general, I think a film like this one conveys the qualities of the whole team as surely as it does, say, the director's personality.

Q: How was the cast assembled?

WH: Here I have to say that this film didn't start with the characters or with specific faces, but rather, primarily, with the locations. All my films actually begin with locations that in a strange way, all of a sudden, appear to me. Afterward, then, I have to find people for my characters. There's no clear typology, even Meinhard is somehow broken, a loud-mouthed boor, who kills insects with his fat fingers and does so with emotion. To a large extent I cast lay actors, and where professionals are used, I tried to approach them in terms of their private personalities and not in terms of their acting potential. In this regard, I think Peter Brogle was a good choice for Stroszek, because he had an unusually close relationship to this character. Brogle is a person who could cry blood, if the role demanded it.

Q: Could your film just as well have been set in Germany?

WH: No, never, because in Pasing [a district in the city of Munich] the people are just people, and the places don't transport us elsewhere. For the film, that is, the quality of the happenings in the story corresponds to the quality of the locations. The fact that I've manipulated and changed most of the locations in one way or another doesn't contradict their reality. I've tried to push the existing reality to the point that other realities, their features and their essence, become recognizable. For example: At the beginning of the film you see the soles of marble feet jutting out of a wall, as though the Venetians, in building the fortress, made an ancient statue like a loaf of bread, inserted head-first into the wall. I had it made by a sculptor, and yet I claim that the feet had always already been there in this spot. Other times I found real existing locations that were so remarkable that I had to represent them as though they never could have existed. I'm thinking of the valley with the ten thousand windmills. It looks like a dense meadow where all the flowers begin to spin. Like ten thousand flowers gone mad.

Q: How did you come across these locations in Greece?
WH: I don't show Greece, but rather very specific places. I lived for a while in the country, and I got to know the island of Kos through my grandfather [Rudolf Herzog], who made his life's work there as an archaeologist. I just wanted to see what kind of a job he did. I don't have the right sense for archaeology, but perhaps one could describe the film's way of seeing as archaeological, because I'm less interested in the surface of things than I am in the cracks that open up in them.

Q: Can you give an example?
WH: Yes, the dream sequence, or better: the evacuation scene, where part of the town has to be cleared out because Stroszek poses a threat. The essence of this scene lies in the very strange and rigid family photos that are suddenly brought out of their houses. What's that about?

Q: Are these the things that cause Stroszek to explode?
WH: Yes, exactly, he's surrounded by them. You see, Stroszek is always someone who's affected. He never acts, he just observes. And then, all of a sudden, he takes tremendous action, and from that point on I'm no longer interested in him as a private person and his personal reaction. From then on, I show only his signs and the banal things that he manages to shoot. From that moment on, when he holds five thousand people in suspense, wondering what's going to happen, he can only be seen at a great distance, as small as an ant. And yet, the film never really creates true distance from the main character. It's more discretion,

because our sympathy for the character remains to the very end, even for the misery of his actual successes. Stroszek shoots into a crowd of people, but only a donkey is killed. Then he tries to annihilate the town with Roman candles, but only manages to set a chair on fire. Discretion is an essential element of the film. It's the only way I could keep the story from becoming a psychological thriller. In the most decisive moments, the camera pulls away from the people.

Q: How would you characterize the film's general structure up until Stroszek's breakdown? Isn't it really just an accumulation of scenes?
WH: In a way, that's correct. This film comes together in the final shot. Only then, looking backward, do the episodes gather to form a clear, coherent image; only then do the events coordinate with each other. This bundling starts with Stroszek's madness. From then on, the film is really narrated chronologically. Then it's only about a half day, a night, and another day, that Stroszek holds his position. In a way, the rhythm of this passage also corresponds in its contingencies with the unfolding of the plot. The extreme act actually comes from extreme inactivity, since the task of guarding the fortress is really just a nominal one. By contingencies in the passage of time I mean, for example, the final shot of the film, a traveling shot on a plain, where you wait for something, but nothing ever comes; there's just an empty plain with a trail of dust. The shot lasts almost three minutes and it covers a stretch of, let's say, two and a half kilometers, and yet it's exactly the right length. This treatment of time is what characterizes the film, and in that respect I've learned a lot from Indian music. I'd argue that [Alexander] Kluge is the best among us working in the modern style, and I'm the best in the Indian style.

Q: Can we draw conclusions from your film, statements that would have meaning for us?
WH: You certainly can, just not in historical or political terms.

Q: So you weren't out for a political interpretation of your film?
WH: I give a whole series of clues in the film that it's not about the historical situation at the end of the Second World War. It's about the situation of the individual person. The situation could just as well be that of the Seven Years' War, which essentially depended on putting the instruments of war into the hands of an individual person. Maybe it could've been firemen who guarded the munitions. The historical details in the film, regarding the occupation of Kos, are false and there are a whole

series of anachronisms and historical falsehoods. The soldiers that I show almost always run around barefoot and shirtless; nobody salutes; and when the captain tells them to fall in, one of the soldiers is chewing on a roll of bread. And all that has nothing to do with either the Third Reich or the Federal Republic.

Q: Does it have to do with the present situation in Greece?
WH: No. The locations and the land are more powerful than the current government.

Q: Does the film take issue with the classicist image of Greece?
WH: That is a layer that is embedded in the background, and you're right, it's not a classicist image. The things you encounter there can't be apprehended in color slides or with the tools of humanistic education. My image is a rather inhuman one, it tends toward folly, and for me it's not just about Greece. You must be thinking about the inscription that Becker, one of the fortress guards, tries to decipher, where it says that all the sailors have been hanged, their captain hanged, even the captain's dog has been hanged. This text is of course pure invention, but it's true that, in ancient Greece, boxers in the Olympic games wrapped their fists in metal and leather and then beat each other's faces into pulp. Only you don't learn that from a humanistic education.

Q: What is your background, then? Have you worked anywhere as an assistant?
WH: I was never an assistant or a student at a film school, aside from the fact that I've been using some equipment from the former Institute for Film and Television in Munich. Nor do I come from anywhere, neither from literature, nor from the theater, nor from photography, nor from any other discipline.

Q: Then how did you come to make films?
WH: I think it began like it does with children who begin playing the piano from one day to the next. In this regard, I never really had a choice. From the moment I could think independently, I knew that I would make films.

Q: And what films did you know at the time?
WH: Chaplin films, later Méliès, then Japanese films, *Rashomon*.

Q: Where did you see them? Were you living in Munich then?

WH: I lived in Munich, but I was very often away because I never felt that I quite belonged here. But it was never easy in other places, either. I almost think the fact of my birth is just a rumor. At eighteen I was in the Sudan during the Congo crisis. Later I lived in the USA and in Mexico. Those were complicated times but also the most important to me. Then again, when I was seventeen, I tried working with a small company to make a commissioned film about penal reform. That was very difficult back then, and fortunately the project was never funded. In 1962, I made my very first short film [*Herakles*].

Q: Do you have any filmic role models?

WH: Not directly. I very much admire [Satyajit] Ray, [Akira] Kurosawa, [Georges] Méliès, and [D. W.] Griffith, though I only know one of his films. [Vsevolod] Pudovkin's *Storm Over Asia* is one of my favorites, and I generally admire Pudovkin and [Alexander] Dovzhenko much more than [Sergei] Eisenstein, who in my opinion is way overrated. Pudovkin is more of a visionary, whereas Eisenstein puts much more emphasis on construction. Of the filmmakers who are closer to me, I most admire [Michelangelo] Antonioni and [Luis] Buñuel, and then [Vlado] Kristl's short *Autorennen* [Car Race].

Q: Do you plan to ever make a film in Germany?

WH: That's totally conceivable. My first short films were made in Germany and Austria. At the moment, though, I don't know of a project that I could shoot here in the neighborhood. It partly depends on whether the current film will bring any money that would allow me to keep working. I have some projects, but again they're strongly tied to locations, some of them in Africa—projects about failed revolutionaries, people like [Nicholas] Olenga, [Antoine] Gizenga, [Pierre] Mulele, [Christophe] Gbenye, John Okello. . . . Logistically, though, without some financial backing that would be sheer folly.

Hope for Berlin

Film in Berlin / 1968

From "Hoffnung auf Neukölln," *Film in Berlin* 6, no. 4, special edition for the eighteenth International Film Festival, Berlin (June–July 1968): 54–55. Reprinted by permission.

Director Werner Herzog (*Signs of Life*) showed festival films in the Berlin suburb of Neukölln with free admission. Public interest surpassed all expectations.

Question: Mr. Herzog, you have organized an event in Neukölln, using films from the Berlin festival—in order to give the *festival* a wider audience or in order to give its *films* a wider audience?
Werner Herzog: Yes, I did it because I fear the Berlinale has lost contact with the people. At the Zoo-Palast and the Festspielhaus [two of the largest, most prestigious festival theaters], a counterfeit public holds sway. Journalists, delegates, and film people are lured there for 280 marks a head. That's why I tried this experiment. It's *for* the Berlinale, and not opposed to it. I will demand that this model be adopted.

Q: What is the model?
WH: We basically created a branch of the Berlinale in a working-class district of the city. For the housewives, workers, and students who live there, we show the same films that run in the Zoo-Palast and in the Royal, only for free. That's the decisive point. Free admission bridges the divide that has opened up between the people and the Berlinale.

Q: Is the model adequately characterized by this one condition?
WH: Yes. Already on day two we had such a crowd—there is such an enormous interest for these films—that we have been totally overrun. For each screening there are hundreds of people left standing in line, they can't get in. They are the best and most open-minded audience that

I've ever encountered. Elderly people are so touched by the event that they intensively engage with even the most difficult films and evidently understand them, something that otherwise never would have happened, for lack of willingness.

Q: So you think the usual consumer-like attitude of spectators has also been diminished by this event.
WH: Yes, definitely. After the screenings, we have had spontaneous discussions on the street. At one show, for example, we were lucky enough to have the film's director and his team present. You should've seen how intense their discussion with the audience was. The discussions at the press conferences at the Europa-Center are nowhere near as vital and incisive as the discussions that take place spontaneously on the street. I'm totally surprised and excited by the response to my idea.

Q: What would you, then, demand for the future?
WH: I demand that the Berlinale adopt this model, which has already proven to generate such great interest. To that end, obviously, they must change the status quo. Should the Berlinale fail to do so, in 1969, I shall call upon the people of Neukölln to come with me to the Zoo-Palast. And together, in protest, we will gain free admission.

South American Experiences:
A Conversation with Werner Herzog
on *Aguirre, the Wrath of God*

Peter Schumann / 1973

From "Südamerikanische Erfahrungen: Ein Gespräch mit Werner Herzog über seinen Film *Aguirre, der Zorn Gottes*," *Frankfurter Rundschau*, January 13, 1973. Reprinted by permission.

Werner Herzog is one of our most important young filmmakers. Since *Signs of Life*, his films belong among the most controversial experiments of German cinema—not because they are fruitless formal experiments, but rather because Herzog's magical, archaic gesture, with which he describes the world and people, tends toward mythological thinking. At the same time, his peculiar films (among them, *Even Dwarfs Started Small*), most of which, unfortunately, have appeared [in West Germany] only on television, are among the better films of our current cinema. Herzog's latest film, *Aguirre, the Wrath of God*, takes place in the age of Spanish conquistadors. This too will have its premiere (January 16) on television. After that, hopefully, we will also be able to see *Aguirre* in theaters near us.

Peter Schumann: Werner Herzog, how does a West German filmmaker come to make a feature film about colonial history in Latin America, above all in the jungle, moreover with Klaus Kinski?

Werner Herzog: That has to do with the history of the film, with its story, which takes place in Peru in the sixteenth century and deals with the search for El Dorado, the land of gold. To be authentic, I had to go to Peru, to the original locations. So pre-production was intensive. I was in Peru for half a year, scouting parts of all the major tributaries of the Amazon. I looked for rapids that were the most spectacular, but not too dangerous to cross with the cameras, with several hundred people, and with all the props, rafts, and horses. I found some unbelievably beautiful locations. Some of the most beautiful parts of Peru are in my film.

PS: Why such a historical topic, one that the Latin Americans themselves have yet to address?
WH: That isn't entirely true. The Brazilians, for example, have made a whole series of films about their history.

PS: Yes, but those are films that reach back at most to the turn of the [twentieth] century, with one exception—
WH: —highly political films, just like *Aguirre*, although it takes place around 1560. And yet, as a theme, this horde of imperialistic adventurers performing a great historical failure, this failure of imperialism, of the conquerors, the theme is really quite modern. The method by which history was then made is actually one that can still be found today in many Latin American countries. History there is staged as theater, with theatrical coups. Think of the banana republics and their dictators. What's fascinating is that their theater tricks made world history. And even [Hernán] Cortés, as far as I know, thought of himself as staging history. He took historical examples like Alexander the Great and tried to stage history accordingly.

PS: Weren't you afraid of the difficulties, which scare even the natives, when you think of the jungle there?
WH: You know, I've filmed in Black Africa, and during the shoot I was jailed five times in a row, I had malaria, we almost died—nothing scares me anymore, neither a jungle nor a Klaus Kinski, nor costumes, nor being with hundreds of Indians. There were in fact extraordinary difficulties, financial problems too. When you see the film, it looks as though it must have cost $2 million to make. But it cost maybe a tenth of that.

PS: An extraordinary achievement, logistically as well as physically.
WH: I'm quite proud of it.

PS: Did you finance the film yourself?
WH: Generally speaking, yes. German television made a small advance contribution, but I'm the sole producer. There was a very small investment by a private source in Peru, and an even smaller one by an American distributor.

PS: An underdeveloped cinema such as that of Peru helps a developed one further develop?
WH: I'd put it this way: there's actually no real involvement. The Peruvian film industry, as it relates to projects like this one, has yet to emerge. In that regard there were no real partners.

PS: In Peru, did you find support or opposition from government officials?
WH: The Peruvian army supplied us with an amphibian aircraft and set up a small radio station, so that we always had contact with the nearest bigger city, assuming the electricity didn't fail.

PS: You filmed with several hundred people? Where did they all come from?
WH: Mostly from Latin America. Ninety-five percent of the extras were Peruvians. And a fifteen-year-old Peruvian girl from Lima played one of the main roles. Then we had around 250 highland Indians from a co-op not far from Cuzco. These Indians made extraordinary contributions to the film, because they always worked with joy even under the most difficult conditions, and they represented the fate of their people in an unusual way [that is, by making a film]. And that's how they understood it. All the Spanish adventurers were played by people from the Cuzco area, the wildest people I could find anywhere. One of the main actors is a very well-known Mexican, Helena Rojo. Then there are two Brazilians, one of whom is a very famous director, Ruy Guerra. For me, he's one of the five most important filmmakers in the world right now and a terrific actor as well. Two Americans, one of them played the lead in Dennis Hopper's film, *The Last Movie*. In all, we had four hundred people from fifteen countries thrown together, though of course that number decreased over time.

PS: Wasn't it decimated by the production?
WH: Luckily, no. We were pretty well prepared for everything. The greatest danger was actually the rapids.

PS: And Klaus Kinski, presumably?
WH: Yes, he was much more dangerous. The man is actually crazy. One evening, one of the extras spoke too loudly in his house—we had to build

a whole village, to house everyone—and Kinski got so worked up that he took his Winchester and shot a hole through the roof.

PS: So Kinski was armed?
WH: Yes, he was the only one, but probably more for fun. He was outfitted with a half-ton of equipment, as if he were on a big expedition.

PS: And how did you get along with him as an actor?
WH: Let me put it this way: Kinski is a very difficult man. His behavior was impossible, and he raved like a lunatic at least once a day. He also wanted to leave the set—for him, that wasn't new—he wanted to go home. So I threatened him with his life. He saw that I was serious, that I really would have killed him. From then on, everything went very smoothly. But that shouldn't really interest you. Only that which you see on the screen should interest you. And there you'll see a totally new Kinski, a very domesticated, well behaved, and yet very dangerous Kinski. To his credit I also have to say that he worked for a much lower fee than usual, out of pure fascination for the role and for the script.

PS: I want to come back to the support by the Peruvian government. Was it contingent on any copies of the film? Did you have to submit the script for review?
WH: A big panel of officials read the script in advance and was extraordinarily moved by the story. The Peruvians currently have a rather unusual form of state: It is a military dictatorship, but a liberal one that has nationalized certain industries—the banks and oil companies of the Americans—and [enacted] a huge land reform, with confiscations from large private owners. They noticed very clearly that my story revolves around the same problem of identity for the Peruvian people, the identity they're searching for, as well. How do you shake off the last vestiges of this imperialism, of Spanish conquest, to achieve a sense of "Peruvianness." And that's the theme of my film. It shows that the strong and the enduring are the Indians and their culture.

PS: Do you want to show this film now in Peru and in other Latin American countries, where the same problems exist?
WH: I'd rather show the film there than I would in Germany, because it fits there much better than it does here. Quechua, for example, is spoken in the film, and it remains in the German version too. It is a film that's

largely meant for Latin America. But the topic may be of interest everywhere. It's also a film that's meant to be understood as a "movie." It's thrilling, it shows unusual locations, and there's lots of action.

PS: So it's an anti-Herzog film?
WH: At any rate, it's my first film that will be more widely accepted. None of the others found a larger audience; they remained in the circles of cinephiles.

PS: Are you seriously counting on the West German market?
WH: Because the film will first appear on television, only smaller cinemas and 16-mm distribution are left. But it couldn't be helped, for economic reasons. I'm setting my hopes more on foreign distribution. *Even Dwarfs Started Small*, for example, has a Mexican distributor, but not a German one. It's playing in Algeria, in Paris, in the USA, in England, just not here.

PS: What experiences have you had with screening your films in Latin America? You showed them in Mexico, in Caracas, in Lima.
WH: They weren't so much screenings of my own films. That's just how it began. I was invited to bring my films to Peru, if I was going to be shooting there. And I suggested that I bring some of my favorite films by other people as well. So I took along with me Werner Schroeter's *Eika Katappa*, [Peter] Fleischmann's *Hunting Scenes from Bavaria*; I had [Rainer Werner] Fassbinder's *Katzelmacher*, and [Jean-Marie] Straub's *The Chronicle of Anna Magdalena Bach*. And I have to say it was huge success in Peru, because German cinema is totally unknown there. We prepared everything very carefully, and it turned out to be the biggest success they'd ever had at a national film festival in Peru. The films resonated in Mexico, too, especially with the press. Then they played in Guatemala, in Rio de Janeiro, in Uruguay, and in Chile. And they'll probably continue to circulate.

PS: Were there different reactions to the film among the individual countries?
WH: No essential differences. Mexico obviously has other political problems, and people there interpreted the films much more directly than they did, for example, in Peru. The only real differences were with *Eika Katappa*, a film that's exceptionally innovative and very difficult, and poses considerable problems for audiences.

PS: That may be due to the difference between the two cinemas. Mexico: a film country steeped in tradition, albeit mostly commercial production, and a vibrant group of cinephiles. Peru: a relatively underdeveloped film country, with only occasional feature film production, but one of the best film journals in Latin America. How did the Germans there react to films like *Hunting Scenes* or *Katzelmacher*?

WH: Negatively, extremely bad, because in Peru there's a whole group of escaped Nazis, who brought with them an image of Germany from the thirties, and were to some degree outraged by these films. Even the head of the Goethe-Institut there and people from the embassy left in protest during the Fassbinder film, right when two men begin kissing.

PS: The film also caused some difficulties for the [West German] embassy in Mexico.

WH: Yes, the German colonies aren't worth discussing, that goes without saying. Unfortunately, however, I must say that the embassies are not well staffed, much to our disgrace. What we currently have in the way of cultural officers in Latin America is a real catastrophe. The kinds of films that are being sent there. . . .

PS: Export Union films.

WH: Yes, but they should be representative. And what passes for German theater there, or contemporary German literature, it's frightening. A cultural officer or a Goethe-Institut leader may have heard of Heinrich Böll, but a man like Thomas Bernhard is a total unknown to them.

Werner Herzog: "Like a Powerful Dream . . ."

Noureddine Ghali / 1973

From "Werner Herzog: 'comme un rêve puissant . . . ,'" and published in *Jeune Cinéma* 81 (September–October 1974): 12–16. Interview conducted August 1973 in Munich. Translated by Japhet Johnstone. Reprinted by permission.

In preparation for the upcoming release of *Aguirre*—the strange and somber chronicle of a sixteenth-century conquistador, filmed in the Amazon jungle—here are some comments by the film's author regarding his oeuvre.

Werner Herzog: When I made *Even Dwarfs Started Small* people would ask me all the time, "What did you want to say with this film?" And I would reply, "I didn't want to say anything." I made the film to free myself from a nightmare, from a bad dream. The film took shape all of a sudden and I saw it in its entirety. I kept it inside of me for two or three years and held back from filming it. In the end it affected me so deeply—there was this drive inside of me to show it to other people. Only after I had finished the film, did I begin to think: "What is this? What was going on inside of me? What was that?"

I am not an intellectual. I do not belong to the ranks of intellectuals who have a philosophy or a social structure in mind and then make a film about it. Nor do I think that I succumbed to literary or philosophical influences. I can say, for the most part, that I am illiterate. I haven't read much and am therefore utterly clueless. In my case, making a film has much more to do with real life, with living things, than it has with philosophy. All my films were made without any reflective contemplation, or hardly any. Reflection always came after the film.

On Landscape

Many of my films have begun with landscapes. Ingmar Bergman, whose films I don't like for the most part, begins with faces. His starting point is the face. For me, my starting points are landscapes or imaginary places and aberrations, hallucinations. . . . When I speak of landscapes, I don't mean landscapes in the provincial sense. It's something different. If you take *Fata Morgana*, you will see that there is profound truth in the landscape. I would have liked to find the same landscapes near Munich. It would have been easier to make my films, to organize them, and I wouldn't have had to go to prison and I wouldn't have gotten sick. If similar landscapes existed near Munich, I would have certainly filmed near Munich. I have a very precise sense for landscapes. It's not something that I can explain.

A landscape always adapts to a given situation, like the arid island in *Even Dwarfs Started Small* with its very stylized landscape of vast lava beds, which really suited the framework of the film. The story could only take place in this setting and nowhere else. The same goes for *Fata Morgana* or *Aguirre, the Wrath of God*—there was no other choice of locations. Take, for example, the windmills in *Signs of Life*. They are in a valley in Crete. No one has counted, but there are about ten thousand windmills on a plateau in Crete. That's a reality. When you see them in the film, you think it's a trick. I'm thrilled by this because it makes reality become strange, you can no longer trust it. And there is something in that which is similar to insanity.

I would like to add something else. I always try to introduce a different aspect, a different character into a landscape. For the windmills in *Signs of Life* sound is important. Here's what I did: I took a recording of nearly a thousand people clapping at the end of a concert and distorted it electronically until it sounded like wood banging. Then I added another sound over it—what you hear in the countryside when you put your ear on a telegraph pole and the wind passes through the wires. You hear a humming that children call "angel song." Then I mixed the banging wood with the "angel song" and used the resulting sound as if it were the noise from the windmills. This changes the windmills. I am not saying that it changes them physically, but it changes the image and our perspective. And this new and very direct perspective on things is what I am trying to show and render visible. It's a way of perceiving that might become a part of your consciousness and intuition. Regarding landscapes in general, what I am looking for is a decent place for human beings, a place that measures up to humanity.

Dignity. Despair. Revolt.

In *Land of Silence and Darkness* the most radical and absolute human dignity can be found in Fini Straubinger or in the man who caresses the tree at the end of the film. Their dignity belongs to those people who are not capable of understanding themselves but who still keep their identity. When I see my films again after they are finished, I realize that many of the figures and people do not possess a language to express themselves and suffer because of it. There is a lot of pathos in that, but it's a sublime pathos. I try to be very gentle and very delicate with the people in my films. I do not attempt to deform them and I do not want to strip them of their identity. I like people the way they are, with all their suffering and destitution, and if I sometimes seem to direct them harshly, it is in their best interest, so that they can bring out the best in themselves. Sometimes I even tell them lies in order to lead them astray, because if I tell the truth they would begin to perform like actors, instead of being themselves.

In *Aguirre, the Wrath of God*, there is a clear distinction between the dignified people and the cruel ones. The dignity of the Indians in particular is very present—for example, the flute player. There are a lot of broken people in my films, and perhaps *Aguirre* is a film without hope. I find despair in many of my films. It is not my goal from the start to make them so, but by the end they just turn out like that. *Signs of Life* also has an atmosphere of despair: The hero's revolt is over the top. Aguirre's venture is on an even larger scale and therefore must fail even more so.

In *Even Dwarfs*, the dwarfs are not outside of society, they are society itself. Everyone is a dwarf. The world is made up of nothing but dwarfs. That's why we see, for example, a very strange woman getting out of a Chevrolet. She gets out of the car . . . and she, too, is a dwarf. The film is not about an isolated community of dwarfs. . . . We are all dwarfs. There was a lot of controversy surrounding the film. No one is indifferent. Either people like it a lot or they really hate it. There's no happy medium. I think the hatred comes from having to recognize your own inner dwarf and realizing for the first time just how small we are. There's a rebellion in *Even Dwarfs*, but not a revolution. It's an insane, senseless revolt without end. I love this film because I was able to make it just as I envisioned it from the very start.

On Animals

I included chickens and a rooster back in *Signs of Life* and the short film *Game in the Sand*. In *Even Dwarfs* they reappear, a bit like veterans from my early films, but they have a different quality. In *Signs of Life* there's a hypnotized chicken and a rooster buried up to its neck in the sand. There is no other meaning behind it. There is something that really frightens me about chickens. There's a flat, incredible stupidity in their eyes. If the devil existed, he would appear in the form of a chicken. But I am completely certain that the devil does not exist. Or if so, then the devil would be stupidity. I once had a dream. I was sitting in a church during a wedding. A friend of mine was getting married and the priest was asking her standard, classic questions from a book: "Do you reject the devil's powers!" And she had to reply: "Yes, I reject the devil's powers!" And the priest added: "Do you renounce the devil's evildoing!" And she had to say: "Yes, I renounce the devil's evildoing!" Then the priest asked, "Do you believe in the existence of the devil?" Then I got up and before she could answer, I came up, closed the book, and said in her place, still within the dream: "I do not believe in the devil. I just believe in stupidity." Then everyone started to chase me. I ran out of the church and found myself nose-to-nose with a donkey. I was so distressed that I mounted the donkey and got out of there.

Now a monkey, that's an animal I can like, as opposed to chickens, which frighten me. A situation always becomes clear with monkeys. Their presence makes everything clear. In *Aguirre* all ends well thanks to the presence of monkeys. Or rather, it isn't so much a happy ending as an exact one, a suitable ending—there is no deeper meaning in it. As for the monkeys on the raft at the end of *Aguirre*, that was the only way to end the film, the only way to give it an appropriate ending.

Images and Commentary

In *Fata Morgana* the text used in the voice-over renders things more visible. It lends the film a certain perspective while viewing. It adapts to the image. And sometimes the commentary is in counterpoint with the image. The text is important for the rhythm of the film, for the entire movement and the tensions. An image can sometimes create tension, a kind of pressure against the other images. The text can release this tension or intensify it.

German Cinema

I don't really feel that I am part of the German cinema. I work alone for the most part without a lot of contacts. There are filmmakers here in Germany whom I admire: Werner Schroeter, Fassbinder, Fleischmann, [Rosa von] Praunheim, Kristl. It is hard for me to recognize my own position, and sometimes people tell me that I'm eccentric, that I'm out there. But that's not true because I feel I am at the crux of certain things that I can't explain. For example, Kaiser Wilhelm II's contemporaries thought that he was at the crux of his times, but if you read his speeches and know about the end of his life—he had two hundred trees cut down for no apparent reason—you would rather say that he was eccentric for the times. On the other hand, a man like Robert Walser, a Swiss writer who later went mad, was unknown during his lifetime. But when you read him, line after line, you get the feeling that he was truly a man of his time. I think it goes the same for me. I'm not saying that I am at the crux of the times here in Germany. That would be idiotic. But I know perfectly well that I am not eccentric. I feel that I am a part of the times and that I am motivated by the same things that motivate other people. For example, like other people, I have no private life.

One of the problems with German cinema is its provincialism. Too many Germans make provincial films. Cinema Novo films from Brazil, by contrast, can be shown all over the world. They have a national character, not a provincial one. Truly national films would be, for example, *Hunting Scenes from Bavaria* or [Reinhard Hauff's] *Mathias Kneissl*. Schroeter and Fassbinder make national films. This provincialism is a problem with production and with the German cinema industry. I am independent. I produce my own films, so I am not forced to do specific things for a producer. It's difficult work, but that doesn't matter because it's necessary to do.

My films are fairly personal and I think you can get a sense of the person behind them, but the character of the person who made the film doesn't matter. The only thing that ought to count is the film that you are watching. I would have liked for all my films to have been posthumous—films made by a man who has been dead for years. I consider myself more a craftsman than an artist. Painters towards the end of the Middle Ages, for example, did not consider themselves artists but rather artisans. For them it was a real profession and they had apprentices for instance. . . . And I feel like my work is roughly the same. It has nothing to do with Art. It's a very direct kind of work.

I am captivated by making films. It is the only way for me to make myself understood and to also have friends. All my new friends from the last ten years I have met thanks to my films. Sometimes I am so very captivated and I feel this drive and want to share my fascination with others. It's like when you have a powerful dream and want to tell it to your friend the next day. It's like a burden, but that's also the reason why I like to carry film reels—they're heavy, you know; one copy weighs about twenty-four kilograms—despite the fatigue. That way I get to feel the *weight* and *material* of the film.

On Physical Labor

I always begin with very precise physical work. I believe that I have gained a physical sense for movement. Of course, it's also intellectual work since I have a clear vision of the scenes, images, and dialogues. But for me—and you might not believe it—making a film is really physical labor. I like to arrange the set myself and I like working on costumes and building a raft. I want to traverse the rapids myself in order to get a physical sense of the rapid when going down a tributary of the Amazon. I tried out all of that. I approach filmmaking through the real, by touching the film with my hands during shooting. That's why I mentioned craftsmanship before. And then some day I'll be old and sick; my legs will be weak, and my body won't be able to move; and then I won't be able to make films anymore.

Every Man for Himself and God against All: A Conversation with Werner Herzog on *The Enigma of Kaspar Hauser*

Hans Günther Pflaum / 1974

From "Jeder für sich und Gott gegen alle: Gespräch mit Werner Herzog über seinen neuen Film," *FILM-Korrespondenz* (Cologne) 20, no. 11 (November 13, 1974): 9–11. Reprinted by permission.

Werner Herzog's new film tells the story of Kaspar Hauser, the foundling discovered 1829 in Nuremberg. Around eighteen years old when he was discovered, he became a pedagogical case study for society, and in 1833 fell victim to an unexplained murder.

Hans Günther Pflaum: Mr. Herzog, two years ago you told me that you would like to make a film about Kaspar Hauser. You also mentioned [François] Truffaut's *Wild Child* and said it was unfortunate that this film had already been made. Now, *The Enigma of Kaspar Hauser* is no doubt a very personal film, which is unmistakably yours, but it may be your first film that permits comparison with that of another.
Werner Herzog: It might not actually do so. I would have also liked to have made *Wild Child*. I think Truffaut's film is really good, even if there are some things in it that I don't like. For me, it's too condescending.

HGP: And with Truffaut there are certain pedagogical intentions.
WH: Yes. Those, I think, I wouldn't have had. The situation in *The Enigma of Kaspar Hauser* is different. Kaspar Hauser is a Passion figure. Like the Passion Play, it is a story of abuses.

HGP: The structure of the film, which is clearly divided into stations, also corresponds to the Passion Plays, above all to the martyr plays of the Jesuits.

WH: There may be something to that. Another important reference point for me is the Passion film, especially [Carl] Dreyer's *The Passion of Joan of Arc.*

HGP: There also must be a close relationship to *Land of Silence and Darkness.*

WH: Sure, that's even closer. It may even be that *The Enigma of Kaspar Hauser* summarizes everything I've done so far. There are plenty of clues within the film itself as to when characters from my earlier films appear.

HGP: How did the script come about?

WH: I was at a friend's when I came across a book containing Kaspar Hauser's documents and testimonials. I had wanted to read it for years, then I did so all of a sudden, and it fascinated me so much that I immediately knew I had to make a film about it. I brooded over it for a while, and then, making one big push, I wrote a screenplay in two and a half days. It's a very loose version of the Kaspar Hauser story. Only the basic features adhere to the authentic case.

HGP: How about the lines of dialogue, which are indirect in the script, when they appear at all—where did they come from? Were they created during the shoot?

WH: Sometimes, yes. What I didn't want was some actor to have all the lines in advance and to start learning them. I wanted to have spontaneous, direct life in the dialogue, too. Normally I write the dialogue maybe fifteen minutes before we shoot a scene.

HGP: But there are parts of the dialogue that appear to be very literary. They hook into you almost like sayings. Were those also spontaneous?

WH: Some of them were already in the script, but there were others that came about more spontaneously. I write best when I am under pressure, when fifteen people are standing around me, setting up cameras, with no going back. It forces me to concentrate.

HGP: So how were the images created, like that unbelievable long shot when Kaspar first emerges from the cellar into the open?

WH: Those were thoughts that then developed. The script was written like a prose text, but it described images and atmospheres very precisely.

HGP: While you were writing, did you already know which landscape you were going to shoot?
WH: No, I looked for that later. You just mentioned the scene when Kaspar is carried out into the open. For me, that was the decisive aspect in searching for locations. I wanted to have the whole landscape, sort of like in pictures from the late Middle Ages, where a Madonna sits with the Christ child in the foreground, and an open window in the background shows an enormous landscape, in which total harmony prevails—cities, rivers, the ships that navigate them, wine growers reveling in the vineyards. . . . I tried in vain to find a garden situated on a slope, to use for the entire second half of the film, so that when you see two people talking, you can see about sixty kilometers beyond them into the landscape. I really wanted to find something like that, but it was too difficult.

HGP: So you created the garden yourself?
WH: For the most part. I had some help from a man who did extraordinary things for the film: Henning von Gierke made all the props and costumes. We worked extremely hard, and there's an unusual amount of detail in there.

HGP: Maybe that also explains the rather high production cost of 850,000 marks?
WH: Two circumstances made the film expensive: The actor playing Kaspar Hauser is not a professional, so we needed almost double the amount of time. And then there was the sync sound recording, which also took a lot of time. The decision to cast Bruno S. as Kaspar was also a decision to use sync sound. We had to cordon off entire districts of the city just to get really perfect sound. That makes a project expensive. We had a shooting ratio of about one to eight. And when you pan with the camera just once over the rooftops of the city, then you have to remove maybe fifty antennae; cars, traffic signs, power lines all have to go; in the streets, we had to cover the asphalt with dirt, etc.

HGP: These strange landscape shots were already in *Signs of Life*.
WH: All my films have views like those from a window, where all of a sudden you see something in the distance that's never been seen before,

that defies reality. They can also be found in *The Enigma of Kaspar Hauser*, but some of them are very simple and unspectacular.

HGP: It seems to me that you must have approached the Kaspar Hauser story with certain intentions, because the film brings together themes that run throughout your work: the character's isolation, but especially the unseen image, or the image that's seen for the very first time. And then there's the dream. Only here this theme is more closely connected with the main character.

WH: Yes, that's true. It's actually the first time that these kinds of images closely relate to one of the characters from my "family series," as I like to call them.

HGP: This intensive relationship between humans and landscape is nowhere to be found in films by any other German director, not at the moment, anyway.

WH: I can't explain the role of landscapes in my films. I just know they have great significance. I also have a very strong bodily relationship to landscapes.

HGP: But the relationship to landscapes in your films isn't just positive. In some way, they are also always shocking or threatening.

WH: That's true, I sense that as well. I wish I could say more about it. I see it, and I want to show it, but it eludes description.

HGP: Within your work, are there films in which the landscape came first, and the script or the story then followed?

WH: Yes, *Signs of Life* and *Fata Morgana* in its present form. Originally, there was also a science-fiction story, but that dropped out, leaving only the images, the views.

HGP: And if one day you no longer find the landscapes for your ideas. . . .
WH: Yes, that could happen. . . .

HGP: Perhaps you would try filming on the moon?
WH: Yes, but then only because of the situation here on Earth, to make something visible that only a lunar landscape could show.

HGP: What was it like shooting with Bruno S.? Did he change the film, and did the film change him?

WH: Bruno changed the film, because he completely brought himself into it. It was extremely intense and difficult work. As a consequence of his upbringing, Bruno carries within him devastations of a kind that I've never seen in another human being. He really gave to the film all of himself that he had to give. I think he changed in the course of filming, even physiognomically. He changed his living conditions; he no longer lives in such clutter, as he did previously. Even at his work, he's become more important. And he's much more easy-going. But his fundamental problems can't be solved, certainly not by the film. From the very beginning, I told him: Bruno, it's not in the film's power to make your isolation and hatred all of a sudden disappear.

Interview with Werner Herzog

Kraft Wetzel / 1976

From "Interview," *Herzog / Kluge / Straub*, ed. Peter W. Jansen and Wolfram Schütte (1976), 113–30. © Carl Hanser Verlag München Wien. Reprinted by permission.

Kraft Wetzel: Your previous interviews give only a partial sense of your autobiography. Were there certain experiences you had that were important to the development of your films?

Werner Herzog: I was often away and alone. I was in Africa, for example, although I never really wanted to go there. I had always been scared of it, of Black Africa. There are people who have such an appalling Hemingway-like desire for Africa, with Kilimanjaro, big game hunting, and manliness—I'm certainly not one of them. I've always seen the dreadful in it, the unpredictable. . . .

KW: In what sense?

WH: Just go to the Central African Republic, and then you'll know what I mean. When you're driving in a Land Rover and all of a sudden it's surrounded by a screaming mass of people, there's only one thing to do: step on the gas and get out of there, because you might not survive five minutes. In the Central African Republic or in the Eastern Congolese provinces, where there has always been tension—before we arrived, five Germans were shot and killed near Uganda, and nobody knows why— God knows what they'll do just because it's a full moon and they want to eat liver.

In the USA, I lived for a while in an old VW that was rusted right through the floor. It was winter and there were snowstorms, only terrible, much worse than here. When they have blizzards, it is twenty-five degrees below zero, and snow blows in through the bottom of the car. I had a cast on my leg, up to my hip, and it was always on the verge of freezing because I couldn't move it. I wrapped thick bundles of newspapers around my feet so they didn't freeze off.

29

At night, when it gets really cold, at three or four o'clock in the morning, there are people in New York City who live like Neanderthals—they come out at three o'clock, when it gets so cold they can no longer bear it. People gather in an empty, totally deserted street and set the trash cans on fire just to warm themselves, and they do so without saying a word. That's how it is there, only nobody sees it.

KW: So all these years had little to do with globetrotting and wanderlust?
WH: It's really like a desperate search for . . . well, for some place I can exist. By existence I mean something different from life. I've become increasingly more aware that there's a big difference between life and existence, and that it's important to even have an existence. There are many people for whom life and existence diverge and apparently have nothing to do with each other. It's easier to say it in biographical terms: Take [Franz] Kafka or Robert Walser. Kafka was just an employee of an insurance company. I also think there's something like a modern tendency for life and existence to deviate more and more. That happened earlier as well, but on a much smaller scale than it does now. Now you have people without existence—that is, they have lives but no existence.

Let me put it this way: I was recently in Brittany, where they have big old farm houses, each with just a single room, where the family and the cattle all live together. There are many legends and poems, which they sang, that come from there. I can imagine that for someone who lived back then in such a family community, there was no such thing as life and existence, but rather something that constituted them together and without separation.

KW: You say that you've produced all your own films. But according to your filmography, the first film, *Herakles*, was not self-produced.
WH: Yes, it was. I produced it myself, and then a producer took it over, around the time when I won the Carl Mayer Prize for the screenplay to *Signs of Life*. The producer thought he might get a prize too, so he invested money [in *Herakles*] retroactively, and had a sound-on-film version made, which I edited again, this time a bit differently.

KW: How did you arrive at this topic? First films tend to have everything thought out in advance. . . .
WH: That was alright, because back then I was fascinated with how images can be juxtaposed. It's a montage of materials that could never actually go together and yet they are supposed to make a film. In that respect,

the film was important, because I learned so much in the process of making it. I've never learned anything from someone else; I never went to film school or worked as someone's assistant. From all that I only learned how it shouldn't be done. I've never learned from good films, only from bad ones. I learned immediately, in the most radical ways, from the first embarrassment, and that was *Herakles*. I'm glad that I made it, because from that moment on I knew how I should really go about it.

KW: Can you say something about your second, unreleased film, *Game in the Sand*?
WH: There's a rooster in a cardboard box and some children. The theme appears in *Signs of Life*, albeit in milder form.

KW: Where does this fascination with chickens come from? They also appear prominently in *Even Dwarfs Started Small*.
WH: Chickens frighten me terribly. I am the first to show that chickens are cannibalistic and horrifying. The most horrifying thing is when you look at chickens straight in the eyes: that is stupidity staring back at you, death and stupidity. What makes this type of stupidity so terrible is that it's completely vacuous.
[. . .]

KW: How did *The Unprecedented Defence of the Fortress Deutschkreutz* come about?
WH: From the location. It's like that with almost everything I do: all of a sudden, a location begins to take on a life of its own. First comes the location, then the characters and the story. The film doesn't show reality, none of my films do; it shows the reality of dreams. I see so many people complain about this or that film having nothing to do with reality. A very simple example: Why do the women in *Aguirre*, at the very end, where everything is rotten and decayed, still have such beautiful clothes? People come up with all sorts of ideas and get all upset. I think the real power of films lies in the fact that they work with the reality of dreams.

KW: Power in what sense?
WH: I mean their staying power, and that they are the true chronicle of what our inner condition is. Even now, when we look at musicals from the thirties, we know that they are truly the chronicle of that time. That's how we know what people were during this time in the USA, not from

the historians, not from the newspapers that we get from the archives, but rather from the films—that's the most intensive chronicle of what the inner condition of these people is. Films that try so hard to capture real life, they don't have the power to do so . . . it doesn't go so well with film. (Documentaries are different; I'm talking right now about feature films.) I feel strongly about that, perhaps also because my own films go in this direction. It's self-defense, when I say that.

I also think that academics have yet to get a handle on what constitutes the staying power and the whole substance of film, and that precisely such things as comics and film—things that very powerfully reveal inner conditions, that come from down low, from the fairground and such—were at first totally overlooked by academics as phenomena, and then, when they later tried to analyze it and examine it academically, they failed. That shows me that real life is in there—in film.

I'm delighted to see that people who try to make films and take an academic approach to it fail. The film medium itself resists such attempts. Another example is how *Cahiers du Cinéma* corrupted itself in one fell swoop by putting itself in the service of structuralism, which is just one approach to film anyway—it's absolutely overblown academic nonsense. Within two years, the journal had slowly committed suicide. To observe this suicide, which actually wasn't intended—which, in a way, film itself forced them to commit—I watch it with enthusiasm.

KW: Was *Last Words* also a negative learning experience, like the first short films?
WH: No, that's my best film. Without that one, *Fata Morgana* would have been unthinkable, the very narrative forms and stylizations that I later went on to develop would have been unthinkable. This film was really a breakthrough. And it went so easily. I shot it in one or two days and edited it in one. Everything was perfectly clear and right.

KW: *Last Words* is actually the un-portrait of a man, about whom we learn very little.
WH: The film is based on a sort of backstory: There once was a deserted and decaying island where lepers had lived, and the island was completely evacuated. A single man remained, he refused to leave the island, and his relatives had him declared insane. He was deprived of his rights, and forcibly taken by the police to the mainland, to a decent, respectable life, so to speak, and since then he refuses to speak—except at night,

when he plays the lyre. You can just catch a little glimpse of all that. But the story itself isn't told, there's only . . .

KW: Reflections . . .

WH: Yes, and compulsive repetitions. Instead of argumentation there are compulsive repetitions. For example, the man who tells the tale of the last Turk's last footprint. He tells this story of the last Turk, who jumps off a cliff into the ocean, leaving a footprint behind him, on the edge of the cliff, and the Greeks build a chapel there. He has hardly finished telling the story when, in the same breath, he begins telling the same story again, and no sooner does he finish than he begins telling it a third time.

All of a sudden, beyond the compulsion in which he's caught, through all the agony, you get a sense of who this man is. This man, who also plays the lyre, is so close to me, he fascinates me. And yet, of course he speaks normally and is a very normal person, who's not crazy and constantly talking to himself, but then he says for several minutes straight: "No, I'm not saying a word, not a single word. I won't even say no. You won't hear a word from me. Not a word. If you tell me to say no, I won't even say that." For several minutes straight, he says he won't say another word.

KW: Turning to *Signs of Life*, your first feature-length film: How did you become interested in radical rebellion and radical failure, which runs throughout your work?

WH: I've actually tried to reflect on that. I think I'm just limited to that kind of theme. I've always wondered how other filmmakers have a range of themes, and how they decide which book they should now turn into a film. For me, I've never had the opportunity to do either this or that; it's always only this one. Looking back, I see there's a common theme.

KW: Do you notice that during the production or only after the films are done?

WH: I see it most clearly afterwards, of course, but I also know that the characters have a lot to do with each other. That's why I called the whole family together for *The Enigma of Kaspar Hauser*. There's the smallest dwarf from the dwarf film, a character from *Aguirre*, the Indian, Walter Steiner appears from the ski-jumper film [*The Great Ecstasy of Woodcarver Steiner*], the pianist from *Signs of Life*, who also composed the music for *Aguirre*, he appears once again as a pianist. The whole family is there.

KW: Symbolically, at least, but Kinski should really be there instead of the Indian.

WH: Right, but he doesn't have to be. The decisive figure in *Aguirre* isn't Kinski but the dull-witted man who plays the flute. The film is even dedicated to this man, though hardly anyone here knows that. He was a beggar we met at the market square in Cuzco, Peru. He was selling a few shears, and he was playing the flute and drumming on a tin can. He was slightly retarded, didn't even know his own name, which is why they called him Hombrecito, little man. He fascinated me so much that I told him I'd like to have him in a film, if he'd like to come along, and he could earn more money than he'd earn in ten years from begging here. He said, no, he can't, he's not allowed, because if he stops playing, then the people here [in Cuzco] will die. Every day I tried to convince him, but it was no use. And then, all of a sudden he came to me, full of joy, and said: yes, [if I come along] then the Indians who are dying out in the jungle won't die. In a way, he was a figure of suffering, because he was a bed-wetter, and nobody wanted to sleep in a hammock next to him. He was like a saint, a wonderful guy. He always wore three big alpaca-wool sweaters and wouldn't take them off, no matter how hot it was in the jungle. Every time we filmed, I had to persuade him to remove his sweaters. Yes, but somebody will steal them, he said. So we gave him a plastic bag, to put them in, and he buried it somewhere in the jungle, and later couldn't find it. Then the whole team had to fan out and dig for these buried sweaters, which was fine.

Sometime after the shoot I saw him again in Cuzco, he was back at the market square, begging. But instead of three sweaters he was wearing three jackets, one on top of the other. I asked him, because it had interested me for a while: "Hombrecito, why are you wearing three jackets at once?" He said it was protection against the evil breath of the gringos.

KW: You said that an idiot would've turned *Signs of Life* into a psychodrama. What's wrong with a psychodrama?

WH: I have something against idiots and against psychology too, of course, because it acts as though it were an established discipline, as though it were something like history or medicine. And yet the knowledge base they've secured is no greater than that of, say, cranial surgery in ancient Egypt. The second thing is this frivolity and a sense of what can and should be done with people, a sense they've yet to acquire—that people who are too preoccupied with themselves can become uninhabitable, unbearable as a result.

KW: What do you mean by "uninhabitable"?

WH: Like a room becomes uninhabitable—that is, horrifying and dreadful. Let me put it this way, if one were to illuminate everything with neon lights, under the bed and in every last corner, then I can no longer live in that room, it becomes uninhabitable. Such uninhabitable people are everywhere now, and that's something that psychology did.

But it's not just psychology's fault. It began the moment when people first looked into the mirror. Only now it's become a symptom of helplessness, like the centuries-long practice of blood-letting documented the helplessness of medicine, a document of helplessness in dealing with oneself and in living a decent existence.

I can't stand psychological films at all, that is what I can't stand about Bergman's films, all these parables and this excruciating psychobabble.

KW: Which came first in *Signs of Life*, the story or the location?

WH: The location. I went to [the island of] Kos very early on, when I was fifteen or so. My grandfather had done his life's work as an archaeologist there. He excavated there as a young man, from 1901 to 1907, approximately. Only later, in his seventies, he went mad, and I only really got to know him as a madman.

My grandfather is really very important to me, because he had a wonderful instinct for terrain. People had already spent eight hundred years searching for the asklepieion [an ancient healing temple] on Kos, and he's the one who found it. The last surviving worker from the dig, the Turk named Achmed, who appears in *Signs of Life*, a holy man—he led me around an enormous flat field. They had excavated ten different sites there and found nothing. For some reason my grandfather dug in the middle of the field and discovered a late Roman bath. Why did the man dig there, on this site alone? Somehow he was able to picture it: How did it look back then and where would I build it? The man had imagination. At a very young age, he became a professor of ancient philology, he was a man of books, who actually changed overnight. He left everything behind, grabbed a spade, and became an archaeologist.

I named my son after him and, incidentally, after Achmed too. Those are people who are very important to me. His name is Rudolph Amos Achmed. Amos comes from Amos Vogel, but that's another story.

KW: You began *Fata Morgana* before *Even Dwarfs Started Small*, but finished it only later. Did the films interact with each other as a result?

WH: I began *Fata Morgana* much earlier, first in Uganda and Kenya, while

I was making *The Flying Doctors of East Africa*. More than anything, we wanted to film John Okello. Okello was a man who came from Uganda, an outrageous figure, who led the 1964 revolution in Zanzibar, after a few months was expelled, then roamed around East Africa, and wanted to liberate Rhodesia and Mozambique and South Africa, and had only three loyal men. I wanted to make a film with him, but he was in prison.

Okello delivered these incredible speeches from an airplane. He circled around Zanzibar—he declared himself Field Marshal, I corresponded with him, and "Field Marshal" was printed on his letterhead—and before he landed, he had the aircraft's radio switched to the local radio station and delivered a short speech: "I, your Field Marshal, am about to land. Anyone who steals so much as a bar of soap will be thrown in prison for two hundred and sixteen years!" A bit of that obviously went into the figure of Aguirre.

For *Fata Morgana* I actually first had a screenplay, a science-fiction story—you can still find traces of it in the film—the story of a space-ship crew that lands on a strange planet and records what they see there—even though we know, of course, that it's Earth. People see trees, mountains, and human beings for the very first time. The film is like the very first awakening and astonishment. Without this film *Kaspar Hauser* would've been unthinkable, this amazed state of being awakened and suddenly seeing things for the very first time, which is also a very painful process. The film [*Fata Morgana*] is an attempt to see things differently, an attempt to understand people in a new way . . . like the dream sequences in *Kaspar* and the visions in the film I'm making right now (*Heart of Glass*).

Very briefly, then, after I got back from Africa, I shot the dwarf film, and this backstory is important, because it explains how the dwarf film became so radical and naked in its frustration. The other films are much more discrete and decent, but here it really screamed. That's why I always say, shoot it loud, the film has to shout at the spectator, and it hardly works if it isn't loud. That's why, at the retrospective, I said the format is important to me, 1:1.66, and turn the sound up as loud as it'll go.

KW: Did you think of *Even Dwarfs Started Small* as a dwarf film from the beginning, or were the story and the cast conceived independent of one another?

WH: I always saw the dwarfs very clearly before me. That has to do with something I always say: representing humanity, what we are on the most basic level, that there's always a search—with Kaspar, with *Land of Silence and Darkness*, with Aguirre and Stroszek—those are all figures where I try to probe into who we are and what our vision is. I want to be clear about what we are.

The laughter from the smallest dwarf at the end of the film—the laughter that goes on for several minutes—it's laughter per se. Just like there's vinegar and vinegar essence, the dwarfs in this film are the essence of humanity, in concentrated form. It's the acidity of the essence that allows us to see more clearly what we are.

KW: This desire to find out what we are, does it run through all your films?
WH: Yeah, I think so. *Kaspar* is a prime example, *Land of Silence and Darkness* is a prime example, even the film I'm making right now, because the actors are performing under hypnosis. I'm doing that in a most unspectacular way, never exploiting anyone; it's all done very safely. And yet, it's elevating in a particular way, which has never been made so fully or completely visible as it is here—not for me, at least. What exactly will come of it isn't yet really clear to me; at this point, I'm still experimenting. But I already know that it's a further step toward what I've been searching for all along, only coming from a different direction. It's really like the dwarf film, only sneaking around from the other side. [. . .]

KW: Where does the music in *Even Dwarfs Started Small* come from?
WH: One is a piece of folk music from the Canary Islands, but I altered it, taking away the entire instrumentation and changing the text a bit. I found a thirteen-year-old girl who could sing, and we recorded the music ourselves in this amazing cave. I paid her quite well, but then I said to her: "You have to scream your lungs out. Your soul should fly ninety-five kilometers out of your body, that's how loud you have to scream." The others, the choral pieces in the film, we recorded those when we were making *Fata Morgana*. On the Ivory Coast there's a man who claims to be the messiah. He works miracles and preaches at a lagoon, where fishermen live, and there he's created a theocracy on a very small scale. The fishermen built him an enormous temple on the sand, which holds four or five thousand people. On Sundays they gather and sing together in the temple, and that's what we recorded, because I immediately thought, that could be the music for the dwarf film.

KW: As far as *Fata Morgana*, why did you name the last two parts "Paradise" and "The Golden Age"? Those are rather facetious names for what we actually see there. . . .

WH: Yeah, that's right, because you see of course that it's not at all like paradise, you see what we've actually made of everything that is available to us. Where can you find a decent place to live? Where can you live at all? What remains and what has already been wasted?

There is also this religious rage in the film. For me, this is biographical. It can clearly be traced back to this intensely religious phase of my life, with conversion to Catholicism followed by a radical antitheism. I was really preoccupied with those things to a much greater extent than my peers. This rage against the meaningless of the world, against all these flaws, these innate inadequacies, that's in there too, of course.

KW: To me, *Precautions against Fanatics* seems like a humorous romp, like it was shot in a single afternoon.

WH: I learned a lot of important things from it about people who are put under intense pressure. The pressure comes, first of all, from the fact that they are prominent people and see themselves that way, and second, that they have been put under the external pressure of a foolish task. And then, all of a sudden, you catch a glimpse of something! Like physicists experimenting with materials, they learn something about a metal alloy only when it's exposed to extreme heat, extreme pressure, or extreme radiation.

KW: Is that what you did with the actors?

WH: A little, yeah. Anyway, all my films have people under considerable pressure—that is, people being sounded and tested under pretty extreme conditions.

KW: Next to *Herakles*, your least favorite among your films is *Handicapped Future*. Why?

WH: The film is too well-behaved. It's too polite and totally conventional. Today I probably wouldn't even make it, and if I did, then I'd be pushing much harder, without mercy, no longer shying away from a certain truth.

Land of Silence and Darkness, for example, doesn't shy away from anything. We went into an insane asylum, where we weren't even allowed to film. We just filmed everything we wanted to film, until the doctor there was called and threw us out.

KW: To what extent does *Land of Silence and Darkness* go beyond *Handicapped Future?*

WH: To the extent that we went there at all, to the extent that we were tapping and feeling our way ahead with Fini [Straubinger], pushing into areas she would never talk about, areas she'd never discussed before. For example, the farmer's son, who lived five years in a stall among cows, and who touches the tree [in the final scene]. That's where I thought: We can't film this anymore, you can't begin to approach that, it has to remain unfilmed. But then I said, "Oh, yes we can, and we must!"

KW: The most terrifying scene for me was the one with Vladimir—

WH: —because you stay with it so insistently. Truth always has its moment, and it always has a way of empathizing, and also of finding the right limit, and on some occasions you can only show it, venture forward, and subject the audience to it. That's what makes it so problematic. Aside from the dwarf film, this is the film that wore me out the most every day, because of what I saw and filmed. [. . .]

KW: Do you see a connection between Vladimir and Kaspar Hauser?

WH: Yes, it's obvious, the same kind of figure.

KW: Because I've always wondered where Kaspar Hauser begins.

WH: Look, it begins with me. There's always obviously a strong relationship between me and my protagonists. To me, Kaspar is like my own existence.

KW: And Fini Straubinger seems like a savior-figure. Was that intentional or . . .

WH: That is in fact what she is, and it somehow radiates. Those are people in whom a fire burns, it glows, and you can even see it from a distance. You can also see it with Bruno [Schleinstein, the actor who plays Kaspar], this powerful inner radiance. With both of them, there's this radical dignity they emit, and its radical quality comes from the tremendous sufferings they've endured. They radiate, like saints in the Middle Ages were painted with haloes. That's how I see them. And I always seem to find these people. That's what I want to see in the cinema, real people—people I want to be associated with.

KW: And yet, those are highly unusual figures, Fini and Bruno. . . .

WH: But we learn infinitely more about ourselves from them than we do from anyone else. Those are the ones who give us insights. For me, Fini and Bruno and Steiner are points of orientation.

KW: Aguirre's downfall gives much less reason for sadness than that of Stroszek, which you've described almost coldly.
WH: Friends who know me relatively well and who've seen all my films identify me most closely with *Signs of Life*. And that's why there's this somewhat harsh and awkward distance, I bring it into the film myself.

KW: Because it's too close to you?
WH: Yeah, a little, sure. Anyway, I want to make a film called *Stroszek*. It's going to be crazy, and I want to work with Bruno, with [Clemens] Scheitz, who played the scribe in *Kaspar*, with Burkhard Driest, and with the Prince of Homburg [professional boxer Norbert Grupe]. The film will mostly be about this constellation of people. It ends at a chair lift, which has stood still for the entire summer. Stroszek sets it in motion. The police arrive at dawn, but they can't shut it off, and the lift runs all day. Yeah, that's how it ends.

The one I'm doing now (*Heart of Glass*) also ends beautifully: I saw a place west of Ireland, a cliff protruding like a pyramid almost three hundred meters out of the ocean, the greatest natural drama imaginable. On top there's fog and steam and a slanting plateau. Thirteen hundred years ago, on this dramatic plateau, monks built cells like igloos. Hias [the main character] has a vision of a man who stands on top of the cliff. It's like the last place on the very last coast, where the people have yet to learn that the Earth is round. The few inhabitants there still believe that the Earth is flat and that it ends in an abyss somewhere far out there on the ocean. One man, insane, stands there, staring out over the ocean for years on end. After many years, a second man joins him, and together they stare out over the ocean. After two more years, two other men join them, and they all stare out over the ocean. One day, they decide to risk everything. They take a boat and row out to sea. A few women are wringing their hands in sorrow and four musicians appear on top of the cliff playing "The Waves of the Sea of Vigo," a composition from 1270. They sing of the waves and of this abyss that's shrouded in mystery. A castrato voice sings and they play the music. In the last shot you see the darkening ocean, big thick clouds, endless waves, and these four men rowing their boat out into the open sea, the water completely grey. That's how the film ends.

KW: One more question about *The Great Ecstasy of Woodcarver Steiner*: Is that even a documentary?

WH: Categorical questions like, "Is it or isn't it a documentary? Is it or isn't a feature film?" They actually don't interest me. But of course *Steiner* isn't a documentary film in the sense of *cinéma vérité*. I would love to go down in history as the one who gave *cinéma vérité* one last kick, and sent it tumbling down into the abyss, but that's not me, of course.

KW: Have you ever ski jumped?

WH: Yeah, I was really good. I jumped until I was fifteen, sixteen years old, and I was involved in some competitions. Sometimes I told Steiner, jokingly: "Walter, if I had continued, I would've been your only true competition." But he would win, because he really is the greatest.

Ski jumping is not just athletic. It's a mentality—that is, how one has already overcome death. It is a question of solitude, of surrendering oneself to the outer limits of what is still conceivable for a human being. That's what distinguishes the great ski jumpers, a mentality. You see it in Steiner, and that's why I say that I would be his only true competition, because those who think they're his competitors are really just athletes who think they can beat him athletically, and they can't.

KW: To me, *The Enigma of Kaspar Hauser* seems like your first "truly" German film. . . .

WH: The Kaspar film is dedicated to Lotte Eisner. That is very important because it creates a bridge to what was then the legitimate German film, in the twenties and thirties, with [F. W.] Murnau above all, and with [Fritz] Lang, [G. W.] Pabst, and others.

KW: Do you see yourself in this tradition?

WH: No, it no longer exists, it was completely cut off. We had to start from scratch, without tradition. Maybe it's a good thing that all the younger filmmakers had to begin working without this historical continuity. What's important to me is that there is legitimate German culture again. The right person, who blessed and sanctioned it, so to speak, like the pope used to crown the emperor—in our case, that was Lotte Eisner. If she says, "Yes, you're legitimate," then that's what we are, and no one can take that away from us.

Hypnosis as Means of Stylization:
An Interview with Werner Herzog

Horst Wiedemann / 1976

From "Hypnose als Mittel der Stilisierung: Ein Interview mit Werner Herzog," *Medium: Zeitschrift für Hörfunk, Fernsehen, Film, Bild, Ton* 6 (December 1976): 27–28. Reprinted by permission.

Horst Wiedemann: Do you think, with *Heart of Glass*, you will find success this time in German first-run movie theaters?

Werner Herzog: Yes, in Munich, the film should play at the "Eldorado." In other countries, though, I've been making it into first-run theaters for two or three years. In Paris, even before the German premiere, *Heart of Glass* is starting in ten theaters at once, including a very large cinema on the Champs-Élysées, two or three cinemas in the Latin Quarter, and so on.

HW: You once described yourself, from an economic standpoint, as being "on artificial respiration." Is that still the case?

WH: It's actually worse. Film funding is an instrument that is never even used on me. My previous films, including *Kaspar Hauser*, haven't brought in enough to be financially rewarded, but that's the principle of film funding. And the project development committee of the FFA [*Filmförderungsanstalt*, or German Federal Film Board] rejects my projects as a rule. *Heart of Glass* actually received funding, but only after the third attempt.

The fight never ends. Look at it this way: Last year, the number of movie-goers dramatically declined by around 15 percent. So theater owners, who have a sort of blocking minority on the project funding committee, now want to fund only so-called commercial projects, and yet they don't have the slightest idea what's "commercial." So they fund films like [Alfred Vohrer's] *Das Schweigen im Walde*, Hans Habe's *Netz*, or [Johannes Mario] Simmel's *Lieb Vaterland, magst ruhig sein* [*Dear Fatherland Be at Peace*, dir. Roland Klick, 1976], and all these films go on to play even less than *Kaspar Hauser*. For twenty-five years, they've been co-funding their own ruin, because they always appeal to the stupidity of viewers, instead of carefully and systematically cultivating a cinema public. While theaters here annually lose about 10 percent of their viewers, for the past six years I have personally gained 10 to 20 percent more viewers every year. So there's a dangerous, even fatal tendency behind all this, if all you fund are those types of films. It will end in catastrophe.

HW: Do you still draw the largest audiences abroad?
WH: Yes. In France, the theater owners have even developed a core audience. *Aguirre* ran in Paris for one year and eight months continuously, even though it never had a proper distributor and the film started in two tiny theaters.

HW: Will *Heart of Glass* be dubbed for foreign distribution?
WH: Half of the French copies are subtitled, but for the outskirts of Paris and for the suburbs—that is, for people not accustomed to subtitles—I want the film dubbed, in order for it to reach this part of the audience. And the language, instead of a Bavarian dialect, will be stylized as "biblical." Of course, you always lose a lot in translation, but at least *Heart of Glass* is easier to dub than, for example, *Kaspar Hauser* or *Even Dwarfs* . . . , films I didn't sell to people who wanted them dubbed.

HW: What was the purpose of hypnotizing your actors?
WH: That was done for reasons of stylization, and not for the purpose of gaining total "control." It's not about "making puppets dance," it's the fascination with seeing people as they've never been seen in the cinema. Ultimately, it could enable new insights into our own inner condition. Here we should recall *The Tragic Diary of Zero the Fool*, which was filmed by Morley Markson with a theater group at an insane asylum in Canada, and *Les maîtres fous*, which was filmed by Jean Rouch in Africa. At a mountain hideout, in Ghana, a group of Africans enter a trance, after taking some heavy drugs, and mimic the arrival of the Queen and the English governor. It's a film that, when you see it in the cinema, makes your heart stand still. Our situation, too, was largely experimental, although we took precautions by conducting preliminary experiments.

HW: What was the aim of these experiments?

WH: The aim was to develop a catalog of suggestions which would result in a stylization [of behavior] that approaches somnambulistic unconsciousness. So it was about "programs" that are retrievable—not: "You are the most talented singer in the world," but more like: "You are moving in slow motion because the room in which you find yourself is filled with heavy water. You have an oxygen tank, of course. Under water it's difficult to maneuver, although your body has become almost weightless. You're drifting. You're not walking, you're drifting." Or: "You look at your partner, but you look right through him, as you look through a window." Or: "Your partner is emitting so much heat (or coldness) that it makes you feel warm (or shudder)."

HW: What's the point of all that?
WH: Maybe I can better describe this idea in terms of its origin. There's this probing for new images—windmills in *Signs of Life*, dream visions in *Kaspar Hauser*, mirages in *Fata Morgana*—and this probing for new insights into ourselves. The attempt to make inner conditions transparent from a certain perspective takes nightmarish form as a vision of horror in *Even Dwarfs Started Small* (where the dwarfs were like an essence, a concentrated form of humanity), and it takes different forms under ecstatic conditions (*The Great Ecstasy of Woodcarver Steiner*) and under the condition of non-participation in everyday social activities (deaf-blind children in *Land of Silence and Darkness*, Bruno S. in *Kaspar Hauser*).

It's important to say that, in all these examples, none of the people are deformed, not even the dwarfs. In that case, it's the objects that are monstrous, the forms of oppression, the education models, the table manners. With none of these people did it ever affect their identity. They merely represented themselves on a very high level of stylization. It's the same thing in *Heart of Glass*. Their identity was never even touched, nobody was deformed.

HW: How did it work in practical terms?
WH: Over a certain period of time we searched for a core of actors (professional and non-professional), first according to type and second according to their hypnotizability, which widely varies in terms of its depth and its outward appearance. Some people, when hypnotized, sink into a sleepy, apathetic state and lose their mobility as a result. Others are so somnambulistic that they can hardly find their bearings. Still others are so normal in their attitude that they can hardly be distinguished from people who aren't hypnotized.

HW: Have you ever shown films to hypnotized spectators?

WH: I showed *Fata Morgana* and *Aguirre* to a hypnotized audience and discovered that there really can be a new viewing position—that is, a visionary position—which of course varies individually.

But I have to add something very fundamental. Hypnosis only works so long as there's a rapport between the hypnotized and the hypnotizer. But there's no one to create that rapport in a one-and-a-half-hour film. The big question, then, was how to delegate that role to the occurrences within the film, to specific situations, to the voice of a person in the film, and so on. Before showing *Aguirre*, for example, I played a piece of music that the audience would hear several times in the film, and I told them: "Whenever you hear this music, it will give you a very strong impulse, and then you will sink back down into a deep hypnosis." In hypnosis, with the help of music, such as theme music, you can give very strong signals.

Then I tried to create the rapport myself for the duration of a film. I said: "So long as this film runs, you will constantly remain deep under hypnosis." On the first attempt, we had about thirty-five people under hypnosis, three of whom fell asleep during the film. When I called them out, these three all protested, claiming they had seen the entire film. In recounting the film, then, they embellished almost the entire second half in the most imaginative way. For them, this thing went in a direction that they couldn't entirely reconcile with the film. For many of the others, however, it was an incredible visionary experience, one that they'll never forget.

HW: Could that also be verbalized?

WH: By analogy. One person had the feeling he was in a helicopter and was flying around within the film, circling around the characters. Of course you have to be very prudent and careful with the whole thing. I would say that putting an audience under hypnosis in order to thoroughly explore this thing—that should never be a public event, under no circumstances.

HW: And yet, you wondered in *Heart of Glass*, if you appeared on screen at the beginning of the film, whether you could hypnotize the audience by addressing them directly.

WH: Correct, and you can do that. But then I said to myself, you mustn't do that for any reason, because I am not there during the hypnosis to observe what's happening. It carries certain risks for one in every thousand people, and that's why it's not allowed.

HW: You've given hardly any interviews on *Heart of Glass* until now, and at first you were also very reluctant to give this one. Why?

WH: With this film, everyone's searching in vain for comparisons, because there's no precedent for hypnosis in film. Here [in Germany] almost nobody views a film spontaneously, like one can experience music spontaneously; there is always this tremendous burden of cultural associations. The second reason is that I worry about an obsessive gawking at the whole hypnosis phenomenon, even though what I've done is quite unspectacular and inconspicuous.

An obsessive gawking at hypnosis and an obsessive gawking at the prophetic word, that's what people have come to expect from me. The press kit for *Kaspar Hauser* included a half-page explanation of the Kaspar Hauser phenomenon, which I had written. And in one form or another it reappeared in 80 percent of the reviews. In their uncertainty or in their laziness, critics simply copied it. None of them had their own ideas, and I am tired of being taken for a prophet. The seduction is so great that this time, in the press kit, I decided to say nothing at all about the film.

Interview with Werner Herzog

Eric de Saint-Angel / 1978

From "Entretien avec Werner Herzog," *Lumière du cinéma* 11 (January/February 1978): 12–14. Translated by Japhet Johnstone. Reprinted by permission.

With his searing gaze and vibrant voice, Werner Herzog looks like a character right out of one of his films. Something about him is reminiscent of Aguirre, the superhuman adventurer, or Kaspar Hauser, a stranger to this world. The thirty-three-year-old Bavarian belongs to a breed of grand dreamers. He does not belong to any school or any current trend. All alone, with the "obstinacy of an ox," he pursues a powerfully original body of work punctuated by disconcerting parables. He says again and again that his own life is of no importance—only his work is important and he must devote himself entirely to it, whatever obstacles and risks might stand in his way. Until now his compatriots have shown little but indifference towards his work. With his most recent film, *Stroszek*, all that has changed.

In his office on Karl-Theodor Strasse in Munich, Werner Herzog gives the impression of being a researcher haunted by a quest for some ultimate goal, instead of a filmmaker who has recently gained notoriety. His reputation as a difficult director comes above all from *Heart of Glass*, even more than from *Aguirre* and *Kaspar Hauser*. An obscure legend from Bavaria, where Herzog spent the first eleven years of his life with no knowledge of High German, the film seems to sound the depths of dreams while concealing its illuminated meaning only for rare initiates. There was even a rumor that the director hypnotized each of the actors in order to get them to perform with a supernatural air. That was almost going too far. . . .

Eric de Saint-Angel: *Stroszek* is surprising in its simplicity and even mundanity. Are you aware that some of your other films have not been so easily accessible?

Werner Herzog: I believe all my films are immediately comprehensible. *Stroszek* is simply the most narrative of my films. Personally, I don't think that the cinema should subject itself to the imperatives of narration. In *Fata Morgana*, one of my first films, or in *Heart of Glass*, narration is less important than visions, stylization, or prophecies. It's a deliberate choice.

Q: *Stroszek* achieves an authenticity in its agony that is rarely attained in the cinema—no doubt due to your demand for this physical expression of reality. It is as if reality were constantly trying to outdo fiction. It's a simple story: three outsiders, a fool, an old man, and a whore, leave Germany and a society that rejects them for America, the land of liberty, tolerance, and happiness. But this is a mere illusion, and the American dream becomes a nightmare. Is there symbolism here?

WH: Of course not. Bruno, the main character, who played the hero in *Kaspar Hauser*, is a human being, an authentic being, not a symbol. And the agony that his gaze expresses is authentic agony. I discovered him thanks to a television documentary made about him by a young German director. His face immediately struck me, the face of a man who had spent most of his life in prisons and psychiatric hospitals. I had never met another human being who had been so destroyed by society. I knew then that he was the only one capable of becoming the character Kaspar Hauser, who himself spent his life locked in a cellar, where he was fed by an invisible jailor, and was then suddenly set free. The extraordinary thing is that in spite of his suffering Bruno kept his dignity. In that respect, he is like a saint. And this type of extremely painful dignity can be seen here for the first time on a movie screen.

Q: After *Kaspar Hauser* you insisted that Bruno S. receive an Oscar for Best Actor.

WH: It's an injustice that he didn't receive anything. Instead, John Wayne was given an award in his place. But I will demand another Oscar this time for *Stroszek*. You understand, I am not asking, I am demanding because I am proud to be among those who are erecting a monument for the glory of the only unknown soldier that the cinema has ever known.

Q: The heavy silhouette of Kaspar Hauser appears again in *Stroszek* with that dazed look turned inward and his strange way of emphatically reciting the most common phrases—like a child repeating adult words. He is like an illiterate person accustomed to the Berlin dialect who is forced by you to say the lines in High German. . . .

WH: It was very difficult to get in touch with him. His life experience taught him to be suspicious of everyone, above all new people. During the filming of *Stroszek* and *Kaspar Hauser,* Bruno refused to quit his job at the steel factory where he worked in Berlin and requested unpaid holiday time. But his true calling, the job that he loves, is that of a street musician. Like in the film, he sings old songs in courtyards accompanied by an accordion. Bruno is undoubtedly the last street musician in Berlin.

Q: Does the film include other autobiographical details?

WH: Yes, the apartment in Berlin that we see him in is his. He bought the three-room place with his pay from *Kaspar Hauser* as well as the piano, which appears in the scene where the hooligans humiliate Bruno on top of it. Of course, the story itself is made up. The real Bruno never immigrated to the United States. He never had problems with pimps or prostitutes. And Stroszek is not his real name. Bruno wanted to remain anonymous. . . . But his own proper identity shows through in the "background." You remember the scene in the mobile home in Wisconsin, where Bruno is in despair because Eva—the prostitute with whom he is in love and whom he snatched from the hands of the pimps—no longer wants to sleep with him? It caused an old memory to resurface: As a child in a detention center, a youth worker forced him to hold out the sheet he soiled at night to dry it with his arms. He had to do this in front of all his peers in the courtyard and did it until his arms hurt so bad that he began to cry from the pain. That's also part of what makes up Bruno S.'s "background."

Q: What about the two other actors, the old man and Eva?

WH: Clemens Scheitz, the old man, is also a marvelous human being outside of the film. He's not a professional actor. But let me emphasize this again, I do not differentiate between professional actors and other actors. . . . Like in the film, Scheitz is an old man who is a bit disturbed. And also like in the film, he is obsessed with the idea of a world that can be completely explained through mathematical formulas, which, according to him, proves that Einstein and Newton were fools. As for Eva Mattes, she is one of the best actresses of her generation. She has done a lot of acting in the theater and in Fassbinder's films. I am happy to have made a film with them that touches the heart before troubling the mind. I say that because I always see a sort of spontaneous sympathy between the audience and the three heroes whenever I have gone to a screening of the film.

Q: So it's not an intellectual film?

WH: *Aguirre* and *Kaspar Hauser* weren't intellectual films either. They are works of spontaneity, like all my films. But certainly, if what you mean to say is that *Heart of Glass* was a much more difficult film, even impenetrable in certain aspects, and much less accessible than *Stroszek*. . . . Well, *Heart of Glass* demanded from the viewer the same kind of effort that a mountain demands from a climber. But once he arrives at the summit, he can indulge in his view of a rare landscape with drunken pleasure.

Q: Are aesthetics a fundamental concern of yours?

WH: It's not something I worry about. I don't map it out like an engineer with graph paper and a ruler. The aesthetic is something that impresses itself on each individual film—necessarily so, it is not arbitrary or gratuitous. For me, making films is not aesthetic work but athletic, in the sense that it is my body, my "body instinct," with which I apprehend the space that I can then organize and dominate, and in which I get the actors moving. Before filming *Kaspar Hauser*—in Dinkelsbühl, a small, sleepy city with old gable buildings—I spent a month plowing a potato field in order to turn it into a vegetable garden. And while I was planting strawberries and green beans I got a perfect sense of the space—a physical and instinctive sense for the space. This became useful when shooting scenes there.

Q: Speaking of scenes, the closing scene of *Stroszek* is really intriguing. America was a mirage. Bruno has just committed suicide. Then for three long minutes the camera focuses on musical chickens and ducks in a strange zoo run by Indians. Is this sequence intentionally ambiguous?

WH: The people who watch this and laugh are right to laugh. Those who do not are right, too. I like laughter that is a spontaneous reaction to an image in a film. And I really like it when people laugh while at the same time wanting to bite their tongue to keep from laughing because it's sad. . . . In any case, it is not up to me to provide a recipe or some ideal rule for a behavior pattern when watching the final scene.

Q: But why this scene then?

WH: I don't know. I can't understand what drove me to shoot it. Like with the beginning of *Aguirre* (the slow march of the conquistadors through the tropical mountains) or the end of *Heart of Glass* (that protruding rock in the middle of the ocean where the world-weary recluses live out an experience of absolute solitude), as with these sequences, the final sequence in *Stroszek* is also a perfect one. It's beyond me. It contains some part of me that escapes my own analysis. It's this dream moment, like in soccer, when you score a goal from an angle that is theoretically impossible. . . . I don't ever regret filming these sequences. In any case, I love all my films with their qualities and their faults. It's like the love one has for crippled children.

Q: How was filming in the United States?
WH: The first thing that comes to mind is how cold it was in Wisconsin and North Carolina. But apart from that inconvenience, everything went very calmly. Toward the end of our stay, the unions wanted to send a representative to us. We made an appointment to meet in Death Valley, where we never actually went for filming, and then we lost touch.

Q: In *Kaspar Hauser* there is a sense of German heritage in the romantic tradition. In *Heart of Glass* there's a sense of Bavarian tradition. Are the Berlin scenes in *Stroszek* an effort to reconnect to pre-war German expressionist cinema?
WH: What you are saying is accurate. Expressionism was part of German cultural heritage. But you must not forget that thirty years of barbarism irreparably severed the path of tradition in Germany. For thirty years we had the worst cinema in the world, after having had one of the best. This phenomenon of rupture was not as definitive in France, Italy, Russia, or even Japan. This means, however, that German cinema today is very fresh because it is starting from scratch. . . . And besides, I am Bavarian, not German. And that's a difference as big as the one between a Scotsman and an Englishman.

Interview with Werner Herzog on *Nosferatu*

Simon Mizrahi / 1979

From "Entretien avec Werner Herzog," *Écran 77* (February 15, 1979): 44–46. Translated by Laura McKee and Japhet Johnstone. Reprinted by permission.

Simon Mizrahi: You have said that, for you, Murnau's *Nosferatu* is the most important film in the history of German cinema.
Werner Herzog: Yes.

SM: So why remake *Nosferatu?*
WH: I did not want to remake *Nosferatu.* My film stands entirely on its own. It is a completely new version that we're dealing with here. The context and the characters are different, and the story is somewhat different. But you're right, I feel very close to Murnau. He is my favorite German director. In fact, I rank him well above Fritz Lang. He sees things much too geometrically.

Murnau's *Nosferatu*, made in 1922, is the most visionary film in all of German cinema. It's a premonitory film that prophesized the arrival of Nazism with its depiction of the invasion of Germany through Dracula and his plague-infected rats. He gave German cinema a legitimacy that was lost during the Hitler era. That is why the film has taken on such importance for me. We belong to a generation of orphan filmmakers with no recourse to tradition, with nothing to fall back on. There is no equivalent in France, the Soviet Union, or Italy, where they were able to secure cultural continuity. In Germany, by contrast, there was a hiatus, an emptiness that nothing will ever fill. Before the war, we had important philosophers, composers, and mathematicians. All that came crashing down. The missing links in the chain can never be replaced. But a certain affinity exists between our current cinema and that of the twenties. It is not so much about a similarity in style as it is a similarity in attitudes toward film production. There is a collective way of envisioning cinema as an art, as a serious mode of expression.

SM: All over the world, we live in fear. It has become our daily fate.
WH: Yes, without a doubt. Personally, I am not afraid, but I find that our society is becoming terribly oppressed and repressed. This climate of oppression consequently reflects itself in literature and cinema.

And then there is this strange phenomenon—we are witnessing the birth of a counter-culture that is reacting against a society that has become highly sophisticated, rationalist, and hyper-mechanized.

It's no accident that English literature at the beginning of the last century offers so many vampire and mystery stories. It was an age of "light." It was the same during the 1920s, when the machine was booming but simultaneously depleting itself. And vampire films often tend to appear after failed revolutions.

I have not studied the question in depth, but I am sure that works in this genre are propelled by exterior elements. I myself cannot escape the influences exerted on a society like ours.

SM: And yet, you insist on telling audiences that your film, in its tone and concept, is not a remake of Murnau's work. Could it be said that this is *Nosferatu* revisited?
WH: It's difficult to explain. One thing, however, is clear: The two films are inspired by the same novel, Bram Stoker's *Dracula*, which is, in my opinion, a bad novel. It's a sort of compilation of all the vampire stories from the period. Of course, I don't live in the twenties, and my ideas are not like any that one could have had back then. I wouldn't have had any trouble making *Nosferatu* if Murnau's film had not existed. But I feel so much respect for his films that I even tried to literally cite him one or two times by deliberately filming the same shots as him. For example, the vampire's lair—the only setting that still exists—is in Lübeck, a city destroyed during the Second World War. There I found the famous salt storehouses that served as Dracula's hideout. And I tried to frame them the same way Murnau did. But the shrubs that were there in 1922 have now been replaced by large trees.

SM: Lucy can come across as quite perverse. She hates the vampire, and yet she feels a strange desire and a distinct erotic attraction for him.
WH: She is indeed an ambiguous character, split between attraction and

repulsion, between horror and love. You see this very clearly in one of the final sequences, when the vampire goes to find her in her room. She then gives herself to him with horror but also with revelry and sensual delight. It was extremely difficult for an actress to express sentiments as contradictory as these, and I believe that Isabelle Adjani did an admirable job.

As for Klaus Kinski, he is sensational. He is the Vampire with a capital "V." After Murnau's film, no one has seen anything like him, and I am certain that for the next fifty years no other actor will be able to equal his performance. I can't imagine there ever being another vampire as superb as him.

SM: Why did you give the role to Kinski? Strictly speaking, that decision couldn't have been easy or obvious.
WH: No, it's true. Kinski has something very special about him. He is the only genius that I know. I insist on putting it this way, even though it must seem outrageous.

SM: What is surprising, and what constitutes perhaps the main difference between your film and other vampire films, is that your *Nosferatu* expresses a vampire's unhappiness, his pain, his suffering, what one might call his existential angst.
WH: Of course, it is an attempt to push the "genre" in a new direction. My vampire comes across as so profoundly human, so parched for love, so miserable in his solitude, and so incurably sad that two minutes into watching the audience no longer sees the ugliness in his long nails, his pointed ears, and his snake-like teeth.

There is still something else that differentiates this film from other vampire films: namely, the freedom that I give to fantasy, to the imagination. The gypsies warn Jonathan about the dangers of the Borgo Pass because that is where the land of phantoms, the kingdom of the imagination, starts. They tell him that the castle is nothing more than a heap of rubble, that it only exists in men's imaginations, and that anyone who has ever ventured past the Borgo Pass has never returned.

In fact, I never show a real castle in my film, but only the ruins of a castle and that creates ambiguity. You catch yourself asking, does this castle really exist or is it just a pile of ruins? Is the vampire real or is he an imaginary creature?

SM: It's tempting to say that *Nosferatu* as well as *Kaspar Hauser* and the hero of *Stroszek* all belong to the same family, whose members are rejects, humiliated and slandered. Nobody seems to try to understand Nosferatu, and yet there is something so human about him that his death saddens us.

WH: That's because on top of bringing desolation to a city by introducing ten thousand rats and the plague, he also brings joy and something like redemption to that same city. I even filmed a scene where Isabelle Adjani, in a moment of clairvoyance, tries to prevent two men from stealing furniture thrown onto the central town square. "Why are you stealing this furniture, poor fools!" she says to them. "You will no longer have any need for this furniture or for your good manners, because, along with the rats, we have ushered in the era of redemption!" But I ended up cutting this scene because I thought it was pointless to beat the audience over the head. Still, Nosferatu's presence is perceived as the presence of a savior, but a savior with an ambiguous message, because he brings both disaster and redemption.

Interview with Werner Herzog on the American Reception of His Films

Jörg Bundschuh and Christian Bauer / 1979

From an unpublished transcript of an interview conducted at Francis Ford Coppola's house in San Francisco, California. Deutsche Kinemathek—Museum für Film und Fernsehen, Sammlung Werner Herzog. © Werner Herzog Film. Published by permission.

Question: In America, German filmmakers are subsumed under the notion of "New German Cinema." Do you like the fact that you all fall under one category?

Werner Herzog: I think being pulled into the vicinity of other filmmakers isn't such a bad thing in itself. Here in America it's called "New German Cinema," but at the same time people here know that it's not a single stylistic or thematic trend, but rather a strong movement by young people working with very different themes and styles. That's why people speak less of a "school," as they do with the Italian neo-realists, than they speak of individual names. The trouble is, the Americans aren't in a position to absorb more than three or four names. The rest don't exist for them. There are actually fifteen or twenty really good filmmakers among us. Why, then, don't people talk about Reinhard Hauff or Werner Schroeter, or others?

Q: What significance does the Pacific Film Archive have for the reception of your films in the United States?

WH: It is somewhat like the Cinématheque in Paris. I mean, the Cinématheque at the time when [Henri] Langlois still ran it. America is very difficult for German filmmakers, because it is a completely self-enclosed cultural area, which actually doesn't open its doors. The Pacific Film Archive began showing my films here very early, which allowed me to build up a particularly strong base. From there, word began to spread—and it spread like wildfire—that something special was going on, and that somehow kept me going.

But the Pacific Film Archive should not be seen so abstractly, as if to say, "There is the institution of such and such." That sounds so fusty, like some elite cinématheque, when in fact it is fundamentally different. It is a person: Tom Luddy, a relatively young man, who has now grown into the role that Langlois once had. Langlois was something like the world's cinematic conscience. And there has yet to be a successor.

So who is our hope? Who is the man who can support and reveal entire stylistic movements? One day that will be Tom Luddy. Of that I'm completely convinced.

Q: How has Tom Luddy been important to you?
WH: Many years ago, when I had made only one or two films, he invited me to present them. He introduced me to the audience and said: "Pay close attention, because what you're about to see is going to be something very special. And if you don't like it, I'll hack off my own arm." He actually put his reputation on the line, and he did so in order to reveal something that had previously been forgotten in this country [what Herzog elsewhere calls "legitimate" German cinema].

Luddy managed to show my films in a way that was consequential. All my films have found distributors here. And now, for example, I have produced a film that was in part financed by Twentieth Century Fox—namely, *Nosferatu*.

Q: Luddy obviously has good connections to the American film industry?
WH: Many people call him a director's director. Maybe that is the best way to describe him. There were finished films, such as [Hans Jürgen] Syberberg's *Hitler*—Luddy arranged for Coppola to buy it—and there are many similar examples. He has yet to directly broker any financial deals. He probably never will, and shouldn't, but he has prepared the ground for them. I can give you a specific example.

Right now, I'm working on a project in Peru, a really big film called *Fitzcarraldo*. I always wanted to have Jack Nicholson as the lead. It was Luddy who put me in contact with Nicholson. He actually showed him three or four of my films, and they made such an impression on Nicholson, that he said he absolutely wanted to work with me and wanted to meet me. I am not yet sure whether he will actually play the role, but the conditions have been created, which will certainly have an effect on any financial deal. If I were to sign a contract with Jack Nicholson today,

I would have the money that I need within forty-eight hours. It would take only three or four phone calls.

Q: But Luddy has also introduced you to independent filmmakers who work outside of Hollywood.
WH: Yes, inevitably. You can hardly go a day in the Pacific Film Archive without stumbling over Glauber Rocha, Dušan Makavejev, Jean-Luc Godard, Les Blank, or some other filmmaker. Somehow they're always there and some even stay at Tom's house.

But how should I put it? I often don't know where to begin with them. There are some people whom I personally like very much, but I don't know what I should say to them. I actually never speak with other filmmakers about film. I may say to Glauber Rocha, "I like your tie," or maybe we talk about soccer.

Q: To come back to the screenings that took place at the Pacific Film Archive: Were there any reactions that surprised you?
WH: I first got to know the American public much earlier, with *Signs of Life*, at the New York Film Festival. But there's something special here in Berkeley, and you can actually feel it: An audience that understands so much about film, it's like no other audience in the world. I always thought there would only be smug, bored reactions from people with academic training who then go out and write something smug for some journal. But here in Berkeley there was actually a very spontaneous and lively reaction. A few years ago, when I had difficulty financing a new film, people asked me about it, and I said: "I don't have enough money. I don't know how to raise it." For days, people in Berkeley tucked money into my pocket or cooked meals for me. In Germany, nobody has ever put a ten-mark bill in my pocket.

Fitzcarraldo: A Conversation with Werner Herzog

Bion Steinborn and Rüdiger von Naso / 1982

From "Werner Herzog: *Fitzcarraldo*: Ein Gespräch," *Filmfaust* 26 (1982): 2–15.
Interview conducted January 16, 1982. Reprinted by permission.

Question: In the brief preliminary conversation we had just a minute ago, you said: "I just want to take a break and not make any more films for a few years. I want to do something else." There was something in your tone that sounded like exhaustion. Was that perhaps a sign of resignation or have the years of shooting *Fitzcarraldo* taken an inner toll?
Werner Herzog: No, no, not at all. I definitely want to continue making films. I can't do anything else, apart from writing. But, of course, you have to be careful. It's just like with top athletes, who train so hard over a very short period of time that they end up destroying themselves. Professional soccer players, for example, have to learn how to rest and how to get into shape. The work of filmmaking cuts to the very core of existence. Indeed, it has already ruined too many lives. So you have to be careful. You see it more clearly in actors who've been working intensively for years. They become clowns. . . .

Q: Do you mean their ability levels off? Or are you trying to say the creative essence somehow gets lost?
WH: No, I wouldn't say that. It's something else. You're an illusionist—filmmaking is the work of illusionists. And at some point the work of illusionists should be interrupted by the real. When I return to Germany, after so many years abroad, everything here seems bizarre to me, and not right. The prevailing condition here is insane. Everything is totally sick and insane. And the people who make films suffer from a similar illness. One should really be doing something tangible on the side.

Q: Does "tangible" mean a more direct confrontation with reality or with nature?

WH: No, it doesn't necessarily mean that at all. During the shoot, for example, we had direct confrontation with nature there, as well—so direct that I lost my shoes. In the jungle they quickly fall apart. So I just walked around barefoot like the Indians. For months I slept in hammocks, felled trees, removed stumps, mucked around in the mud. You see what I mean? It was all concrete, tangible work.

Q: And yet you view this work as illusory?

WH: You can't really classify it that way, because in fact we hauled an enormous steamship over a mountain. That's no longer an illusion; it's real work. And yet it's work that can't really be done. It's difficult for me to explain. All I know for certain is this: I need to get some distance, to do something else for a while, in order to find solid ground again, to regain a clear relationship to film. I really want that. And if I pull out, then I won't be doing so in order to go on vacation, but because I have another project, a very specific one in mind, one that I would really like to do. Rather than lead me away from film, it will bring me back even closer.

Q: So you're burned out and you want to gather new energy from some other activity?

WH: No, not at all. That's certainly not what I need. I can't even speak in such terms. Energy, for me, comes from eating. From food.

Q: And not from the imagination as well . . . ?

WH: No. Energy is something gained from the ingestion of a foreign substance, which is then transformed into a bodily substance that produces energy so I can move. When I walk up the stairs, I use energy. And it comes from food and from nothing else. I can't stand it when people talk about vibrations, energy, and such nonsense. That's an utterly stupid concept, and I'll have no part of it. My energy comes from food.

Q: Already with *Aguirre*, but maybe especially with *Fitzcarraldo*, I had the sense that for you the process of work is so important—as opposed to the results, however great they may happen to be—that I have to ask whether the results are ultimately what matter for you. You once said—

WH: —I'm interrupting you, because I don't want you to continue. The result has always been the only thing that counts. Nothing else has ever really mattered, not me, not the work, not the process, or anything. And that's what makes it bearable. I've always said that my personal feelings, my exhaustion, my doubts or whatever, none of that counts, it doesn't exist.

[. . .] I hate it when people hype up films—how incredibly difficult it was to make, how expensive, and so on—and then the films are bad, like *Apocalypse Now*, for example. That's basically how it went. Incidentally, *Apocalypse Now* was like kindergarten compared to what we had to do, overcoming obstacles, for example. In the end, Coppola solved every problem with cash money. The resulting film is all that counts, and that's what you should be looking at. That's what it's all about and always has been. I've always had problems showing journalists that they should really be writing about the film, and not about how long it took to make, how much money was spent, whether I shaved my mustache— all of that is totally irrelevant. It doesn't matter.

Q: Elsewhere you once said that film is your ticket to life. . . .
WH: I wasn't referring to myself personally. Filmmaking is the only thing that connects me with other people, brings us together, and connects me with life.

Q: In that case doesn't the process of work become indistinguishable from one's personal life?
WH: There's never been a distinction. I've never distinguished between them. That's why I never take vacation, for example. Vacation is something I simply can't understand. It's a completely foreign concept to me. Not that I'm a workaholic—of course, I've worked a lot and very intensively—but what taking vacation really means is that you step out of your work and say, here is work, and there is life. On vacation, then, you live out the desires you have in life. At any rate, I don't have any life goals. I have existential goals.

It always seems odd to me that people want to be happy. Happiness is a life goal. The question why isn't so essential to me, why am I unhappy, why am I happy? And the reason why isn't ultimately decisive for me. There's no distinction, for me, between life goals and existential goals.

Q: What you're calling happiness is, for you, really the concept of existence as opposed to that of life in general.
WH: I don't want to get philosophical now. But believe me, I've thought about this question for a long, long time. And I'd have to go into way too

much detail, in order to explain what I understand by existence, by life, by existential goals, and by life goals.

Q: We're not asking you to do that. But maybe you have ideals? Life ideals?

WH: For me, this word is too hackneyed. It's suspicious. But let's say I have questions of faith or a clear vision and I try to follow it and make it visible for others. But even that's too abstract. For years now, I've really been working like a madman knee-deep in the mud. That's what we should be discussing. But you shouldn't think that I don't know what I'm talking about. I've really given it a lot of thought.

Q: This exhaustion, which you said will keep you from making films, at least for a while—

WH: —Excuse me. I'm not exhausted. When you look at me, you can see that I'm healthy and fit. In fact, at the end of these four years of filming in the jungle, I was in such good condition that I immediately—after the team and the actors went home—wanted to begin shooting the next film. My Peruvian assistant [Jorge Vignati] and I were about to begin, when we realized it needed more preparation than we had thought, so we postponed everything.

We had a number of misfortunes [while making *Fitzcarraldo*]. We had a plane crash, and who knows what else—earthquakes, the most terrible things happened that we all had to endure. And then, after the negatives were developed in New York, all the material had to be shipped via airfreight to Germany. So I said to my second cameraman [Rainer Klausmann], a Swiss: Let's just assume the plane crashes and the negatives are lost, the entire film is lost—something similar already happened to us once. We'd shot half the film when the main actor became seriously ill, so I had to start all over, from the very beginning. So let's just assume the worst will happen—especially now, at the very end, after four years, now that everything's done—and the plane crashes. I'd immediately begin shooting the film all over again. Are you with me? And he answered, Of course. I'd do it all over again. But it would only work if the insurance covered all the losses. In terms of resolve, though, there's no question. It would take a year to prepare everything, before we could begin filming, but I'd do it.

Q: I don't see how that's related—

WH: —because you thought I was exhausted.

Q: What that represents to me is what you see as existence, something that's associated with a tremendous intensity, which you've always displayed, as far as an outsider can tell. Intensity, as I understand it, has less to do with the body and more to do with the psyche and with the intellect, and for that reason it can't always be maintained with equal strength.

WH: Yes, but the danger is rather different. I can only say it in Bavarian: You become a *Kasperl* [a Punch-like figure from the puppet theater]. This line of work turns you into a *Kasperl*. It happens to almost everyone in the business. So you have to be careful.

Q: Nevertheless, your work seems to assume that filmmaking in essence is also an act of will—in the sense of the creative act or, more precisely, in the Schopenhauerian sense of will. So is it the will as demiurge or the will as defiance? I think of that, because you said, "If the plane with the negatives were to crash, I would immediately begin filming again"—

WH: The project is too good—

Q: Is it that, or is it because once you've begun something, you want to finish it by any means?

WH: The project is too important for me to be able to give it up. My existence was always bound up with it. So long as I live and breathe, I would pursue this project—but obviously within certain limits. Of course I put moral limits on how far I would go. But as far as me personally, what I would ask of myself, there's no question. I'm healthy, I'm at full strength, and why shouldn't I do it?

Q: Since you just spoke of moral limits, I have the impression that your approach to things that interest you is rather amoral. Sort of like how one can speak of the main character in *Kaspar Hauser* as having an amoral approach.

WH: Can you elaborate on that a bit, maybe with an example? I don't understand the question.

Q: By amoral I mean that which is neither moral nor immoral, but rather a position lying beyond both these ideas, from which you make decisions and take action.

WH: Possibly. But it would only apply to that which concerns me personally. You don't make a film alone. You can write alone. But when you make a film, you work with other people and enter a distinct field, where specific categories of behavior—including moral categories—are necessary and must be enforced. You can't just go around them. Personally, though, I'd never ask somebody else to do something that I hadn't myself tried out in advance.

For example, I made a film about a volcano that was about to explode [*La Soufrière*]. We climbed up to the top, to the edge of the crater, and we knew what might come. The entire island had been evacuated and the last scientists to work there had also already fled. There was an earthquake with fourteen hundred aftershocks, and yet we went up there. I said, "I'm going up," and I asked the two cameramen, "are you coming with me? You don't have to; you could also stay here, at a distance of some fifty kilometers, and wait in safety." Both of them replied "we're coming with you." But I would never send a camera team up a volcano, if I weren't already first among them standing on top. Do you understand what I mean?

Q: Speaking of *La Soufrière*—
WH: —the cameramen hadn't been misled; they knew exactly what was going on with the volcano. It's not that I convinced them there wasn't any danger. We all knew the risks. Even for the scientists, the risks were incalculable, because too little was known about volcanoes. We took this risk because we asked ourselves, as we were sitting in a car, what's more important? Is the film more important for us or is it our lives, our own asses? And we were of the opinion that our asses didn't matter.

Q: This "staring into the eyes of death" appears throughout your work. Whether it's the film about the ski jumper, *The Great Ecstasy of Woodcarver Steiner*, or *Aguirre*, and now *Fitzcarraldo*. Is it fair to say that, in these films, death is part of the equation?
WH: No. At least not for other people. *La Soufrière* is the exception—

Q: —for yourself, I mean, for you alone. And isn't that a sort of desire that you have, this searching for confrontations with death?
WH: I don't have any kind of death-wish. On the contrary, I just know what I'm doing and what I'm trying to accomplish. And what I have to do when there's no alternative. Our civilization attaches great importance to physical life. But all that is not so important. We don't need to take ourselves so seriously, to make such a fuss over ourselves. I don't think of myself as terribly important.

Q: Do you think it's at the extremes that people best recognize what's most important for their own existence? This moment always confronts the characters in your films—whether it's the deaf-blind people in *Land of Silence and Darkness* or the old man in *Last Words*. Or is it your will that forces them to find out what it is to live in the face of death, and that what we call life can only be found in the extreme?

WH: I have always been in awe of undeveloped film material. I like touching cans of raw film stock. Every day in the jungle, I thought, this could be the last roll of film I ever shoot. And when you have to ask yourself that question in your work every day, then you do something sensible with it. When this feeling of death isn't there, then the film material has no value either. No, it's not that it has no value. Rather, the film has a different value. If you're sitting in a prison cell, and the next morning you're going to be put in front of a firing squad, and before that you're handed a pen and a last piece of paper, and you write a letter to your wife or to your brother or to your mother or to anyone—this piece of paper has a different quality, a different value.

Q: Would you agree, if I were to say that in order to have good images— good in the sense of intensity and—

WH: I'd prefer if we left it somewhat vague. . . .

Q: We'll just leave it vague—that you also have to put yourself in danger, and not because you're afraid of what people will say (oh, he's just trying too hard to be original), but rather because you need the singularity of directly experienced images (*erlebte Bilder*), in order for the viewer to be able to experience them as well in the darkness of the movie theater? Comfortable images convey the comforts of studio work and arrogant standards of living. . . .

WH: No. You don't have to put yourself in danger. I know lots of films and many, many people who have made wonderful images without putting themselves in harm's way. Some of them even came from the padded chairs of the studios. . . .

Q: I wanted to talk about this difference between studio and location. Would you ever go into the studio?

WH: No, not to film anything, because I feel uncomfortable there. Everything there is so artificial—I've never worked in a studio—it's so sterile that I feel like an alien element. But that's just me. Other people work very well in the studio, because it has very pure, controlled conditions, and they need that.

But putting oneself in danger, I've never put myself in danger, and I would never do so, not even for a film—unless specific circumstances, relating to the film itself, made it absolutely necessary to do so. For example, we're going through the rapids with this enormous steamship. For weeks, we'd been going against the current, inch by inch, using steel cables and winches. There was an accident: All at once, fourteen steel cables broke, and the ship went careening into the rapids with tremendous drama and banged up against the cliffs. And, unfortunately, we didn't yet have the four cameras in position. Nevertheless, we tried it two more times, and on the last try there were seven people on board—three cameras, two actors, an assistant, and me—and we managed to film this whirling ride onboard the ship.

It looked like we would come out of it unscathed, after our previous experiences, when we stood on the riverbank and safely observed the ship from a distance. From there, it looked doable. We said to ourselves, we really ought to be onboard; the film takes on a very different quality if we actually have the cameras and some actors onboard while the ship is whirling down the rapids. So that's what we did. And everyone who participated knew what was coming. They volunteered. And there were injuries—nothing serious, but everyone got injured, actually. But afterward everyone agreed: It was worth doing. And the results were amazing. You'll never see images like that anywhere else.

Q: Was that when your cameraman, Thomas Mauch, injured his hand?
WH: Yes. He went flying through the air, and crashed onto the deck, never letting go of the camera, so when he landed it split his hand wide open, right between two fingers. Up on the bridge, another cameraman strapped himself to a wall, so he wouldn't go flying through the windows when the ship crashed into the cliffs. Strapped in like that, he was able to stand, but the impact knocked him back so hard that he broke two ribs. And yet he stood up and kept filming.

Q: Who was that?
WH: A Peruvian, a wonderful man, by the name of Vignati. He's also a filmmaker. He worked a lot with [Jorge] Sanjinés. An excellent man, Vignati was my assistant director, but also a cameraman. [. . .]

Q: The way you describe your endeavors is reminiscent of how danger is represented in literature. It confirms what I said earlier. To put it mildly: Without great exertion, you can't get great images.

WH: And I would again disagree. Danger is just an inconvenient side effect.

Q: So in your case it wasn't necessary?

WH: In this case, yes. *Kaspar Hauser*, too, has some beautiful images and there was no danger in that case. I'm the last person who would go looking for danger. I'm always represented as someone in search of adventure. But I can't stand adventurers. I'd be the last person to go looking for danger, but I'd also be the last person to shrink away from it.

Q: Many characters in your films have something like the traits or the aspect of Prometheus. They're always in act of stealing fire. In antiquity, they described such acts in terms of hubris. Is hubris for you the opportunity that a human being must seize in order to be able to adapt to an otherwise hostile nature? Could that be a behavioral pattern for your characters?

WH: I wouldn't generalize like that. Those are just my themes, and they can be found in my films. But in this case, to speak of *Fitzcarraldo*, what we did there was definitely approaching hubris. The scope of the work was enormous, there were so many people involved in it, and we were fifteen hundred kilometers deep into the jungle, where every single nail, every medication, every grain of salt, every spoonful of soup had to be brought in under unimaginably difficult conditions. Essentially, nature's overwhelming power and drive forbids this type of work from being done in the jungle—that is, something so highly organized, so sensitive, so easily disrupted. That's the first thing.

The second thing verging on hubris is that we made a film that defies the laws of nature, that is, the laws of gravity. This film is a challenge to something that is actually impossible [to challenge]. Nobody in the history of technology has ever dragged a ship of this scale, all in one piece, over a mountain. And the reason is very simple, because it wasn't necessary. And when, for example, they take a steamship up to Lake Titicaca, at an elevation of four thousand meters, they break it into two hundred pieces, haul them up there by train, and reassemble them in a little shipyard. So what we did was unnecessary, and in that regard my film defies the laws of gravity. But I don't mean it to sound abstract. We actually hauled this ship over the mountain. And don't ask what kind of effort that took. Nobody will ever be able to imagine that.

Q: "Defying the laws of nature" is definitely linked to an idea, such as that of building an opera in the jungle, so Fitzcarraldo can hear Caruso there, so the Indians can hear Caruso. Godard did something similar in *Week End*, where a pianist plays Mozart in the middle of a barnyard, bringing art as it were to the farmers. . . .

WH: It's definitely linked to an idea, because it's about an opera. Something enormous is being wrung from what were then the governing conditions: namely, opera in grand style is being made in the jungle, because that's where it belongs. In the jungle, even fantasy is possible. There, everything proliferates; there's vitality, there's life, rotting, and murder—everything is there. The very biggest feelings and fantasies are there. That's what the film is all about.

Q: So, for you, opera in the jungle doesn't mean "jungle opera." There's no stylistic break in a cultural sense?

WH: No, it's not a break in style. The very lushness of the opera at the turn of the century finds its appropriate place there. Look at the opera house in Manaus, which was built in 1896. Back then, there was nothing but jungle all around and a couple of corrugated-metal huts. And that's where they built this enormous, grandiose opera house. We shot the interior scenes inside of it. This opera house is one big dream of desire and luxury and fantasy. It's unbelievable, and when you walk into this opera house, you instantly know: This is the right place for opera. Caruso belongs here.

Q: That sounds like a doubling of ecstasy. First, there's the jungle, which for Europeans has something to do with madness. . . .

WH: Yes, exactly!

Q: And then there's the luxurious marketplace of feelings, the opera. . . .

WH: Exactly. The human feelings and fantasies and the jungle, they all belong together. And how imaginative the jungle's inhabitants are, too, it's unbelievable. The jungle is a place of spontaneous culture—not in the sense of domestication, as in cleared forests and perfectly straight furrows, but rather culture as agitation of the mind, as fantasy and illusion, dreams and growing and blossoming. Kinski always says that the jungle is enormously erotic. But he's wrong; it's obscene. It's an obscene landscape, a naked obscenity. There's open copulation everywhere—right under your feet, right before your eyes—just everywhere.

Q: Is that what brought about the love scenes in *Fitzcarraldo*? You've never shot a love scene before, until now at least. . . .

WH: Yes, I have. In *Nosferatu* there's a love scene between Lucy and the vampire. . . .

Q: I still find it astounding that the search for extremes in your films is undertaken for the most part by radically solitary male figures. Where love is more a process of change, of becoming more than oneself, of over-coming boundaries. . . .

WH: It's funny, but love doesn't really interest me as a topic for a film, otherwise I would've already dealt with it. There are other people who can do much more with that topic than I can. Love has never really in-terested me—not as the topic for a film. . . .

Q: Not even a "L'amour fou," a madness of love?

WH: It's difficult to answer. I can only say, in retrospect, that it never occurs in my films. Maybe I'm one-dimensional, restricted. I am limited. But Buñuel is limited, as well. I don't think any of his films have love scenes. . . .

Q: Oh yes, they do!

WH: Well, alright. Let's put it this way: Buñuel is also limited to certain themes. And Mr. Buñuel's limitation is probably also his strength. Or in literature—take, for example, Kafka and how thematically restricted he really is. But that's the enormous power and substance that will survive for centuries. I, too, belong somewhere among those who are limited, although I don't really mean to compare myself with Mr. Kafka and Mr. Buñuel.

Q: It seems to me that music plays an important role for you. What role does the music of Caruso play in *Fitzcarraldo*?

WH: The music in *Fitzcarraldo* is an integral part of the story. The screen-play has a list of characters, but before Fitzcarraldo and Molly and other important names appear, at the top of the list stands Enrico Caruso, fol-lowed by, in parentheses, absent for the entire film. And yet he's one of the main characters.

In the film itself Fitzcarraldo is the first to have a gramophone and the first records of Caruso. And he plays them. And he plays them in the jungle. And we hear them. They are original recordings from 1902 and 1906, the earliest known Caruso recordings. They are unbelievably beautiful.

Q: Is the music employed as you just described it, does it structure the film, or . . .

WH: It's not background music. The Caruso music is always there, whenever Fitzcarraldo listens to the gramophone. Of course, there's other music in the film, too. There are two opera performances, one in the Manaus opera house . . .

Q: Did Werner Schroeter create that scene?

WH: Yes. I filmed it, of course, as we agreed. But Werner Schroeter is better than I am, when it comes to staging a turn-of-the-century opera, or at least part of one—all we see is the end. Then there's music from the opera *Ernani*. We chose that one because the tenor dies in the end. And at the very end of the film there's a piece by Bellini from *I puritani*.

Otherwise, though, it's difficult to talk about music, because it can't be verbalized. Who really wants to say why this or that piece of music fits so well with a particular scene? Generally, one could say that hardly any filmmakers take music very seriously and really know how to work with it. . . .

Q: The Taviani Brothers, for example. . . .

WH: Yes, there I have to tip my hat out of respect for them and for their way with music, especially in *Padre Padrone*. [. . .] And then there's Satyajit Ray, whom I also admire. He knows music. Have you ever seen his film *Yal Sagar*? No. That's the story of an aristocrat, who sits in his crumbling and dilapidated palace and spends the rest of his fortune having all the best musicians and dancers of India brought to his palace, and throwing parties there. An unbelievable film. [. . .]

Q: Here's a question we ask every director, and one that we want to ask you as well: Which focal lengths do you prefer to use?

WH: I can give you a fairly precise answer. *Even Dwarfs Started Small* was filmed almost exclusively with a single 24mm lens, which means it was fairly wide-angled. I like to see people up close and at the same time I like to see as much of their surroundings as possible—all in focus, whenever possible. I don't much care for longer focal lengths, I work with them very rarely, and I almost never work with telephoto lenses. And I don't use a zoom of any kind, I don't even bring one along with me when we're shooting.

Q: A well-known director, namely Jean-Luc Godard, said the zoom lens saves works, the actual movement [of the camera].
WH: I have to confess: I once took a zoom along with me, but never used it as such, only with fixed focal lengths. We were looking for a focal length especially for shots of the ship as it went down the rapids, because we never knew what would happen next—would it sink or not, where it would collide with the rocks, or whatever—and we had to work quickly, there was no time to lose. In this case the cameraman was told not to use the zoom, to choose a fixed focal length and leave it there.

It's obviously different when I make a documentary. Generally, I don't bring a zoom along with me then either, but in *The Great Ecstasy of Woodcarver Steiner* I had to use a zoom, because there was no alternative. But all the others were shot with fixed lenses. During the award ceremony, when Steiner was standing on the podium surrounded by three to four hundred journalists, I said, we're not going back thirty meters, setting up on top of a car, and filming from there. We have to take the camera and physically plough right into the crowd, in order to get near Steiner. You have to feel that kind of thing, this sense of physical resistance. I want the camera to breathe and be physically present. Either the camera has to be curious, or what's happening has to be so important that you have to physically immerse yourself in it. Anything else would be too distant. You have to be part of it. Even in *Land of Silence and Darkness*, for example, there are long conversations with Fini Straubinger, who for several minutes tells us about her life. Normally, this type of situation would be filmed from a tripod. But I said to my cameraman, Jörg Schmidt-Reitwein, let's not use a tripod, and he immediately agreed. At the same time, he also understood what the issue was for me. A tripod always corresponds to an inhuman position; it's fixed—especially in this case. So the camera should always be steady as if it were on a tripod, and yet the cameraman actually moves closer to the subject, that's the first thing. And second, it's right that the camera breathes, it's not disruptive. You don't even notice whether the camera is on a tripod or hand held. The viewer doesn't need to know that or see that. And yet, it's something you have to sense. It's another kind of internal involvement, another form of access.

Fitzcarraldo, by contrast, was shot almost entirely on a tripod. There are also some hand-held shots, of course. It just depends on what you're doing. So your question is a good one, because I'm fairly limited in my use of lenses.

Q: In making *Fitzcarraldo*, did you stage everything very strictly or did you sometimes follow what was going on around you, the lives of the natives, cultural gestures, and other things or events?

WH: I didn't want to make an anthropological film. In that respect, I didn't go around filming native ways and customs. That wasn't the decisive issue. And yet the film shows a lot, however stylized. The really decisive issue, in making a film like this in the jungle, is how you deal with contingencies. If a cable breaks and the ship slides back down the slope a bit, then of course I film that, even though it's not in the screenplay. In many ways, we did what was doable, because that had much more power, dynamism, and truth than something that was purely imagined. But we also did everything that we absolutely wanted to do. The ship really went down the rapids. And the ship was essentially pulled over the mountain with bare hands.

Q: Since you just mentioned anthropology—you've polemicized against *cinéma vérité* at almost every opportunity. That was never quite clear to me, because films like those of Jean Rouch, for example, who uses the camera to intensify life, to go beyond the dull mimetic approach to documentary, as he does in films like *Moi un noire* and *Les maîtres fous*. . . .

WH: *Les maîtres fous* is an unbelievable film. It's one of my favorite. You might say this film was the father of my film *Heart of Glass*. That is, people in trance, in real ecstasy. But I would never ascribe Jean Rouch to *cinéma vérité*. He's way, way beyond that. I don't want to get theoretical—for this is something that actually requires theoretical discussion of a broad scope—so I'll put it very briefly: I think in the cinema there are multiple different dimensions of truth that come down from the screen. The absolute truth can never come down, of course, but there are other layers of truth and intensive forms of truth. The truths that come from trance, for example, are different from those that come from holding a camera out in front of you and just filming the ordinary, what you see on the street. *Cinéma vérité*, as I see it, and to put it very simply, shows and only tries to show this one specific layer of reality.

What I've tried to do, so far, is push into other layers of truth. Take *The Great Ecstasy of Woodcarver Steiner*. There of course I filmed a very normal or ordinary event, which I didn't influence: namely, a ski jump competition. But it's not *cinéma vérité*. There are stylized elements. And yet we also tried to follow what was going on there.

Q: When you were speaking of truth, I thought of the tree-frog story in *Kaspar Hauser*. And somewhat tangentially, I think children have a truth in themselves, which goes beyond the mere truth. I believe you made a film, or didn't make a film—I haven't seen it—that had to do with children. . . .
WH: Correct. I made a film with children, my second film. It is called *Game in the Sand*. . . .

Q: That one's unreleased?
WH: Yes. And I'll never release that one. It's horrifying. But then I made a documentary short called *No One Will Play with Me*. It's not that important. But what interested me about it was the following: that it was a film for children, four- or five-year-olds, who don't yet go to school. I don't think anyone has yet to appreciate or understand their imaginations and their interests. We did an experiment, for example, where we made reproductions of some painting and showed them to the children. Then, afterward we asked them, what did you see in the pictures? And they said, a horse, a horse, a horse! I thought to myself, what horse? And sure enough, somewhere in the background there was a little horse. We showed them *Prince Valiant*, and then asked them what happened in the film, what they liked about it, etc. And, strangely enough, fifteen of them—two or three of them saw it separately from one another—spoke of a medieval soldier leaning against a door. And I thought, huh? So I watched the film again. And at one point, Prince Valiant walks out the castle door, with his armor, and a bow, and a quiver with arrows, and— sure enough—there's a watchman leaning against the door. Why did they point out this soldier? To this day, I don't know. I can't figure it out. But it's still peculiar. What do children see? What do they remember? What captures their interest? All of a sudden it's some extra leaning against a door that no adult even notices. It's a mystery. We know too little, and we aren't curious enough. It was also the first time that I made a film for a target audience.

We actually know almost nothing about the process of seeing, about the perception of images, and how they affect us. It's funny, but after I made *Heart of Glass*—where all the actors, with one or two exceptions, performed under hypnosis—I was able to go a step further. There is such a thing as visionary seeing or certain religious experiences in religious ecstasy. What happens, for example, when you have people under hypnosis watch a film? What could that teach us about the process of seeing? I showed films in a cinema where I hypnotized the spectators. Of course, you still have to suggest to them that they look at the screen and that later they recall exactly what they saw. The reactions varied, but some of them were extraordinary and very peculiar.

Memory functions very well under hypnosis. And very often it activates language abilities that were otherwise totally buried. I've hypnotized people to whom I then suggested they were in a totally strange, mysterious, exotic land, like on a totally different planet. No one had set foot on this land for hundreds of years. There's a vast forest, and orchids, and in this forest, many hundreds of years earlier, there lived a holy monk. And if you would take a step further—that is, the hypnotized— then you would suddenly come across a high cliff wall. As you look more closely, you would notice that it's one enormous emerald. There lived the monk, who was also a great poet. And because this stone was so hard, it had taken his entire lifetime, working with chisel and hammer, to inscribe a poem into this emerald wall. Then I approach them, lay my hand on their shoulder, and open their eyes. You are the first to read this poem here.

First I went up to a man, now fifty years old, who had served as a stall boy in a mounted police squadron, opened his eyes, and he said to me: I can't see it clearly, I've lost my glasses. I said, that doesn't matter, just take two steps closer, and then you'll see it very clearly. All at once, he said, yes, now I see it. To which I said, read it aloud to me. And then he began to read in the strangest, most wonderful voice: "Why can we not drink the moon? Why is there no vessel to hold it?" And so it continued. It was wonderful. I didn't know him before or what kind of a poem that was. But he saw it and read it aloud.

And you see, in a similar way, in ecstasy or trance the process of seeing is intensified. I think these intensified forms can tell us something about the mechanisms and effects of seeing as well as about images and visions. Of course, you'd have to use more precise means, develop a whole research program of such tests. We know too little.

Q: In that respect, are you also interested in drugs?
WH: No, not at all. I've never taken drugs. I've also never allowed drugs to be taken while we are filming, by no one, not even Mick Jagger. And he kept his word. . . .

Q: There's that wonderful line from Baudelaire: A butcher on drugs would only dream of butchering.

WH: Yeah, I don't know anything about drugs, but I do have a clear position on them. The people I know who take drugs, I don't know where to begin with them. They aren't the kind of people I really want to be around; I don't want to have anything to do with them.

Q: Do you think life has images that should not be shown—and that can't be filmed?

WH: Yes, that's exactly right. There are a number of things that I would never film. And there are a number of images that can't be filmed, because they can't be organized that way. Even if they have the inner aspect of an image, it might not be realizable.

Q: There I think of religious images, mythological images. . . .

WH: Right. But that's exactly why mythologies exist. We need to keep them alive. Also faith and religious ecstasy are not to be scoffed at, the latter having certain areas and images that should remain. It's like how certain works of literature shouldn't be touched—just let it be literature, and for God's sake don't try to make a film out of it.

Q: Alexander Kluge has criticized Jean-Marie Straub, in the film *Moses and Aaron*, for filming the dance with the "golden calf." To him, it's impossible, so the results are not surprising. . . .

WH: Fine, but Straub made it. I don't have any relationship to this film, not so much because of Straub or the way it was made, but rather because the music doesn't speak to me. The music is repugnant to me, and I can't get over that. It's like, how you don't want to be married to a person who smells bad. [. . .] For me, it's like that with the film—I can't stand the smell of the music. And that's why I have no relationship to it. I have access to other types of music, but not to this one. In that respect it's difficult for me to judge. They [Straub and his partner Danièle Huillet] are just asking for trouble.

But Kluge is probably right about there being images that can't be filmed, be it the dance in *Moses and Aaron* or something else. Take, for example, the Revelation of John. No film can be made of that, for God's sake. It's a religious text and a religious vision and it should remain that way. Period. Whoever wants to film that sort of thing is an idiot, and doesn't know what film is good for, and above all doesn't know what a religious text is good for.

Q: Can your films be understood as a way of coming to terms with Germany?

WH: I can't disown my culture. I don't even want to. I belong here. German is my language. If I work somewhere else, that has nothing to do with my culture. For this reason I could never work in Hollywood. Because Hollywood is not a different place; it's a different culture with a different cinematic mythology. Of course I've already worked with Hollywood, but it was always clear that I would only make German films, never Hollywood films. If the gentlemen in Hollywood are agreeable, then they can be my partners.

Q: There's one question that I have to ask you, there's no way around it. Admittedly, I'm not 100 percent informed, but I've read what's appeared in print. You know what I'm talking about—the many charges, allegations, and denouncements against your conduct toward the Indians in Peru. At one point, Amnesty International intervened and accused you of human-rights violations, but later disclaimed their accusations. One day we'll know what was fact and what was fiction. Do you have anything to say about all this?

WH: I want to focus on a couple of things. You're in a similar position to that of others who published reports in the press—that is, you weren't there. I don't own the truth either, but I have one advantage over you: I was an eye-witness. That distinguishes us, first of all. Second, it has essentially been a media event. It's not my problem; it's the media's problem. And it's not my scandal; it's the media's scandal. When it's reported, for example, that Claudia Cardinale was in a serious car accident, that she was run over by a truck and critically injured, when that's published everywhere, without anyone checking the facts, then all I can say is: Truth be told, she was never even in a car there, to say nothing of having an accident.

Of course there were problems with the Indians. But how it was represented alone—in *Stern* [magazine], for example. A journalist and a photographer were sent to observe the production for a few days. The photographer took hundreds of pictures of me and the Indians and the surrounding area. But what was published? They didn't show the Indians who were wearing blue jeans and John Travolta t-shirts and carrying walkie-talkies on the set. Instead, *Stern* published photos of naked Indians carrying bows and arrows in confrontation with a missionary. This is how the fabrication begins. The press doesn't care about truth. Moral categories don't even apply to them. Have no illusions. In politics it's all about power, and with the press it's all about the story. The amount of truth, the degree of truth doesn't matter. And what they found on the set was an excellent story.

I can illustrate the problem very briefly. Out of geographical necessity—that is, because we needed two rivers located in close proximity to each other—we came to an area inhabited by Aguaruna Indians. We flew over the area—for which I would also be denounced—took photos, evaluated them, and then went into this area on foot. We came to a village and were very warmly received. I asked if I could stay there for two or three days, to present myself and my project before an assembly of all the elders who were eligible to vote. And that's what I did. We began building a camp for ourselves—outside of their territory, incidentally.

And then came the problems that no one could have anticipated, not even the press. The Indians, the Aguarunas and others, had organized themselves politically as an Aguaruna council. And they made things difficult for me. They denounced me before I had even started to work or even be there properly. By this time people were already writing protest letters. You have to see it against a certain backdrop.

Nobody ever looked for rubber in this area, by the way. The argument that the Indians actually defended themselves against Fitzcarraldo is pure propaganda. He was never there. He never exploited rubber or gold, which were nowhere to be found there. The area in which the Indians live was claimed by Ecuador more than a century ago. This area is located right next to the border [of Ecuador and Peru]. A fair amount of oil was discovered there. For this reason, the Peruvian authorities maintain an enormous military presence there. At every turn there are military camps that capture Indians, cut their hair, and put them in khaki uniforms. Then they have to serve three years in the military. Anyone who so much as moves there is closely monitored—I always had to show my passport and say where I was going, where I was coming from, and so on. The Indians, whose land that actually is, have to go through checkpoints every couple of miles and explain why they're even there. Of course, it's terribly frustrating for them, and that's understandable.

The oil explorers, who were there, built a pipeline with unimaginable brutality—accosting native women, and who knows what else they did. There were acts of violence, prostitution, and more. But the Indians in this area are acculturated. The river there is like an enormous highway. It's impossible to traverse the jungle; it's just too much of a swamp. So everything revolves around the river. It was also the case—there was a tendency, which I can't actually prove, but could only hear about second-hand—that the Indians there and related tribes in Ecuador were fighting for their own land, politically sovereign and separate from both Ecuador and Peru. In this area there were political activists, who also campaigned against us. One day, for example, there appeared a German activist with large-format photographs showing corpses and skeletons of Jews, and he said that we are perpetrators and fascists, and that's what we have in store for them. The Indians of course took notice and got upset. It was said that I had denounced people and thrown them in jail, which is total nonsense. As a result, Amnesty International began questioning me. . . .

Q: That's when you said, if they don't take back those accusations, you'll publically set yourself on fire. . . .

WH: Correct. And this lame horse set the whole campaign in motion. Before I could even respond, it set off an avalanche, with people making the wildest claims. I was denounced and criminalized like you couldn't imagine. There was, for example, a young French agronomist working there, who claimed in the French press that I had had him jailed several times and that once we even picked him up in our boat and tried to drown him. He said we threw him overboard. I was then labeled a murderer—only the murderer hadn't expected him to be such a good swimmer. Truth is, I've never seen this man in my life, and he doesn't interest me. I never had an occasion to drown him.

That's how it went. There were reports in France that were reprinted here [in Germany]. Of course, that got totally out of hand; it was a sensational story. Amnesty International did its research and determined that the person who was jailed had since been set free and that nobody who was jailed had any relation to me whatsoever. I went back to the Aguaruna council and said: You'll be named as the source that claimed I denounced the people who were thrown in jail. Because there were supposedly four people who accused me, I asked who they are: What are their names? For a half hour, I insisted. Finally, they gave me one name. And I asked them, Where is the jail? They told me the location. I went there immediately. The *Stern* reporter came along with me. He [the man named by the council] was in fact arrested by the police and held there for two days or two hours—I can't remember exactly. I asked him, What did I have to do with it? He had no idea. It turns out this man owed money to some sixty people and couldn't pay them back. He'd been indicted by about a dozen people and the police then just nabbed him. They tried to force him to pay his debts, and that was it.

Q: And this campaign—

WH: Just a moment. I want to say something else. They put me on a show trial. A little bit like the Moscow trials under Stalin. I fought back and organized a press conference. It was a total flop. For the press reported all the charges made against me, column by column, with only three lines at the very end noting that I had vehemently refuted all of them. And now? Nobody cares about it. If there had been any substance to the charges, I would've long been chased to the devil. I couldn't have lived another day.

I want to ask you a question: Do you believe that, in making a film, I would commit massive and permanent human-rights violations? Do you think I would shoot even one meter of film under such conditions? Everybody wrote, for example, that I had forced the people to get in front of a camera by directing them at gunpoint. But I wasn't even filming then. Production began two years later. I didn't expose one meter of film in that area. I didn't even have a camera with me there, where I supposedly did all that.

Q: You mean in the Indians' territory?
WH: Exactly. But that's what everyone wrote.

Q: Is that why you don't speak highly of journalism?
WH: I just don't trust them anymore. Let me put it this way: If you're going to deal with journalists, then you have to know what you're getting into. You can't be so naïve as to expect that the truth is the one and only thing that would interest the press. That's an illusion. The story is what interests them. That's the only thing that really matters to them. Just like in politics, how the only thing that matters are power relations and securing certain structures of power. That's what it's about. It's not about morals or anything else. That's why I always found it odd that people got so upset about "Watergate," as though it weren't the most normal and obvious thing in the world. In that case, the machinations were simply brought to light. In that respect, I would never denounce politics. If you take politics for what it really is, then it's about power and, above all, articulating a certain image of the enemy. Whoever doesn't understand that doesn't understand politics, how it's used and why it's needed. How does a story come to be? What about it comes to be inevitable? And how does journalism function? Here you can have no illusions. That's why I don't have any personal feelings about it. I just see it clearly. In this case I was slapped in the face and that of course hurts. Sort of like when, as a

child, you got smacked by your parents for something you didn't steal. It is doubly painful.

Q: Did these charges and so on burden you during the production?
WH: Of course. Internally, it's difficult to set that aside and work on something else. But that was the least of my problems. We also had to deal with very concrete problems. For example, one of my assistant cameramen, from Switzerland, almost didn't come, because his friends had said to him, how can you work with such a pig? Why would you participate in that mess? He lost those friends, because he chose to work with me. That sort of thing is very concrete. Or when I was filming in Iquitos with five thousand extras, it was clear to me that, under the circumstances, there could be a militant demonstration waiting for me just around the next corner. That was always a real possibility. And so it went. I was denounced in a way that you couldn't imagine.

But I was able to live with it, because I was at least an eye-witness to all the accusations, and because I know that I never had anyone thrown in jail. Period. I didn't, and that's the way it is. People can make whatever claims they want to make.

Q: You've often said that the insane—in the strict sense of the word—is actually not the so-called eccentrics who have been excluded from bourgeois society, but rather the society that excludes them. How does one live with this awareness?
WH: Yes, it's strange, especially now, after having lived for so long in the jungle. Whenever I was away [from Germany] for a long time, when I came back, I had something like a kink in my vision. But the kink I have this time will never go away. There are some realizations that are irreversible. For example, if you've ever encountered a real idiot, someone who's really stupid, at some point it becomes totally obvious and you realize just how stupid this person is—and that's the impression that lasts, you can't go back and change it.

Now that I'm back again, I think it's a land where only the insane live. The set designer for my film recently called me—he was in the jungle for a long time, as well—and told me that the people in his building, where he lived in Berlin, they got all excited and asked him very politely to park his car not in front of the building but around the corner on another street. It's a totally dented, weather-beaten, run-down, ancient car. And to have that car in front of such a beautiful building—the neighbors asked him to put it somewhere else. And then they asked that his daughter not park her bicycle on the "marble floor." And I think to myself, this is a world of the insane. Those are just two minor but striking examples—it's just like that in many other respects.

Q: But you have to keep living here.
WH: I don't have to, but I belong here. I may be on the fringe of this society, but I'm not on the fringe of this culture. I belong to this culture entirely. I'm even proud of it. But we have to do something about marble floors or about floor gongs. Do you know about that? There are these gongs that hang in apartments and that people use to call the family together for a meal. It's strange, but I've only seen the distorted here—I have a kink in my vision. But that doesn't matter, I can deal with it. I like these people too, even if it's against my better judgment.

Q: Do you think it will remain this way or do you hope things will change here?
WH: Are you speaking of Germany? That's what I'm talking about, Germany. The worst is that there's hardly any more room to maneuver. I don't mean that in terms of expansion, towards the East, for example. There's no mobility anymore because we no longer have a historical perspective. The last great historical perspective that we had was the reconstruction [after the Second World War]—and now it's over. There's no longer any real politics anymore. Everything migrates slowly but surely into management. There's no faith anymore, either, only the church. We're no longer even capable of history. That is to say, we're a country that's irreversibly disappearing into the abyss of history—like Holland, for example, or Austria. The forest there has almost taken over.

But Austria is a totally bizarre place. And because it's so insane, the most amazing literature comes from there, out of pure despair. And I also think that which we're articulating in film also comes from pure despair—for the most part, at least. It rouses the spirits.

Interview with Werner Herzog on *Where the Green Ants Dream*

Simon Mizrahi / 1984

From *Where the Green Ants Dream*, Cannes Festival press kit, pages 9–19. Deutsche Kinemathek—Museum für Film und Fernsehen, Schriftgutarchiv. © Werner Herzog Film. Reprinted by permission.

Simon Mizrahi: This is a project that dates back quite a long time: Does the film have the same shape today or has it evolved over time into its present form?

Werner Herzog: I have some vague memories of the very first stage of this project. I spent some time in Australia for the first time in my life around 1973, at the Perth Film Festival, when I read about Len Wright's battle of some Aborigines against a mining company that did bauxite mining in the Northwest of Australia. And I learned that many such struggles had taken place. It intrigued me and I wrote a story, which already was entitled *Where the Green Ants Dream*. Then, a few years later, I saw some documentaries by a young Australian filmmaker, Michael Edols, and I became very intrigued by the leading character in the film *Lalai Dreamtime*, who was called Sam Woolagoocha. Through Mike Edols I met this old man, who was a very charismatic figure, a saintlike, wonderful, wise old man. We tried to put a film together, partly with Australian money and organization, partly with German, then with all the bureaucratic hassle this old man died. If Kinski had died during the preproduction for *Aguirre*, I wouldn't have shot the film, and at that time I said to myself: That man can't be replaced, I have to drop the project forever, I won't make it now. While I was doing *Fitzcarraldo* the project kept bothering me, again and again, becoming heavier and heavier. I said to myself I shall look in Australia, maybe I can find some people who would be as good as this old man, and I came across a family clan, and two or three of the leaders are now the leading characters in the film.

82

SM: Instead of just one?

WH: Well, there were several characters in the previous project, but it has changed a little according to the real people who are in the film now.

SM: The dying civilization of the Aborigines, the coming of progress and technology that kills the indigenous culture: This ecological theme has been around before, hasn't it?

WH: I don't see it as an environmentalist film, it's on a much deeper level—how people are dealing with this earth. It would be awful to see this film only as a film on ecology. It has a common borderline with that, but it would be very misleading to see it as a film for the "Greens." We must not forget that there is a real struggle going on, a confrontation between two groups of people. It's also a film on a strange mythology, the green ants mythology. It's a movie, that's the first thing. It's kept open towards the end whether the plane has actually crashed or not. . . . I hope that the two Aborigines have flown somewhere over the mountains into the east, into their dreamland . . . even if at the same time some tribal Aborigines from the mountains report that they've found a wing somewhere in the ravine of a mountain. It's left open. . . .

SM: What do you mean by the green ants mythology?

WH: That's not easy to explain. . . . It is basically an invented mythology. We did not want to be like anthropological researchers, strictly following their rules. I wanted to have legends and mythology that come close to the thinking and the way of life of the Aborigines, but I made it clear to them that the film is not their dreaming, it is *my* dreaming. I couldn't claim to make their cause my cause; that would be ridiculous. There are too many fraudulent people around, whom I would call the counterfeit people, who claim to know everything about them and to be their defenders. I am not like that. I think I have a certain understanding of them, but all our understanding is limited; even if you spent twenty-five years with them and spoke their language, your background is still a different one; you don't come straight from a tradition of Stone Age people, and their highly complicated family structure and mythology. You just will not understand them. I can't bear it that there are so many people, missionaries of all kinds, anthropologists, political activists and politicians, who claim they know exactly what has to be done with them, who claim to understand them completely. My understanding of them is limited. Therefore I want to develop my own mythology.

SM: But you respect them very much, don't you?

WH: Of course I respect their identity, and you can see it in the film. I respect them as people who are in a deep struggle for their religious belief.

SM: Is it only religious belief, or, also, a struggle for survival?

WH: That is part of it.

SM: They are on the verge of becoming extinct, aren't they?

WH: They are. Only two hundred years ago, in Australia, there were approximately six hundred different tribes and languages. Now there are less than 150 left. And the tragedy is going on every single day. There are at least eight or nine known persons who are the last speakers of their language, and there's nobody left of their tribe. And only one single person surviving who speaks and understands this culture and language. I've seen one in Port St. Augusta, in an old people's home, who will die within the next few years. The tragedy is irrevocable. I can't protect them. I don't think anybody can, really. We will lose, we will be poor, stripped naked at the end, and we will only have McDonald's culture on this earth.

SM: Are you that pessimistic?

WH: Well, it goes very, very fast. I've seen it with the native Indians in the Amazon, and you can see it very clearly in Australia. It is a great tragedy. . . .

SM: A tragedy for the Western world or for the indigenous population?

WH: For the entire world. It is tragedy enough that there are no more mammoths left on this earth. I don't speak of the Western or Eastern world, it is simply an enormous, monstrous loss, for all of us.

SM: We see very few Aborigines in the film, never more than twenty, twenty-five at most. Why so few? And what are they trying to fight for, in their non-violent way?

WH: One should know that tribal Aborigines do not normally appear in big groups. I remember there was a big fuss about Kirk Douglas who once had a Hollywood project, where he would, as an outlaw, head ten thousand angry Aborigines who were to attack a town with spears. . . . He was immediately told that never in history had such huge numbers of Aborigines ever appeared together! They always go in much smaller clan groups.

SM: And they managed, socially, to survive like that?

WH: That was their only way to survive, because they had to be very mobile, very flexible, very fast.... And they don't run naked with loincloths, and with their faces painted. That doesn't happen anymore. They come in blue jeans, they have their transistor radios or their walkie-talkies.

SM: It's almost as bad as the Indians in Brazil....

WH: Almost. But there are certain groups, whom I would call the fundamentalists, the traditionalists, who have adopted certain elements from Western civilization for their survival. For example, they went to court and sued mining companies, and are getting revenues now. That survival is maintained through such technical means as wireless radio, which they use to call for help and support among other groups, and to activate political groups within the cities. In some areas, it functions very well; medical and legal aid is organized with and for them; there are some astonishing things going on. And yet at the same time there are certain groups—in my film you will see one of those—who are still thinking traditionally, and who have moved a camp now to a traditional sacred site, and they still do their burial rites and their ceremonies and their songs and their drone pipe music....

SM: They seem to be very clever strategically.... Their non-violent way of fighting, and the way they sit, like a modern "sit-in," is this completely invented or does it correspond to a certain reality?

WH: Aborigines have traditionally hardly ever been aggressive.... They don't sit in terms of a "sit-in." They *are* the rocks that you have to move away! They understand themselves as a part of the earth. It is as if there is a universal body, and they are only part of that body. That's why a man like Sam Woolagoocha said to me one day: "Look here ... you see these ditches and this mine here ...? They have ravaged the earth. And don't they see that they have ravaged my body?" That explains everything. They are the rocks, they are the trees and you'd have to shoot them first, or blast them, before they would move. It has nothing to do with modern "sit-in" techniques—we mustn't be confused by that. While we were shooting, only two hundred kilometers away, some Aborigines had blocked an access road to a sacred site which was just about to be explored for mining. For two months they had been sitting there, with their tents, waiting until the bulldozers arrived, and they would not let them pass. And the struggle is still going on. There are only ten or twelve of them there, but as soon as the bulldozers arrive, they will call for help, if necessary, and they will be two hundred or so.

SM: In the film there is this notion of dream, which is very beautiful . . . the green ants dream, the dreamland, the children that have been dreamed. . . . What does this mean?

WH: I have to be very careful here, because I am not an anthropological expert, and as soon as I begin to speak of the Aborigines and their concept of dreamtime and dreamland I will run into trouble and I could probably be proven wrong.

SM: What matters here is your idea of dreams. . . .

WH: I think that the group of Aborigines with whom I have worked have understood that it does not depict precisely their philosophical concept of dreamtime. Their dreamtime is something of extreme importance, of mythological beings in the dreamtime that is still going on. . . . There's a forever continuous present time that is beyond everything that is going on now, in the past, or in the future. Therefore, in many of the Aboriginal languages, you don't have a future or a past tense. There is a vague form of present, the "now time," and much of their life is based on their dreaming. For example, apparently at certain spirit places, such as a pond, a father would sit and dream his child and then the child would be born, and he would be connected with the dreamtime, or a dreamland, or sacred sites. It is very beautiful how the whole continent of Australia somehow is spread over with a network of rivers of dreams or "songlines": They would sing a song when they travelled and by the rhythm of the song they would identify a landscape. A friend of mine who travelled with Aborigines on a truck saw them singing in fast-motion, as if you were running a tape forward at ten times the normal speed, because the car was passing so fast that the rhythm of the song had to be in the rhythm of the landscape, according to the movement within that landscape. There are things that we will never comprehend and that are very beautiful.

They apparently know how to handle their life on this earth much better than many of us do. And they think that we must be crazy; a bunch of crazies has arrived on this earth and is coming to Australia, who do not understand anything anymore, that are just doomed. . . .

SM: Which is what the old Miliritbi tells Hackett: "You white men are lost. Too many silly questions." Is this what they really think?

WH: Many of them are absolutely convinced that this civilization will come to an end, without sense, without purpose, without direction.

SM: What were your relations with the Aborigines? Did they accept your way of depicting them in the film? Or were there many discussions?
WH: Yes, there were discussions. I explained very clearly what my idea was, and asked them whether they found it acceptable or not. Strangely enough, the real objections came from a completely different angle. They immediately spoke almost exclusively about the names that I used in the film. For example, there is a name in the screenplay which is not in the film anymore. Apparently, a man with that name lived, and once a man dies, for at least ten years afterwards, you must not ever speak that name out loud again. They would speak of "that man who died" but never say his name or the secret name of the young men when they were initiated. And they would also change their own names—that's why in lawsuits it is often very difficult to identify Aborigines, because from one day to the next they might assume a different name and would in all seriousness present themselves as someone else under a different name. Second objection, strongest objection, which is visible now in the film— the sacred objects during the courtroom scene. It has actually happened that in a lawsuit, in the Supreme Court of the Northern Territories, the Aborigines produced some sacred objects which they had dug up from the earth, which had been there for about two hundred years, and asked that all the spectators in the courtroom be removed, so they would show them only to the judge. They were wooden objects, with carvings, that were completely beyond the comprehension of an Anglo-Saxon judge. Yet for them it was the proof of why and how they belonged to this special area. In the film, they asked me not to show anything, even though I had offered to fabricate some sort of duplicate, but they refused even that. Therefore it is not visible in the film—you only see that they have something wrapped, which they hold. We respected their wish.

SM: None of the Aborigines are actors?
WH: As you know, I don't make that distinction anyway. But they are not professional in that sense, no.

SM: The ones we see in the film, what do they do?
WH: The man who plays the drone pipe, the bearded old man, is very colorful, his name is Wandjuk Marika, he used to be one of the leading Aborigines in cultural renewal; he was the chairman of the Aboriginal

Arts Council of Australia. He is considered probably the best drone pipe player in the country, and he's one of the finest bark painters (painting mythological scenes on the bark of trees). He has had several exhibitions. He's multi-lingual, like many Aborigines (most of them are bi- or tri-lingual), he speaks nine Aboriginal languages and almost perfect English. He's travelled to the U.S., Russia, Jamaica, England, everywhere.

SM: And the others have jobs in the cities?
WH: No, most of them live in the most northern part of Australia, and they are one of those groups who are still "traditional" thinkers and try to preserve their culture. For the sake of the film, they travelled some fifteen hundred miles on location and I made it very clear to them: "You are not at your place, you are participating in a movie, for three weeks you will not be at home, you will be acting (many of them of course had travelled before to do shows, music or dance) . . . you will not be in your real life. . . ." And they found that acceptable, they liked it.

SM: The film has a lot of humor in it, but this is funny and very strange: The two Aborigines alternately speak their own language and the English translation. And once in a while, one of them says, "What did he say?" referring to the English, and translates, and then to the contrary!
WH: Wandjuk, the bearded one, speaks English most of the time, and the other one refuses to speak English, although we know that he can speak it and understands it. For example, in court, he insists on making his statement in his Riratjingu native language. They do that quite often, and I like it a lot!

SM: But can you explain why?
WH: They insist on their tribal dignity and pride.

SM: Was it improvised or did you discuss it beforehand?
WH: We observed it, we discussed it, and in a few instances, there is a very simple explanation: The one who was supposed to speak in English had difficulties, so I'd say, Okay, say it in Riratjingu and the other one is going to translate it. That happened once or twice, but it was an exception.

SM: There is this strange character, the crazy scientist who is some sort of an ant specialist. . . .
WH: We learned, through him, a lot about green ants! I mean, this is all

invented biology; just as there is an invented mythology on green ants, there are also a lot of invented scientific things on green ants. For example, this ant researcher explains that the green ant is the only living creature on this earth that has a sensory organ for magnetic fields. Like little particles of metal in a magnetic field, they would all face in one direction, like little soldiers in armies. We actually tried to shoot that, but the ants wouldn't behave like that! We tried so long and so hard! We came closest in a cold store, where we kept them at two and a half or three degrees Celsius, so that they were almost immobilized by the cold. But as soon as we switched on a reflector and some light, they started to stir and move and bite.

SM: Do green ants exist? Ants that are actually green?
WH: Yes . . . well, the tail is green, but the rest is brown. And all the things that you learn about green ants, that they grow wings, that they fly east over the mountains, are of course invented. And, you see, these green ants, for some of the tribal Aborigines, are the totem animal, whereas for others it is the green lizard, or the kangaroo . . . the totem animal that has created the world and created human beings.

SM: So there is some truth in it?
WH: Yes.

SM: What is the didgeridoo? Is it some kind of sacred instrument?
WH: It's a drone pipe, which traditionally has been used for ceremonial purposes only, during initiation ceremonies, or when they have burials. It goes on sometimes for weeks and weeks, and they hardly sleep for days and nights. I remember when Wandjuk came to meet me for the first time, he was completely spaced out, very tired because he'd been in ceremonies for three weeks. And he is considered some kind of custodian priest of his tribe. Anyway, he had it in his contract that if someone in the family group within the clan died, he would have the liberty to leave instantly from the shooting location and go for ceremonies for up to three weeks. That was one of the big points of discussion, but we accepted it.

SM: The early shots and the last shot . . . those small pyramids look like anthills. . . .
WH: They are all artificial, of course. Very early in the film, you see how some sort of conveyor belt accumulates one or two such heaps. Yet the

way these tens of thousands of artificial heaps are shown, you start to doubt whether they are man-made or not. It's almost like another world's landscape . . . or a landscape that could only have been created by ants.

SM: And in the last scene of the film one thinks that Hackett goes into those anthills. . . .
WH: He disappears into them.

SM: As though he goes into the ant civilization, becomes one of them maybe.
WH: At the end, he's like a renegade, he disappears into a dreamland, and so have the Aborigines with their airplane . . .

SM: The explosions we hear are those of the mining company?
WH: Yes, the disaster goes on. The mining that had been stopped will continue. The court case in the Supreme Court has been lost by the Aborigines and they have been tricked into accepting an airplane—a green airplane that has the wings of a bird of death.

SM: The smoke we see coming out of the plane, is it some ritual fire?
WH: We never know exactly what it is, but one of the white pilots who is so scared and upset runs into the airplane and comes out saying it's just a camp fire on the floor. The moment they take possession of it, they do a corroboree inside and sing songs and make little camp fires, so the smoke is trailing out from all the doors and windows.

SM: The dream that Lance Hackett tells the old woman bears some sort of relation to the rest of the story?
WH: Not in a way that can be explained like in an equation, yet I know it belongs to the film. And he says it very clearly: "I've never been inside such a situation before . . . it's just a dream." He even, jokingly, puts that dream aside, and yet he knows somehow he is in a situation like that.

SM: Why those stock-shots of tornados at the beginning and at the end?
WH: I wouldn't call them stock-shots, because my cinematographer, Jörg Schmidt-Reitwein, spent four weeks in Oklahoma chasing after tornados for our film. And those shots were always written into the screenplay. Something like "the little end of the world" . . . that's how I see it . . . a tornado that comes and wipes everything away, sucks everything into the clouds. I was very much intrigued by the hurricane "Tracy" that

destroyed the city of Darwin in northwestern Australia. A few years later, I saw some of the destruction still in this place. People showed me a huge water tank, on three legs, and the tank itself, made of steel, was about thirty meters in the air, and there was a huge rectangular imprint on it! What had happened was that a refrigerator flew through the air for a few kilometers and hit the water tank! Everything else was sucked into the air, only this water tank remained standing!

SM: One of the most intriguing shots is, towards the end, the close-up of this little Aborigine girl holding a stone and, by her side, the transistor radio with the voice of the Argentina World Cup coming out . . . like some menace for the future . . . from one extreme to the other: the futile sophistication of Western civilization and the desperate and raw violence of a dying Aborigine in the middle of a desolate desert. . . .
WH: It strikes me very deeply . . . and I must say that I don't know why it's so powerful, I can't tell you why this is so. . . . It is very desperate, and it has a deep pathos, a deep sadness to it, and you can't name it: What is it? A voice in ecstasy about a goal that was scored by Argentina, and a child holding a stone in her hand and not knowing what to do. . . . An image like that is probably as important as the whole story. And that's why I want to make films; I want to show things that are inexplicable somehow. . . .

SM: I like very much, at the beginning of the film, the helicopter shots of the ant-hills with the Requiem by Fauré, then the sound of the machines, then, as if it were born out of it, the sound of the didgeridoo; as if one sound were always born out of the other. . . . It's strange and fascinating and tells a lot already.
WH: You could stop the film right there, and you would know everything.

SM: Speaking of dreamlands, what is your dreamland?
WH: I wish I knew. I wish I could find it, then I could make a film and close the book.

SM: Only one film? You'd never close the book on your dreamland. . . . That would take a whole life!
WH: Well, I would just stop making films and stay there. If I have an answer to that, I'll let you know!

Discussion with Werner Herzog on Staging His First Opera

David Knaus and Beat Presser / 1985

From an unpublished transcription of an interview conducted in Bologna, Italy, March 1985. Deutsche Kinemathek—Museum für Film und Fernsehen, Sammlung Werner Herzog. © Werner Herzog Film. Reprinted by permission.

Question: Why the opera? It seems like that's unusual.
Werner Herzog: Yes, it is, because I have no experience with opera. When I made *Fitzcarraldo*, I had never seen an opera in my life. Only a year after the release of *Fitzcarraldo*, I saw a production at La Scala in Milan, which was the same production we had in *Fitzcarraldo* at the beginning. I've seen a second opera here in Bologna, which I just saw to get an idea of what the stage looked like, what kind of technical possibilities they had. So that's all my qualification.

Q: I thought this morning, it's a little bizarre that *Fitzcarraldo* revolved around opera, and now you're directing an opera.
WH: Yes, well, there are really two elements to this opera I'm doing here. I was asked to come to Bologna to direct *Doktor Faust* by [Ferruccio] Busoni. It was based not just on *Fitzcarraldo*. The lady who invited me here to do this had seen many of my films, and she said to me on various occasions that it was not only *Fitzcarraldo*, but also understanding music in films and transforming how, let us say, landscapes relate to music. It was based on that that she decided to invite me. She has such an enthusiasm I've never seen before. I warned them that I was some sort of a Neanderthal man of opera, I cannot read music or notes, nor have I seen an opera in my life, and so they thought it would be a new approach, someone who was virtually untouched by such a thing. And I agreed. The second reason, which is one of the strong motivations, is the composer, Busoni, who is somehow in between all chairs. Germans don't

consider him German and Italians don't consider him Italian. He had a German mother and lived most of his life in Germany and German-speaking countries. And also his music is between all chairs, he wrote this opera at a very strange moment when the musical world somehow had stopped its breathing for a moment, and then it went on with the theory of twelve-tone and nine-tone music, and Neoclassicists, and I don't know what else. There were a lot of things going on then.

Q: When was it written?
WH: It was written over a period of eight years. It's not finished. They tried to restore the end of it, but what is important is Busoni is a man of considerable stature and completely neglected and it shouldn't be like that.

Q: How do you feel today after three weeks of rehearsal?
WH: It's not three weeks yet, but it's kind of strange to work inside an opera house. If technical things would work straight away, like lights, then we would do it in a week.

Q: How different is it from film? There are technical problems with film.
WH: Yes, but I would not like to compare this work to any I've done before. I try to forget completely that I am a filmmaker. I'm directing always with my back to the house. I'm very well aware of how the house looks. I could blindly, without turning around, see that if this singer makes a step to the right, the whole right side of the house can't see him anymore. Or the people down in the parterre wouldn't see this. I'm aware there are a hundred different angles for the spectators. With a camera there is only one position you take at one time. So I'm directing with all the lines of view behind me that are possible.

Q: Have you found it at this point to be fulfilling? If someone came next week and said we want to do an opera or a stage production, would you do it?
WH: A stage production, I don't know.

Q: How about another opera?
WH: I have to go through this first. I have no idea how it's going to be at the end. Sometimes I have the feeling something very weird is going on.

Q: You mean behind your back?

WH: No, no. I mean particularly when I think about the next things I might do. In ten days, after this production.

Q: Are you satisfied with it thus far?

WH: Yes, if I'm allowed to make some remarks about the opera itself, then I am satisfied. The problem is the opera itself, it's unfinished. There are so many ruptures and gaps in the music itself, inconsistencies in its dramaturgical flow; it has some very embarrassing moments. It is very hard to get beyond those points. I've tried to make Busoni look as good as possible.

Q: But don't those gaps give you more freedom? Can't you take those gaps and do . . .

WH: Yes, but you've got to stick to the music. You can't cut it down. It's the first time, apparently, that a final version of this has ever been shown in the world, so you can't start to chop it down to its good moments. It wouldn't be just. You could do that after the twentieth staging of this opera, [then] you could go and take this big knife and chop it. There are some obstacles we have accepted as they are. I feel alright with it. It's very strange, from the very first day I walked into this work I felt very safe. It's a little bit the way I did my first feature film.

Q: Do you feel comfortable with it?

WH: Yes, I feel comfortable with it. Strangely enough, even though I can't read musical notes and most of the time I hear the music played only by the piano, I somehow sense the orchestration out of it. I work effects according to the orchestration, which is not yet there. The moment we had the whole orchestra I found out most of it was fitting.

Q: Based on what you heard, you can visualize the music, the rest of it?

WH: Yes, exactly. Just one line of music that gives thirty different voices squeezed together into one instrument. There is another basic thing that has to be considered. Opera houses are very institutionalized, so you can't just try whatever you want, you run into those limitations quickly. I can give you an example. The matches—we had one scene where they light some candelabras on the stage and we asked the prop man to give us some matches, because no one had any. So Uli [Ulrich Bergfelder], who assists Henning [von Gierke], the set designer, went to the prop man and asked for matches and he said there were none. Well, there were some lying around but they belonged to another opera—*Madame Butterfly.*

But *Madame Butterfly* was already finished. Because these matches were bought for *Madame Butterfly*, they were not available just spontaneously. This kind of bureaucracy and institutionalization is a way of their hearts and minds already.

Q: You haven't been affected by the strikes in Italy?
WH: Well, there is a general difficulty in Italy with the theaters because all the funds for theaters and opera houses were blocked and some went on strike. Like Milan—for other reasons as well. In Bologna they considered to go on strike, because they got some additional work with additional performances of another opera, but they decided to work for my production. These people are very enthusiastic. They want to do this. Particularly the stage workers, electricians, and the singers and the choir. They feel totally safe, how I work with them.

Q: Did you pick the cast or was that decided?
WH: I had no idea. I have no idea who is singing in the opera world anyway. So, who are the opera singers? I've heard stars on records, but for Bologna of course they are too expensive.

Q: In staging the opera with these people, do you find it different from working with actors?
WH: It's an entirely different world.

Q: Are you dealing with them the way you deal with actors in directing a film?
WH: Completely different. I've completely forgotten that I've ever made a film in my life. I just wipe it out of my mind. I just have to see what the situation is and adapt to it.

Q: Do you find it an advantage that you don't know a lot about opera?
WH: Yes, I think so. I don't make any theoretical approach to it. This one lady, for instance, came to me the day before we started working with a whole catalogue of literature on Busoni and opera and opera theory. I said I hadn't read any of it and I won't read one single line of what you are offering me. She kept asking me the first day, what do I have to say to all these people—in the first scene there are eighty people crashed on an ice shelf—and I said nothing. Tell them to just come on to the ice and start singing. After forty seconds or so, tell them I just want to observe the chaos. She translated, "Please all come onto the ice and have the

party now on the ice." I said, "Please translate the reason—that I want to observe the chaos." Three times she refused because she found it so embarrassing. But the choir likes it that I'm so frank with them. And the next time we had some structure in the chaos, some very clear lines and observations. It goes very fast that way.

Q: How modern are you staging it?
WH: I don't know how modern, or if it's in Egyptian style or whatever. I have no idea what modern opera is or what ancient opera is. I think the opera is in Egyptian style. I have no labels.

Q: When you read the opera, did you instantly have an idea of what you wanted to do?
WH: No, I didn't plot anything out. I walked on stage and worked myself into it. A long time before I made some basic decisions in which scientific epoch *Doktor Faust* should play. The basic sets were worked out by me. I mean, the court of Parma should be on an ice shelf with a ship crashed. A scene inside a church is now outdoors with a Stonehenge-like circle and two thousand candles on the ground—something very sacred. It fits very well.

Q: The opera as such, don't you find it very absurd?
WH: Yes, of course. That's why I had no idea how expensive a production like that was. I had no idea. I was not involved in the calculations for the set designs, for the running costs, the fees for the singers, and so on. It's absolutely out of proportion with box-office returns.

Q: For the same money you could make a movie?
WH: I could make a low-budget feature film for the same money spent on a production that will be shown only six times.

Q: I find that really strange, because you have nothing in your hands after it's staged.
WH: Yes, but that's okay. It disappears in the air somewhere. The same happens to films, only a little bit slower. The negatives of my first films are already fading away. There was no money to pay for a safety dupe negative, and now they're almost gone after twenty-three years. They're just fading away and there'll be nothing left. Maybe some black-and-white copies. Films disappear, I'm aware of that and there is nothing which remains in your hands either. What remains of old films you will

see in books like *The Haunted Screen* by Lotte Eisner. Of some obscure films from the twenties there are two photos, a description of the story, some notes on the director and style, and that's it.

Q: Doesn't it seem strange to you to do opera? It seems to me that opera is somehow beyond absurd, embarrassing.
WH: If it was embarrassing, I would never have touched it. I mean, there is a spirituality that is behind the whole thing. It's like a conquistador of the useless. I wanted to have the experience. I said to myself, "Why shouldn't I try at least once in my life to transform everything into music, every action, every word into music." I have worked in a similar way, to a certain degree, in my films, transforming an image that is physically there into something more intensified, into something elevated or stylized. In that respect it is fine work. And I must say I like very much the people around. You can tell the moment you walk into the theater how I get along with them and they want me there. And it is an important thing, if you sense it so strongly, how welcome you are.

Q: On the other side, isn't it interesting if you do, say, eight performances, that the eighth performance of the opera will be different from the first?
WH: There is definitely a different form of life. And if it changes within the first and second performance, then let it change—there must be a reason for that change, something that comes from the sheer life it has from within itself. I even try to allow a certain amount of life for the singers and the situation.

Q: How far in advance did you know you were going to do this opera?
WH: About eight months ago.

Q: You've been in rehearsals two weeks? Three weeks?
WH: Just three weeks. I started to go into it the way I go into a film: I tell everyone on the set, "Let's pretend we have opening night in a week from now." So in less than a week I went through the entire opera, every scene, and tried to settle things quickly so that if tomorrow was the opening night, then at least all the singers in the choir would know exactly what to do. In the same way I tried to tell [Zoltan] Pesko, the Hungarian orchestra director, who is very cooperative with me, I told him, they are not very well prepared in the orchestra but they are quick in learning, so let's assume that in five days there will be a world war,

but in the meantime we've got to finish this one. He's working very fast with them and they're making rapid progress. I could do it tomorrow if I needed to. There is only technical things missing. Yesterday night for example I had more than three hours of rehearsal time and I was finished after twenty-five minutes. It would be ridiculous to rehearse it to death. It would become stale. From then on we went on into the next set and began building for the technical test.

Q: Don't you in a sense have to become every character in the opera in order to stage it?
WH: In a way, yes, I try it out physically myself. I play stand-in for them before they arrive. For example, yesterday what you saw—the tenor who is murdered. For some reason he wasn't there the night we rehearsed it, so I rehearsed his part with the eight dancers and developed a choreography of the whole thing. The next day, when he arrived, I showed him exactly what we had worked out, and that is what you saw yesterday.

Q: You have one scene which might turn out to be a scandal. Would you like to have a scandal?
WH: No. I don't work towards a scandal. It's simply a scene with Jesus crucified and he transforms into the beautiful Helena. That is already settled in the opera by Busoni, and we do it as it is. Italy in that respect is strange. You can buy pornography everywhere. You can have very explicit sex scenes in films running in regular theaters, but on stage a naked woman on the cross is something which might raise some sort of a controversy.

Q: But they can't stop you from staging it?
WH: They can, yes.

Q: Not before you actually do it, can they?
WH: The house could do it. Yes. I don't have a straight answer to that. They are very nervous.

Q: What would you do if they came tomorrow morning and said you absolutely can't use this woman?
WH: I would say, in that case, they should finish the opera themselves and do whatever they want, because it would be ridiculous to start censorship within their own walls. Let's do it, there's nothing scandalous about it. It's done with all decency. It's an image of beauty that's important. If

some denunciation comes and a court order comes to stop it, fine. Let's wait. But we should not start to censor ourselves before someone comes and tries to stop the performance.

Q: You're scheduled for eight performances?
WH: Six. Maybe London also. We'd take the whole opera over to the Royal London Opera. They seem to be interested. They have discussed it with Bologna and they are thinking of opening it in a little bit less than a year. They asked me if I agreed in principle to come to London for a week or so and put it together, and I said of course, why not.

Q: In doing the opera do you find anything which might be used later in film?
WH: No. I like to do things that I have not done before. I might act in a film now, as a leading character in a film by a colleague of mine. I think it is alright that I do such things.
[. . .]

Cobra Verde

Jean-Pierre Lavoignat / 1987

From "'Tu n'as pas peur de mourir? Je n'ai jamais essayé,' répond Francisco Manoel alias Cobra Verde," *Studio* (July–August 1987): 47–52. Translated by Paul Cronin.

In some ways, you could say it all began when I read Bruce Chatwin's novel *The Viceroy of Oudiah*, but actually the seeds were sown long before that. I'm someone who walks a lot, and who walks great distances. I thought Chatwin's first novel *In Patagonia*, the story of a long walk, was extraordinary, one of the best books I'd read in years, so when *The Viceroy of Oudiah* was published I read it straightaway. I immediately thought it would make a magnificent film, even if it doesn't have the storyline or complexity of a film. It was full of fascinating characters centered on the slave trade, as well as showing a great sensitivity for Africa.

During the filming of *Where the Green Ants Dream* in Australia I met Chatwin, and we immediately became close friends. I told him I wanted to make a film based more or less on his book, but that I couldn't do it so soon after *Fitzcarraldo*. I needed four or five years to get over the trauma of my recent filmmaking experiences before I jumped into something that big again. I told Chatwin that if anyone approached him to buy the rights to the book, he shouldn't make a decision before letting me know. Last year he called to say that David Bowie's agent was interested. Negotiations dragged on and on because, as usual with these Hollywood people, no one was talking about the book or the story, only about the "property," sequels and percentages. Apparently Bowie was more interested in buying the rights so he could play the lead character than in directing the film, so I told Chatwin to sell the book to Bowie on the one condition that I direct it. I felt attached to the project like a dog to a bone. We never got a final answer, even when I tried to negotiate with Bowie directly, and eventually I told Chatwin these Hollywood types were pretty stupid and didn't deserve his book. The more I thought about it, the more I realized that Bowie wasn't the best choice for the role of Francisco Manoel, this poor wretch who becomes a bandit, an African viceroy, and slave trader. Bowie has star quality, forever glowing, but with an artificial brightness and neon intensity. There's no real depth to him. He lacks the dark, dangerous, brooding intensity that the character of Francisco Manoel demands. I decided to rescue the book from their sullied hands, save the story from their machinations, and make the film myself.

I bought the rights and told Chatwin and his agents exactly how I was going to adapt the story and depart from the book. The film would definitely not be made in a studio with African American actors. It had to be shot in Latin America and Africa with real Africans, who with their social and cultural background speak and move differently. I warned them from the very start that I didn't want to work with the big studios because I knew there were elements in the story that every penny in Hollywood could never buy, and also because I would have had to cast a huge star in the central role, and that was out of the question. I couldn't imagine anyone in Hollywood capable of playing Francisco Manoel. I told them exactly how the film would be made, financed, and produced, and apparently this convinced them.

Though he immediately came to mind, and though I tried to ignore him, the only person I could think of for the role was Kinski. If you read the script you'll notice that all the characters, even the secondary ones, are described in very precise physical terms, except Francisco Manoel. This was because I wanted to avoid describing Kinski. I didn't want to allow him to penetrate my imagination and insert himself into the film. But while I was writing the script, throughout that long week when I was working away at my typewriter, he appeared between the lines and wormed his way onto the pages. The script was like a boat taking on water, with Kinski slipping in through every crack. But as I didn't include a description of the character's physical appearance, I at least left the door open for some debate and the possibility of considering someone else. Why was that? Perhaps because I felt that Kinski wasn't young enough for the part, although that didn't really make much sense, as the man is much younger than his physical age. Or, probably more likely, I had a feeling it would be very difficult—almost impossible—to work with him, and I was afraid he would sabotage the production. The fact that we finished *Cobra Verde* obviously dispels that notion, but you wouldn't believe just how difficult it was to make this film. It was certainly my biggest challenge to date.

So in my mind there was never any question of someone else playing the role and by the time I'd finished the script no other possibility existed for me. Sometimes you have to face facts, whether you want to or not. I called Kinski and told him, "If you don't take this role, I won't make the film." I also had the feeling this would be one of my last chances, if not the very last, to watch the genius of Kinski in action. I have to admit that in spite of all the difficulties and problems, Kinski really is one of the wonders of the world, even if we won't be working together again. To start with, he's at a turning-point in his career, and plans to become a director with his film about Paganini, in which he'll also be acting. This will certainly mean a break in his career, and will make any further collaboration impossible. After *Cobra Verde*, more so than on the earlier films, I was left with the impression that Kinski wasn't working per se. Rather, he was prone to bursts of fury, interspersed with brief moments of grace every now and then. It was no longer a case of rehearsing a scene or checking he was on his mark, but simply—and quickly—rolling the camera. I don't remember things being so chaotic on the other films we made together, probably because everything that characterizes Kinski, everything that makes him the man he is, has become visibly more intense in the last few years. But to a certain extent he's still cooperative because despite everything, he did want to make the film as good as possible.

Working with him on *Cobra Verde* was like tracking a wild, unsociable, and rarely seen animal. If we wanted to catch him on film, we had to sit in the bushes for days at a time. Suddenly he would come to drink at the waterhole, and then disappear in a flash of lightning. For sixty seconds it was possible to shoot a sequence and capture a moment, but we had to wait for days. He had never needed such space and freedom of movement as he did on this film. It's true that if you imprison a lion in a small cage, nothing of the true lion remains, but giving Kinski more and more of a wide berth made the shooting increasingly difficult. I always had to creep up on him like a thief. We had no option but to give him this free reign, otherwise we wouldn't have made it through the first day of filming. Of course I knew all this before we started, but this time it went way beyond what I was used to.

I'm happy with everything we caught on film, but you've no idea how draining it was, both emotionally and physically. The filming environment made everything worse. Imagine being confronted with 750 Amazons, armed and in costume, who have been training for two and a half months, and are almost impossible to keep under control because the infrastructure around us is so inadequate, and it's so hot you can hardly touch the burning ground with your feet. And then, in the midst of all this, is Kinski, in a ferocious rage, holding up shooting because one of the buttons on his costume is loose, even though he's not in close-up and everyone else is suffering because of the intense heat.

Though we've played on each other's nerves over the years, there have also been moments of friendship and warmth between us, but God only knows, while we were making *Cobra Verde* they were rare. There were scenes that, before we shot them, no one—not me, not him—knew what was going to happen, but once we were rolling we both knew something incredible was taking place. During these moments Kinski and I had real trust in each other. We felt very close to each other, and to the cameraman. Unfortunately I wasn't able to make this film with Thomas Mauch, who shot *Aguirre* and *Fitzcarraldo*. From the moment filming began, Kinski set about intimidating Mauch and questioning his abilities, which is ridiculous, as Mauch is one of the finest cinematographers I've ever worked with. Kinski managed to put him so on edge that he wasn't able to continue with his work, and eight days into filming I had to find a new director of photography. I chose Viktor Ružička—none of whose work I had seen—simply because I'd heard he was physically very strong. He's Czech, built like a peasant, patient and not easily ruffled. Anyone else would have quit after two hours.

I don't believe, as is often said of me, that I need this kind of tension in order to be creative. I know my failings, faults, and deficiencies. But though, as usual, I don't want to point the finger at anyone in particular, after making *Cobra Verde* I do have to say that if there were problems, it was because of Kinski, not me. Of course I owe him a great deal, not least because he was in my most intense films, but he owes me a lot too. There's something inexplicable behind our relationship, something beyond reason, a bitterness that brings us together, however different we are. There's an intensity and fever in my films that also belong to him, and I can't imagine anybody but him embodying those characters.

Francisco Manoel, the bandit in *Cobra Verde*, doesn't pursue some impossible dream, unlike some of my other characters. He never wanted to be a slave trader. To begin with, he simply wants to escape a life of dire poverty. "I have to get away from this life, even if it kills me," he says. "I'm leaving this existence behind." He comes down from the mountain with the gait of someone who has spent a long time on his knees, and along the way his fate leads him to become a sort of king. But when he agrees to be a slave trader in Africa, he knows these powerful Brazilian landowners are sending him, outlaw that he is, to a certain death. After all, for the last ten years the king of Dahomey has killed every foreigner who set foot on his country's soil. So why does Francisco Manoel agree to go? His motivations are hard to fathom, but the point is that he's not going to back down. He confronts the situation head on, and reaches beyond it. That's what I like about this kind of character. His journey isn't the fulfillment of a dream. The only dream was Africa.

Things we are concerned with become even more visible in Africa. There's an exuberance and sense of fantasy there, an overflowing and stimulating imagination. For example, talking about the twilight of slavery, the last days of the slave traffic, goes beyond a simple account of a historical phenomenon. Francisco Manoel says that "Slavery was not a misunderstanding, it was a great crime. But it will never be possible to abolish it through legislation. It's integral to the human condition." By showing a long line of slaves in the film, the suggestion is that the entire world is implicated in slavery.

In terms of cinema, I've always wanted to show things which up to now have been ignored, including Africa, which has been represented either as a continent of savages or—in "The Snows of Kilimanjaro" and *Out of Africa*—with a Hemingway-like nostalgia. What we tried to do with *Cobra Verde* is show Africa as it is: an organized and sophisticated society with complex structures of kingdoms, tribes, and hierarchies. As far as I'm aware, no one has ever shown that onscreen before. The king in the film is an actual king. I searched for a long time before I discovered him, and I don't think I would have found him anywhere but in Ghana, or perhaps certain areas of Benin. He's a man with immense dignity and a natural authority. In Ghana he's the head of the equivalent of the British House of Lords, and he agreed to appear in the film with his entire court: the guardian of his throne, his dancers, drummers, fetish priests, and his entourage, including the fellow in charge of his parasol. More than 350 people! I was his guest at his palace before we started filming and showed him some of my films in order to explain what I wanted. Nobody could have been more convincing than he was. He doesn't play the part of the king; he *is* the king, which meant he exercised a formidable authority over everybody, even Kinski, who respected him greatly. I can recall an incident when, once again, I thought we were going to have to stop filming because Kinski had physically attacked one of the producers, sent the camera flying, and insulted the thousands of Africans, with their horses and drums, who had shown up especially for us. Once Kinski announced he was going to leave, all the extras decided to leave too. It was impossible to hold him back, so the king explained to him that he had to stay, and that the filming had to continue. He told Kinski there were too many important things being said in the film for the first time, about slavery and the history of Africa, for anyone to halt production. The next morning Kinski was on set, and never again raised his voice to the Africans. The king literally saved the film.

My films are often discussed in terms of risk, but I don't like to take risks, and I've never been in favor of risk-taking. I do like challenges though, both physical and spiritual, and enjoy taking myself to extremes. But in doing this I'm only doing my duty, whereas in the case of risk there's never a sense of duty. I'm only trying to find a way to lead my life, a way of fighting through, which is what my films are about. When I walk it's not to exercise, it's a way of life for me. Walking is as simple and indispensable as breathing. Writing and filming can be looked at in the same way. You don't say of the head of a family that it's his "profession." The same is true for me. Making films isn't my profession, it's my life.

The Mirror of Bangui: According to Werner Herzog *Echoes from a Sombre Empire* Is Not a Documentary on Bokassa but a Portrait of Us All

Danièle Heymann / 1990

From "Le miroir de Bangui: Selon Werner Herzog 'Echos d'un sombre empire' n'est pas un documentaire sur Bokasse mais un portrait de chacun de nous," *Le Monde*, December 2–3, 1990. Translated by Japhet Johnstone. Reprinted by permission.

A diagonal phalanx of red crabs can be heard rustling as they storm an apocalyptic beach. In a deserted zoo, a chimpanzee smokes a cigarette behind bars and casts his keeper a hopeless glance. Between these two symbolically charged scenes spans Werner Herzog's latest film *Echoes from a Sombre Empire*. Under the guise of a television news magazine (documents, interviews, exposé) the film meanders through the reign of Bokassa I, emperor of the Central African Republic, with visits to the palace now in ruins, the walk-in freezers, and the crocodile pond.

In interviews with journalist Michael Goldsmith, a sweet and sensitive man who was imprisoned in the jails of Bangui himself, one witness after the next appears: Bokassa's wives, his daughters, his sons-in-law—a big tragic family saga. We rewatch the grandiose and grotesque "coronation" ceremony for the former captain of the French army, whom we endorsed back then. . . . It is hard to say where Werner Herzog's position is in all of this, where his loyalties lie, or how much of it is fascination for him and how much is disgust. At the same time, his answers consistently offer up generous portions of *malaise*.

Danièle Heymann: Have you been interested in the Bokassa "case" for a long time?

Werner Herzog: Since I was twenty. I was in the Central African Republic, when a German mercenary whose name was very similar to mine had been implicated in a failed coup d'état. They arrested me. I was very sick, malaria, bilharziosis. That was all very unpleasant.

DH: How would you define your film?
WH: First and foremost, it is not a documentary. When you see Andy Warhol's Campbell soup can, it is not a document about soup. In *Echoes from a Sombre Empire* there are a lot of scenes that were directed just like in a fiction film, the scene with the ape in particular.

DH: A dreadful scene . . .
WH: Yes. When we came to the zoo, we saw the animal. The soldiers had taught him to smoke and got him completely addicted to tobacco. He reached out his hand begging us for a cigarette. Mike Goldsmith told me, "I can't take this spectacle any longer." That night we wrote the scene, and the next day we shot it in six takes.

DH: This human, all too human, ape makes one think of men behind bars, the men imprisoned by Bokassa, and perhaps even Bokassa himself. . . .
WH: No, no! That is a Western sickness, always seeing metaphorical connections in everything! Things are clearer for me. They're simpler. An ape is an ape. A cigarette is a cigarette. And Bokassa is Bokassa.

DH: Your images are too powerful to not invite some interpretation.
WH: That's not my doing. I have a problem. I am not capable of thinking in terms of symbols and irony. I take everything literally, to the letter. That's why I have such difficulty with the French language. I can speak it, but I refuse to. The French love their language and they love irony—they revel in it. But as for me, I am completely lost. I will say it again, for me Bokassa is Bokassa.

DH: An obsessive question runs throughout the film: Did Bokassa eat human flesh or not?
WH: The truth of the situation is outside of our reach. But not the facts. You want a fact? Here's one: Bokassa was a cannibal. It is as simple as that. It is of little importance what the tribunal concluded or whether or not the witnesses were lying. It is a fact. However, I have to stress that I am not in possession of the truth and I think it is good that the mystery

remains. And I would add that though cannibalism seems fairly atrocious to us, it is not that out of the ordinary in other cultures. . . . What I find more terrible is the image of Europe that Bokassa reflects back. By appropriating Napoleonic "grandeur" for himself and performing it again as a distorted farce, he holds up a mirror to us, bringing us face to face with ourselves and our darkest and bleakest parts.

DH: Bokassa's life is a real novel.

WH: Yes. He had two daughters. One was his real daughter, the other fake. Both were named Martine. They got married on the same day, both in white. When you watch their marriage, it is a document of the past. Everyone there is now dead. The first son-in-law killed, accused of having conspired against his father-in-law—his wife, murdered. Their baby, just days old, was killed by the other Martine's husband, who was a doctor and was executed after the fall of Bokassa. It's an uninterrupted string of horrors. A Shakespearian tragedy.

DH: What do you hope that audiences will take away from *Echoes from a Sombre Empire*?

WH: I don't have any advice to give. All that I can say is that I really love this film. It is in the same family with *Aguirre* and *Nosferatu*.

Interview with Werner Herzog on *Lessons of Darkness*

Alexander Schwarz / 1993

From an unpublished German transcript of an interview conducted April 7, 1993, in Munich. Published by permission.

Alexander Schwarz: *Lessons of Darkness* is not a pure documentary film. So maybe we should start by talking about the circumstances of its production. The motivation for the film was probably to record a singular event, which is actually a very documentary impulse.

Werner Herzog: Let me first say something about categorization. Obviously, it's something that has always interested the media and academics, and people try to determine a specific direction for the film. I always say it's a great requiem for a planet that is no longer inhabitable, or that it almost becomes a science-fiction film. There's actually not a single frame where, as a spectator, you think the film is shot on this planet.

As for the film's actual impulse, it came about very quickly and unexpectedly. [The German television channel] Premiere, that is Rudi Klausnitzer, called and asked if I would like to make a film about the Texan fire fighter Red Adair. I first said: For god's sake, no, that would instantly be reduced to the glorification of firemen. But then I said, as an aside: To film what is happening now in Kuwait, however, that would of course immediately interest me. If I could do what spontaneously comes to me, and also what must be done—since television worldwide always presented it in ten-second spots, because it wasn't there on location—then I would like to capture the magnitude, the visionary magnitude of this catastrophe. I had always said: Yes, I would like to make a film, one that had to be recorded, whether or not anybody sees it, for the memory of mankind. It had to be done. And then it came about very quickly.

All of a sudden it turned out that the work of extinguishing the fires would be finished much earlier than expected. That caught me off-guard, for it would have taken months to get a permit to film in Kuwait. By chance we learned that an English group, with Paul Berriff, had planned to shoot a film on a similar topic, and we quickly reached an agreement. I didn't know all of them, but within forty minutes it had to be decided, in a hotel room in Vienna. . . . And within four hours the production was practically set, so that Premiere, my producer, ITEL, which was also involved, and Paul Berriff were all working in unison. And that meant immediate departure and shooting, without any preparation.

AS: Paul Berriff already had a concept, which he had developed earlier—to film extensively from a helicopter, for example.
WH: It was clear from the beginning that the decisive things would be filmed from a helicopter. And, you know, in such cases it is perhaps not so decisive who the cameraman is, but rather, who is the pilot. And so they took along a helicopter film team, in which the pilot and the cameraman already knew each other very well from many years of collaboration. In this case, the pilot is the decisive figure—that is, where he flies, at what speed, how he sums up a catastrophe that had previously been unthinkable, and does so without having to cut.

AS: Was the flight pattern actually rehearsed? There is a noticeable searching movement: We repeatedly encounter objects with such emotional force that the gaze then holds on them.
WH: Yes, we first had to go up in the helicopter and see. Much of what we would have liked to film wasn't doable, because we would've been pulled into the hot area of one of these enormous fires. If you didn't come from the downwind side, then the surrounding heat would make the helicopter explode. So it wasn't possible to do everything that one could dream of doing. But there was so much there, so much that was astonishing and unheard of, that it was no problem, in one uninterrupted shot of eleven minutes, to give a summary of things that were simply uncanny. Paul Berriff—yeah, that was the funny thing: Technically, he already knew how to solve things, and that you really had to go in physically, and all these things. But in this case he didn't have the right conceptual framework, whereas I could develop something right on the spot. In that respect we almost immediately understood, even within forty minutes, this was a project that we should do together.

AS: The closing credits name a particular cameraman for the helicopter footage. So it wasn't shot by Paul Berriff?

WH: No, that was Simon Werry. The pilot is also named. But of course they all worked under very specific instructions.

AS: Since you just mentioned the film's concept: The film is called *Lessons . . .* Is that a sort of residue of a documentary film? One becomes aware of a situation, then tries to visually depict it in such a way that one can ultimately convey and explain. And yet, alongside this "documentary track," the commentary is often deliberately misleading—for example, the people whom you describe as having lost their ability to speak, who then speak strange languages, or the story of the fire that's reignited.

WH: Because we didn't want to do *cinéma vérité*. We understood that there is a deeper layer of truth, which under certain circumstances can only be reached by saying what is factually untrue or by doing something incorrect. As for the title, forgive me for saying something different here as well, but it came about in a different way: There is a composition by François Couperin called *Leçons de ténèbres*, it is Jeremiah's elegy for the fall of Jerusalem. And for many years it has been one of my most important and favorite pieces of music, which has always given me consolation. That's actually where the title comes from.

AS: Music plays an enormous role in your film, and it does so in two ways: First, it largely replaces the sync sound, which must have been strange and extremely loud. Second, the music dramatizes and it does so much more powerfully than had we heard whooshing and gurgling throughout the entire film.

WH: The question is always, how much stylization does the truth need? That is the big question that has always moved me—even in the film that I'm making now, *Bells from the Deep*.

AS: During the production, did you already know that the ambient sound would be replaced by music?

WH: No, no, not replaced! It is a great requiem. No, there are many great sound events that you, as a television viewer, cannot possibly appreciate: A great column of fire shooting one hundred meters up into the sky sounds as loud as five jumbo jets taking off at the same time. That for me was the most impressive thing. And you can only notice and appreciate that if you're in a cinema with Dolby stereo. In that respect the television broadcast makes a much less powerful impression than the film, not so much in terms of its images but mainly in terms of its sound. That's why

I appreciate it when this film is shown in a cinema with Dolby stereo. I'm not a big fan of Dolby, but in this case it's absolutely necessary.

AS: In a way, the film creates a fiction, which is actually twofold: first, that of a strange planet. . . .
WH: We know, of course, that it can only be ours. This is the provocation that you have to discover, again and again: It's our planet. Even the images that you can no longer reconcile with the Earth obviously have to be filmed here.

AS: Second, that this is indeed our own world, only dating back several millennia, to the Stone Age. Bones are strewn about. Aerials show traces in the sand recalling the photographs of Erich von Däniken [the popular Swiss author], who claimed to discover the traces of early human culture. In terms of content, all that departs from the actual war, even the ruins that can be seen. And yet, it is precisely that which is strange and alienated here that comes to be seen or understood as an especially powerful document of the war.
WH: Yes, the war that caused this catastrophe is in itself not so interesting. From a military-historical perspective, of course, it was significant and interesting. The Gulf War was also an important step toward the future of war, because it was the first war to be clearly fought for control over diminishing resources, and in that respect it was obviously significant. But the result that is a world in flames could have been sparked by any number of possible things. It seems obvious today, and that's why it is not decisive: Was it the Gulf War or was it the Russo-Japanese War at the beginning of the twentieth century? So it was always clear: This film is not about a specific war. Ours was a different project; we had a different perspective. And that, of course, didn't sit well with some critics, especially here in Germany, because they wanted the villain to be denounced, for Saddam Hussein to be named. But that's obvious; everyone knows that. It doesn't need to be made explicit.

AS: If I can return to the helicopter perspective combined with the use of slow motion. . . .
WH: It's a space-ship perspective, not a helicopter perspective.

AS: But in addition to the extraterrestrial, the perspective is also reminiscent of a bird in flight. And yet there are no animals and no plants that appear in your images, they've all been destroyed. . . . In effect, that creates the fiction of a final creature surveying the destruction one last time.

WH: Only there's no salvation. There's no place to land—even that is no longer possible.

AS: That's also deceptive: The lakes and the lands are no longer what they appear to be. . . .

WH: Yes, but there actually are birds that become disoriented by the lakes of oil reflecting the sky. The lakes, when you look at them, appear to be blue, and the clouds can be seen, too, because the surface is so pitch-black and so reflective. And then these flocks of birds try to land on it. . . . So you don't have the slightest chance as a bird, only as a cockroach or a termite or as certain types of bacteria. They have an excellent chance of survival.

AS: As far as the intertitles, that's a very good means of guiding interpretation and also of deliberately misleading. When did it occur to you to use intertitles in this way?

WH: In the process of editing it first became powerfully clear that there should be chapters of a sort, that it should be organized almost like an enumeration of lessons. But that didn't emerge during the production. There's an opening title, a quotation from Blaise Pascal: "The collapse of the stellar universe will occur—like creation—in grandiose splendor." That too is a quotation that I invented, it doesn't exist; it's not from Pascal. You see, that's how far you have to go in such a film, you have to reinvent Pascal, as it were.

AS: So you're building on the idea that, against the background of the news media, what the film doesn't show will ultimately be decoded. It's provided by the imagination, but it's also produced by means of affect, the film's emotional force, image patterns, noise, music. . . .

WH: And of course a vision that's contained in the film, that is probably the decisive element. I can only compare it to art history, when you look at visions of hell by Hieronymus Bosch, for example, that may be a point of comparison. And I think stylization is also what gives this vision its enduring power. Maybe I'm mistaken, but I think the images of Hieronymus Bosch have a certain actuality, which recurs in very different cultural epochs, because it derives from a certain vision and way of stylizing, which has in itself a certain power and persistence.

AS: Looking at your entire oeuvre, the extremes of primal forces, of the elements, and the extremes of human experience appear to play a major role, as we see in this film with the extreme of absolute destruction.

WH: That would perhaps make sense if I had planned everything exactly in advance, as you may be just assuming. And it would perhaps make sense if this project hadn't been proposed so spontaneously. Sure, of course I think I've recognized something in the project, that it suits me, and that I can do it well—otherwise I probably wouldn't have touched it. It was clear that I also wasn't going to have anything to do with a film about Red Adair.

AS: But it must be very problematic for someone who thinks and works so visually, as you do, that wherever you begin to look you find destruction, and that you always have to be dealing with the "aesthetic of horror," as you've described it. There's also Godfrey Reggio's film *Koyaanisqatsi*, which argues that—

WH: Yes, yes, but I can't stand that film at all. Everything about it is so terribly artificial and it has this stench of New Age spirituality, which is something I just can't bear. Let's just leave that film out of the debate entirely, because it would only make me angry.

AS: The argument is also much too simple: natural beauty here, destruction there. . . .

WH: Yes, that's never interested me.

AS: If you don't want to render something mimetically, on a one-to-one basis—that's how I saw it, and that's exactly what I'm showing you— then you have to shape and interpret the footage through the editing. What's the status of this film, which acts like a documentary to a large extent, but also gives non-documentary signals? Is this an answer back to the unfortunate discussion about "reality TV"?

WH: I don't even know what reality TV is. But it doesn't matter. Ever since I could think for myself, ever since I took my first breath, actually, I have always said: We have to rid ourselves of this unsatisfying and inadequate *cinéma vérité*, because it can only represent a superficial layer of truth, of visible truth in film. The cinema however can register very different, much deeper layers of truth, and that's what we have to work on. When you mention reality TV or *cinéma vérité* or whatever you want to call it, I want to be one of its gravediggers. I've been working on it for a long time.

Werner Herzog

Edgar Reitz / 1995

From *Bilder in Bewegung: Essays, Gespräche zum Kino*, by Edgar Reitz, 64–74.
© 1995 Rowohlt Taschenbuch Verlag GmbH, Reinbek bei Hamburg. Reprinted by permission.

Edgar Reitz: Do you remember what the first film in your life was?

Werner Herzog: I remember it very well, because I grew up in a remote mountain valley in upper Bavaria, where a car was a sensation, where a banana was totally unknown, I didn't even know the word for it. Nor had I ever seen an orange, so I had to learn all that, and I first had to learn High German. Later in school, when I was eleven, they showed two films, both documentaries: Eskimos building an igloo, followed by pygmies building a liana bridge across a jungle river somewhere in Cameroon or in the Central African Republic. One of them was swinging across the river on a vine, just like Tarzan. They were hanging from the suspension bridge like spiders. For me, that was sensational.

ER: Is that what started this yearning for distant places?

WH: I don't think so, because I was very happy with where I grew up and I had a wonderful childhood. My father wasn't around. I think many of the directors who worked in the New German Cinema were fatherless in the sense that they had no teachers and no continuity in terms of film history. We were orphans. I never yearned for distant places, but I did want to go someplace else, to find a place that is worthy of human beings and where we could live an almost utopian existence. That came later, maybe when I was fourteen. That's when I had an intensive religious phase and began skipping school. I wanted to go to Albania, and when they didn't let me in the country, I followed the border all the way to the Adriatic Sea, always remaining so to speak in Kosovo, always with the border to my left, sometimes only fifty meters away, but I never let myself cross the border. And this was when I came to the clear, unconditional, and unwavering realization that I would make films. Even though I had seen hardly any films. I had seen *Dr. Fu Manchu* and *Tarzan* and the *Zorro* films. And a few special films like *Ugetsu Monogatari* by [Kenji] Mizoguchi. Those were moments of enlightenment.

ER: So it was a film experience that awoke in you the desire to make films.
WH: There wasn't a particular experience, where I could say, that was decisive. Rather, for me, it was totally clear that that was my destiny, and I would carry it on my shoulders. I had this feeling very early on, and it has never left me.

ER: Do you feel you have an artistic mission?
WH: I would be careful with the word "artistic." Filmmaking is essentially a handicraft. It has a lot to do with athletics. Not that it requires endurance or special physical abilities. When I say "athletic," I mean more like "a feeling for space." How do you move in a given space? How do you put people in it? How do they relate to one another? How does a gaze move, a camera? How do you use spaces that aren't even visible? I always played soccer, not very well, but intelligently, because I always had a sense of space. I always wanted to do things that aren't really possible for human beings, for which we're not physically built. I always wanted to be able to fly. I wanted to be a ski jumper, the world champion ski flyer. I still do. During the Olympics I sit there, in front of the television, with sweaty hands and watch how the people fly almost without any equipment.

ER: You love the extreme, you look for challenges.
WH: It is something ecstatic, I wouldn't call it extreme. This feeling of complete ecstasy—to step out of that which we physically are, in a figurative sense, too—that's what excites and fascinates me. What we can do in the cinema is show images that are pure fantasy, that lie dormant deep inside us—images we awaken with a camera and we can also awaken in the spectators. I think it's always images that lie very deep inside us and are suddenly awoken, like siblings we never knew we had. All of a sudden we have gained a brother or a sister.

ER: Where does that come from? Do we have memories of lost abilities?
WH: Maybe I can explain it most clearly with Michelangelo. The Sistine Chapel: I was really shocked by the scale of this human achievement.

Pathos has existed for as long as there have been human beings, but Michelangelo was the one who could articulate it. Ever since he painted the Sistine Chapel, we know much more about who we are. Michelangelo showed us a side of us that we hadn't seen before.

ER: I always see you in foreign landscapes in your films, in extreme landscapes, which are actually not suited for life. What are you looking for there?

WH: Landscapes play a major role in all my films, including most recently *Lessons of Darkness*. The film was shot in Kuwait, where an entire world basically went up in flames. For sixty minutes, there's not a single image where you recognize our planet. It's a landscape that is uninhabitable and it has lost all dignity. When I watch Hollywood films or commercial films on television, all I see are used, embarrassed landscapes. They only use landscape as background. In my films, landscape is always an inner landscape. The jungle in *Aguirre, the Wrath of God* or in *Fitzcarraldo* is a human condition; it's a fever dream, a delirium, an almost invented landscape. Landscapes can be "staged" to the extent that they are properties of our souls. That connects me to Caspar David Friedrich, who tried the exact same thing, with other means and in a different time, of course. The question was always: How can we represent landscapes of the soul?

ER: With the paintings of Caspar David Friedrich—the people in them are always very small—it often feels like in the landscape one is closer to God. You say that landscapes can be "embarrassed." Who "embarrasses" them?

WH: I think something has gone awry in our relationship to landscape and in our spirituality. You can name the moments in our civilization, going way back, when things went wrong. The trial against Galileo Galilei is an important example. The church knew that he was scientifically correct, but the question was: What's more important, faith or scientific truth? Back then, they decided in favor of faith and Galileo was condemned. Maybe Petrarch made one of the decisive mistakes in human history, when he climbed to the top of a mountain. No one had previously thought of climbing a mountain. Mountains were just left alone in all their dignity and inviolability. None of the mountain peoples on Earth, not the Tyroleans, nor the Sherpas, nor the Baltis, nor any other mountain people ever climbed to the top. Petrarch was the first, and he described his anxiety in a letter: He knew he was breaking new ground for the sake of progress, and he knew that he was probably going too far. I think it was an original sin, to speak now in religious categories. There's another original sin that can't be dated so exactly: Somewhere between the Palaeolithic and the Neolithic, the first pig was domesticated. In the Palaeolithic there were only hunters and foragers, who lived as nomads. It wasn't an original sin to domesticate the first dog, because dogs accompanied hunters. The same goes for horses, because they were a means of transport or of going forward. But domesticating the first pig was truly an original sin. It started an evolution that bothers us to this day. And, to come back to your question, I'm trying to find in landscapes a place that reflects our dignity and our balance.

ER: When you take a camera and a team up to a mountain or into a jungle, are you able to reproduce this dignity or aren't you also sinning?
WH: All the sins have already been committed. I sin too, of course, but I can render a memory of the landscape's dignity. I think I can, anyway. But you have to be careful with such statements; you shouldn't brag.

You can only really experience a landscape on foot. To measure distances by foot! That's why, when it comes to all the really decisive things in my life, I always travel by foot. If I love a woman and I want to have children with her and marry her, then I go by foot [to propose to her]. It doesn't matter how far the distance is.

ER: The role of human beings in nature is actually one of violence, isn't it?
WH: Someone who travels on foot is never violent. A tourist is violent. He destroys cultures. Just look at Greece! Tourism is a sin. Travel on foot, that's a virtue. And that's how the cinema can be, too, with a dignity and a certain truthfulness that's unique and cannot be made in any other way, not by technical tricks or anything else in the world.

ER: And yet your films often show people who are perpetrators of violence. Is there a certain fascination with violence?
WH: Violence in my cinema is different from that of Hollywood films like *Rambo*. But of course there are people who practice violence: Aguirre, for example, and yet he ends in colossal failure. All these perpetrators ultimately fail and they meet a spectacular end. I wouldn't speak so of violence as I would of original sin.

n you say "sin," are you thinking of "God"?

WH: The question of religiosity was decisive for me, because I come from a family of militant atheists, and in spite of everyone I converted to Catholicism at the age of fourteen. In that respect I was really preoccupied with such questions. But that's what happened, and it must have a distant echo in the films. [Andrei] Tarkovsky would understand me, if he were still alive. He spoke very similarly about original sin. No one understands me, because no one travels on foot anymore. And that's why sometimes I'm just talking to myself; it echoes as it goes out one ear and into the other, and nobody hears it.

ER: Earlier you said that as German directors we were "fatherless." We're "orphans," because in the Nazi period our fathers were monsters for lack of conscience. When you think about the cinema, if you had to define your relationship to the film history of our fathers—is there a German cinema, beyond all these discontinuities, that means something to you?
WH: When I look at German film history, a feeling of pain sets in almost immediately. There is no continuity for us. When I began [making films], I always had the sense of being an orphan because the generation of our fathers took sides with barbarism—the barbarism of fascism. It was such a loss—a void of fifteen years or even more. You can't work in the cinema without having a relationship to your own film history, which is why we searched so intensively for connections to the grandfathers' generation. Lotte Eisner was a sort of bridge, that is, a person who knew the entire film history from the very beginning, as though she were the last woolly mammoth—a person who knew everyone who had worked in film, from the Lumière Brothers to Méliès and Pudovkin, Eisenstein, Fritz Lang, Murnau—everyone. And everyone loved her. It was Eisner who first put me in contact with the films of the twenties. For me, the most significant filmmaker, the director of directors, has always been Murnau. Fritz Lang thinks too geometrically for me. It's similar to Eisenstein, who's too geometrical for me as compared to Pudovkin. Of all the films, *Nosferatu* is the one that has touched me most deeply, because he [the vampire] is such a nightmarish image of terror, almost robotic, like an insect that is irreversibly creeping closer to you and there's no way to stop it. A visionary film! It was only when I made a new version of *Nosferatu* that I had the feeling I was standing on solid ground again. For Murnau, the vampire is a figure without a soul, a forward-crawling insect because he has such long fingernails and holds his hands so strangely at his side. Those are powerful images of horror lodged deep inside me. In *Nosferatu*, I tried to break through this soullessness, this lifelessness with

Kinski. The vampire tries to partake of human passions, of love, of human companionship, of daylight. Kinski was of course a wonderful vampire, with this extraordinary presence of horror. I think he is on-screen for only eighteen minutes in the entire film, and yet it's as if he were there from beginning to end.

ER: Was Kinski the vampire in your life?

WH: Not really, because we had some great moments with each other. He's the most difficult person I can imagine. At the same time, he had a presence and a charisma on the screen that is unprecedented. Nobody in the history of film had what Kinski had. But you could never really see it in the proper light, because whenever people spoke about him, they spoke about scandals, and that's totally immaterial. But the films remain.

ER: Are you looking for a similarly difficult person?

WH: I am not looking for any difficult people. I'd prefer it if they were easier to manage. And yet, precisely because it took so much crazed fury and strength to domesticate this man for the screen, maybe we can sense something beyond these images.

ER: Is filmmaking always a feat of strength?

WH: I'd be happy if that weren't the case. My films often just come about through extraordinary feats of strength. Take *Fitzcarraldo*, for example: We had a ship that weighed 340 tons and had to be dragged over a mountain one and a half kilometers wide, over a very steep mountain. At first it was sixty degrees steep, and we flattened it out to forty degrees, but that was still unimaginably steep. And we were in the jungle, where the nearest inhabited place was fourteen hundred kilometers away. But it was always clear to me that a "plastic solution" was not an option, like you have in Hollywood, pulling a model over a mountain and pretending it was an actual ship. Today, even six-year-olds know a trick when they see one, and they even know how it was done. It's a question of truthfulness, which is decisive in film and will play an even greater role in the future. The more technical tricks we can do, with digital images, the more important the question of truthfulness becomes: that the audience can trust their eyes again. In the early sixties, I went to a movie house in a Mexican village, and I saw how people talked with the screen and cursed at the villain. One guy took his pistol and shot into the air, to scare him. In the cinema, there are other layers of truth, which one can explore and establish, and they're wholly unique to the cinema. There are plenty of examples from German cinema, almost all Murnau's films would count, above all *Nosferatu*. And the films of Fassbinder, for example, *The Bitter Tears of Petra von Kant*, such a wonderful film, which cost almost nothing to make—everything in just one room, with four or six people. Or the early films of Schroeter, *The Death of Maria Malibran, Eika Katappa*. Today, nobody remembers that film, but for me it was a revelation, something special, which could only be done and accomplished in the cinema.

ER: Is poetry, which is actually a literary concept, a criterion for your selection?

WH: Direct comparison with literature should be avoided. I mentioned *Ugetsu Monogatari* by Mizoguchi. That one has what you're calling poetry. I just saw *Where Is the Friend's Home?* by Iranian director Abbas Kiarostami. A boy, who accidently took his friend's notebook, tries to return it, because the teacher has threatened to expel his friend if he fails to submit his homework again. This boy, who has his own responsibilities at home, buying bread for the family and taking care of a baby, suddenly breaks through the iron discipline that has been imposed upon him and runs away, traversing a mountain in search of his friend. It's a fascinatingly beautiful film. Or *Close-Up*, also from Kiarostami. A poor man imagines himself to be a major filmmaker, he even resembles a major Iranian filmmaker, and so he pretends to be him when he enters the home of a family, promising them a part in his next movie. He develops a project and they let him live there. But he's a fraud, a doppelganger, and he's arrested. He actually would've made the film with this family, who were then financing it. But he's arrested and three quarters of the film shows footage from the trial, an authentic case. Rarely have I seen something so moving, of such beauty and poetry.

ER: We carry within us the memory of such events and others we experience in our lives. Is filmmaking also a way of remembering?

WH: We're becoming more isolated, and I think the next century, if one can already characterize it, will be a century of isolation. The cinema is different. It brings us out of this isolation; the cinema brings us together with other people. Above all, it brings us in line with ourselves and with our images, which lie dormant in us.

ER: I very much agree. But in searching for traces of German film within us [namely, Reitz, Herzog, and other prominent German directors and actors of the late twentieth century], I want to briefly touch on a sinister time. There are a lot of films that we find truly noxious.

WH: When I began making films, I didn't want to just take a position against Nazi films. Back then I hadn't seen any of those films. Rather, I was in the situation that I had to invent the cinema for myself. I came to films without film school, and I was never an assistant. So I invented a lot for myself. Of course that's an illusion. You can't invent that from scratch. The Nazi films, like *Kolberg* [dir. Veit Harlan, 1945] and the newsreels, led to a negative boundary, which only played a role much later in my life, at a time when I already had enough negative examples, such as the negative definition of the German film of the fifties and sixties. I always knew how I felt about films made in the early sixties: That's *not* how to do it. Those aren't images and those aren't people I'd trust for a second.

ER: What do you think about Leni Riefenstahl?

WH: Leni Riefenstahl never particularly impressed me. I see, of course, that she knew how to work with images, but the false tones—they can easily be heard. How she used the cinema, that's where I'm very sensitive and where I look very closely. You have to be careful that film doesn't play a role in everyday political developments as it did with her.

ER: But was she an artist?

WH: I have no doubt about that. I wouldn't deny that even in a fascist dictatorship there are creative people like Leni Riefenstahl. But she was never important to me. To this day I have seen maybe two or three of her films—one of the *Olympia* films and *Triumph of the Will*. That didn't particularly impress me. For example, I wanted to hear Goebbels's Sportpalast speech for once in full length. It was a two-and-a-half-hour speech that ended by asking, "Do you want total war?" Goebbels was an extraordinary speaker, [and it was] undoubtedly a remarkable rhetorical performance. That's how you sharpen your feeling for how word, image, speech, and cinema can all be misused and how even false tones and a language can lead to catastrophe.

ER: You've directed many operas. Is there a relationship between opera and the cinema?

WH: Opera and cinema are only somewhat related. Competent people have tried to film opera on original locations. But it always fails. I think opera and cinema are like cats and dogs. There are a number of reasons why. When a question is asked, for example, it's followed by ten minutes of music, before the answer comes, and then that's repeated five times. That doesn't work in cinema, and the emotional world functions differently in opera. The opera works more with archetypes. It evokes the most unbelievable, the purest of all emotions, which don't even exist in everyday life—almost like mathematical axioms, extremely reduced and concentrated, as they never occur in the world. They originate from somewhere, of course, and we recognize them—I can cry my eyes out in the opera. Emotional worlds are built differently in the cinema. But the way music is received, how we open our hearts and let feelings inside, that's in the cinema, too.

ER: Opera's greatest theme—that's what I'm calling it, anyway—is death. It defines the outermost limit of what is even conceivable. Doesn't that link opera and cinema?

WH: There's always been a certain feeling of death in the cinema, as well, on the big screen. I'm thinking of films by Kurosawa, by Pudovkin. Dying is nowhere more beautiful than it is in *Storm over Asia*, where the main character is shot, and yet he survives and is resurrected. Dovzhenko's *Earth* begins during the apple harvest with the death of an old man, who peacefully lies back and passes away on a pile of apples. It's wonderful in a way that only the Russians could do. There are also feelings of death in many of my films. In *Lessons of Darkness*, it is the death of landscapes, the death of an entire planet. And *Fata Morgana* is actually a requiem, although it looks as if it were a film about the creation of the world and paradise. Or *The Great Ecstasy of Woodcarver Steiner*: A man steps beyond that which we are as human beings, and he is immediately threatened by death, because he's flying. Were he to land on the flat [beyond the ski-jump landing area], he would be dead on the spot; he'd be struck dead. But he flies so far that he reaches the very border of death. And this border of death is even marked in the snow, a red line. Cross it and he's dead. And he flies and flies. At the end of the film he tells of a raven he raised and who was his only friend. He fed him, but the raven began losing his feathers and he could no longer fly. The other ravens then pecked at him until he was injured, and Steiner had to shoot his own raven, because he could no longer fly. And then we see how Steiner flies. That is one of those moments where I have the feeling: Yes, that worked.

ER: One hundred years of cinema have passed. Measured by the other arts, one hundred years is a short span of time. Music and poetry have been around for at least four thousand years. In another hundred years, will the cinema still exist?

WH: In the cinema's immediate future, one thing stands out: Images will continue to develop. In the last fifteen years, sound underwent extraordinary developments through digital recording, through Dolby and the like. Now, all of a sudden, it's possible to make dinosaurs come to life through digital images and computer animation. I'm speaking only about the immediate future. We'll go back to that which is remote from television and from all these virtual possibilities, which at first will be used excessively. I actually have a project, where I'm using digital images of necessity, but it's not decisive. Decisive will be a certain spirituality, a truthfulness and a vision that we can only experience in the cinema.

ER: Closing question: What is your favorite season?

WH: Autumn. But I'm often in areas that don't have distinct seasons like we do.

Werner Herzog in Conversation with Geoffrey O'Brien

Geoffrey O'Brien / 1996

From *Parnassus: Poetry in Review* 22, nos. 1 & 2 (Spring–Summer 1997): 40–54.

I met Werner Herzog in late October 1996 in Washington, D.C., where he was rehearsing a production of Carlos Gomes's 1870 opera *Il Guarany*, starring Placido Domingo and scheduled to open at the Kennedy Center a week later. The opera (which Herzog directed previously in Bonn) is something of a curiosity: Based on a popular Brazilian novel by Jose de Alencar, it was turned by his compatriot Carlos Gomes into an Italian opera which enjoyed tremendous success before dropping completely out of the repertoire in the early twentieth century.

With its bizarre plot, an impenetrable tangle of conspiracies and abductions pitting European colonists against two different tribes of Indians, and its gaudy settings, ranging from castle vaults to a clearing in the jungle, *Il Guarany* clearly has some resonance for the director of *Aguirre, the Wrath of God, Fitzcarraldo,* and *Cobra Verde*. Delighting in the multiple absurdities of the libretto, he was determined to play it absolutely straight in order to extract the somewhat demented grandeur at the heart of the enterprise.

Characteristically, Herzog was in the middle of any number of projects in addition to the opera: a film about a German-born pilot who was shot down in Laos in 1966, another film about the conquest of Mexico told from the Aztec point of view. While in Washington, I got an opportunity to watch on tape Herzog's recent documentary *Bells from the Deep,* filmed in Russia. Subtitled "Faith and Superstition in Russia," it makes no judgments and provides little in the way of background information as it presents a series of scenes ranging from deep-voiced throat-singers chanting by a river in Siberia to a self-proclaimed Jesus ministering to his faithful followers, from a rather terrifying exorcist talking about fire and death to a haunting image of people staring through thin ice, supposedly to catch a glimpse of the legendary lost city of Kitezh. *Bells from the Deep* belongs recognizably to the same genre as other Herzog documentaries such as *Wodaabe: Herdsmen of the Sun* and *Lessons of Darkness*, films structured like poems, and that allow themselves tremendous freedom in the use they make of the "real." As Herzog notes in our discussion, *cinéma vérité* is far from his goal.

Herzog had agreed to talk about the relation between poetry and film, with the proviso that academic discussions are not in his line; abstract definitions interest him far less than story and image. We ended up agreeing that, if we cannot usefully define the essence of poetry or filmmaking, we can come up with names, with examples.

It remains to be noted that Herzog's recent work—unconventional in genre, subject matter, and running time—has fared poorly in the hands of American distributors. His extraordinary film on the aftermath of the Gulf War, *Lessons of Darkness*, needs to be much more widely seen, while others have not been released at all in the U.S.

If Herzog is one of the filmmakers who really merit the adjective "poetic," it is not in the sense in which the word (as he notes in the course of this interview) is conventionally used by film publicists and critics. The pivotal images and situations in his films are not interpolated symbols or decorative frills; they have, rather, the bareness and often the harshness of the most ancient poetry. In the freedom with which, in his ostensibly documentary films, he juxtaposes separate realities (including those he has invented), he confirms his kinship with those visionary poets he most admires.

Geoffrey O'Brien: I've just seen a recent movie of yours, *Bells from the Deep*, about faith and superstition in contemporary Russia. It's a wonderful example of what you do that's so different from most filmmakers today: to present without explaining, without commentary. Wallace Stevens said that poetry tries to explain the inexplicable, and in a way that's the feeling I got from your film: It gives us the world without an explanation.

Werner Herzog: It's a very difficult task, obviously, to depict the soul of the whole country on film, but it was what I had to do in this film. How do you show the Russian soul in fifty-five minutes? I felt that it could be done, and that there were a couple of elements that had to be focused upon, and that one of these was the very major question of "truth."

Cinéma vérité can only capture the surface of truth; and yet in filmmaking there is a deeper stratum of truth that I have tried all my working life to reach. This deep inner truth inherent in cinema can sometimes be discovered only by not being bureaucratically, politically, and mathematically correct. In other words, I start to invent. Through invention, through imagination, through fabrication, I become more truthful than the little bureaucrats.

GO: This is very close to what I think of as the truth of poetry. Take [Geoffrey] Chaucer, for example, in whose work you have story, song, scientific and religious information, history—
WH: Let's not forget great characters.

GO: And it's all part of the same thing, which is poetry. It's not a question of fiction or nonfiction, documentary or imaginary.
WH: Chaucer is a very good example because he was a great filmmaker, in my opinion. He has qualities which are needed to make a movie. And then many good filmmakers have written poetry—[Bernardo] Bertolucci, for example.

GO: [Pier Paolo] Pasolini—
WH: Yes, Pasolini as well.

GO: Your own book, *Of Walking in Ice*, strikes me as in effect a poem.
WH: Well, we shouldn't get too deep into definitions. It's a prose text but has qualities of poetry, like *Lenz* by Georg Büchner. *Lenz* is only thirty pages long, but has such a condensed reality and such a condensed beauty in it; it's what poetry is all about.

GO: He raises language to the highest pitch of intensity and compression. In your book, the overwhelming sense I had was of forward movement through space, of such intensity that the whole world is carried along by a person walking.
[. . .]
WH: Of course, when you travel on foot with this straightness and intensity, mostly it isn't a matter of covering actual ground; it's always a question of inner landscape. I want to underline that, because *Bells from the Deep* is largely about inner landscape, as is *Of Walking in Ice*, which I consider better than any of my films. Much of what you see when you read Büchner's *Lenz*, or [Heinrich von] Kleist, or [Friedrich] Hölderlin,

is the innermost landscapes of human beings, and that is why they will outlive everything else.

GO: What struck me in *Bells from the Deep* is that the outer landscape—the ice, the lake, the river—is inextricably bound up with the inner one; the same is true of all your films.

WH: Space is very important to me. In the United States, you often hear a film described as "poetic," and what is meant is only the camera work, which normally has the quality of TV commercials.

GO: You mean slow motion or hazy light. . . .

WH: The crane flying majestically towards its nest. . . .

GO: Yes, that's what they call poetic in the advertising business.

WH: But many people who see films, including professional film critics, take that for poetic filmmaking, and it isn't. There are many other things: the question of truth, of inner landscapes, of rhythm, of space. What sort of space can you create?

GO: In your films I often get a sense of space being presented in a raw or almost brutal way, exactly without the poetic touches you're talking about.

WH: I have never tried consciously to create style. The crudeness comes as naturally to me as breathing or writing; it doesn't constitute a quality per se. I sometimes "operate" or "direct" a landscape as I do animals or people. There are others, like Kurosawa in *Rashomon*, who use space in a geometrical and well-balanced way; there are no clearer strictures and balances than in his pictures. Through this completely different approach, he achieves the enormous depth of poetry.

GO: We keep coming back to this emphasis on space, which I think is crucial for poetry also. You mentioned Chaucer as a potential filmmaker; I think of all the great poets as having some of those qualities. Certainly in Virgil or Homer we experience the creation of complex environments through language, with the voice of the poet navigating them. This is one place where film has taken over what was the function of poetry in ancient societies.

WH: Yes, I think the same way. Why poetry isn't in the forefront of things right now is almost inexplicable; of course, the evolution in our tools has probably caused certain shifts. But I must say that although I believe Chaucer, Virgil, Homer, and so on would have been great film-makers, those are not my favorite poets. I love to read them, but I prefer Hölderlin's poetry, which fathoms the outermost borders of our language. From him, I get the sensation of the Hubble telescope probing the very depths of the universe.

Another German poet, whom nobody knows, is Quirin Kuhlmann, a very strange Baroque poet, in constant religious ecstasies, totally, totally mad, and who took everything very literally. Around 1680, when alchemists were still searching for the philosopher's stone, Kuhlmann was digging in the ground for it with a spade. Like Hölderlin, he was a great voyager on foot. Hölderlin walked from Nürtingen to Bordeaux (six hundred kilometers!), and went insane. (He was already on the brink of insanity.) Kuhlmann crisscrossed Europe on foot, preaching; he wanted to engender a new David, who would establish a new kingdom. He met two hysterical women, a mother and a daughter, and set out on his last crusade with them. He travelled on foot to Venice, where the women abandoned him for some sailors. He swam after their ship as it sailed away and almost drowned before they picked him up. He made it to Constantinople, where he tried to convert the Sultan and was arrested. Ultimately, he was burned, along with his books, at the stake in Moscow, after having incited a religious riot, which was misunderstood as political.

Kuhlmann's writing is really extraordinary, because it goes into unspeakable ecstasies of language, to the outer limit of what the German language is. I truly like these people—[Arthur] Rimbaud would be another—who fathom and explore the depths of our poetic senses and our language.

GO: Have you ever read the journal of the English poet John Clare? He was a nineteenth-century poet of peasant origin who wrote incredibly ecstatic nature poetry. He was more or less self-educated and extremely poor, but was briefly discovered by some literati in London, who made a great fuss over him for a year or so, then abandoned him. He went mad and was confined to an asylum in Essex, but ran away from it and walked a hundred miles or so to Northhamptonshire looking for a woman who no longer existed, to whom he thought he was married. You should read it—it's an extraordinary document.

WH: I don't know him. Of course, there was François Villon, constantly travelling on foot, *en vaguant*, like a vagabond—

GO: In earlier periods, that was how poets gathered material and disseminated their work: by going from one place to another. It's so much a part of poetry, that physical rhythm of breathing and walking.

WH: Yes, I think that some of the very best poets have been people on foot.

GO: Whereas now most of us are working on computer terminals, which to some degree is creating a very abstract poetry—I don't want to say mechanical, but a poetry that is highly conscious of machines, in a rather nightmarish way.

WH: We aren't made to sit at a computer or travel by airplane. Destiny intended something different for us. We've been estranged from the essential, which is traveling on foot. While it would be ridiculous to advocate traveling on foot in our time, I would rather do the existentially essential things in my life that way. It was this love of traveling on foot that made me an instant friend with Bruce Chatwin, for example. I still carry his leather rucksack that he used all his life; when he was dying he gave it to me and said, "You are the one who has to carry it on." I carry it with great honor, knowing it is much more than just a tool to transport little necessities.

One of the things I did on foot, or tried to do, was in the mid eighties, when Germany was still divided and nobody much believed in reunification. I had a strong, clear vision of the historical inevitability of reunification, and of the people's need for it, although many politicians, including Willy Brandt, had declared publicly that the book on German reunification was closed. I felt that only the poets could hold the country together, could keep it unified. So I started to travel on foot all around my own country, following the sinuous border demarcations through the mountains of Austria, then along Switzerland, France, Belgium, Luxembourg, Holland, Denmark, Poland, Czechoslovakia, and Austria, then back to the village where I grew up, which was right on the border. I never completed the journey because after more than a thousand miles I fell ill and had to be hospitalized for a week. The idea that an artist can hold the country together by traveling around it on foot sounds very odd, yet three of four years later, all of a sudden and against all expectations, Germany was reunited.

GO: As you were speaking I couldn't help thinking of several American poets. Of Walt Whitman, obviously, and of the contemporary poet Gary Snyder, whose new book I'm reading. It's called *Mountains and Rivers*

Without End, and evolves very much out of that type of experience—walking around America on foot over a period of many years.

I want to talk a little more about space. My overwhelming impression when I first saw *Aguirre* (the first film of yours I saw) in the early seventies, was that the world had come into the theater. Suddenly, you're not watching a movie—you're actually being transported to these extraordinary places. I've had that experience over and over watching your films.

WH: Yes, I think I'm pretty good at doing that, although how and why I have no idea. In Hollywood and on TV, a scenic landscape is always some sort of a backdrop, like a beautiful postcard. In my case it's always something different. The Peruvian jungle in *Aguirre* isn't a backdrop—it's an inner landscape, like a fever dream. It has a human quality of madness, confusion, voracity, hallucinations, malaria, and the yellow fever that sweats it out.

GO: Do you not, then, see yourself as a documentary filmmaker in the usual sense?

WH: Even though strictly speaking I make documentaries, no, I don't see myself as a documentary filmmaker. It's something different, because I stylize my documentaries highly; I fabricate, I stage. In my last "documentary," *Death for Five Voices*—on [Carlo] Gesualdo, a mad Italian late sixteenth-century composer who happened to be a murderer as well—every single shot was written, rehearsed, and shot a number of times. Yet for anyone who sees it, it looks like a straightforward documentary. Or for example in my film *Lessons of Darkness*, the very first thing you see on the screen is a quote: "The collapse of the universe will occur—like creation—in grandiose splendor."—Blaise Pascal. I concocted it. When people ask me where I found that quote, I'd say, "I don't have the book anymore; it's not from the *Pensées*, but from one of his other works."

The audience steps into the film at a very high level, and I never allow it to go below that; I step into the building at the 34th floor. One of the first images in the film is of a vast, wonderful, outer-space landscape. The commentary says: "Wide mountain ranges, the valleys enshrouded in mist." What I actually filmed were little heaps of dust and soil created by the tires of trucks; the mountain ranges weren't more than one foot high. It's an invented landscape, yet it builds something beyond these little accountants' truths. It immerses you in the cosmic.

When I first saw those burning oil fields in Kuwait, I instantly knew that I was being called to duty. This was something of momentous significance, which had to be recorded for the memory of mankind. It sounds—how shall I say it?—very pathetic. But I felt a deep sense of duty. This was an event which only the poet, not the TV documentary film-maker, could preserve for our memories.

GO: I had a similar response seeing *Bells from the Deep*: the sense of being privileged to participate in scenes I need to know about. I felt overwhelmingly that for you to make visible this kind of hidden reality in a film is really to open up another world. It is, as you said, outer and inner at the same time.

WH: It's probably the first film I ever made with real balance. *Lessons of Darkness*, in contrast, was thrown a little off balance by the fact that I got to film only two people who had lost their speech, and they are outweighed by the flames and firefighters. I was planning to shoot more such people, like the mother who was forced to witness the torture and murder of her two grown-up sons and lost her speech over it, and who struggles to explain to the camera what happened. I had four more such people lined up, but was not allowed to continue shooting, and was expelled from Kuwait. If I had gotten to film those four people, the film probably would have been a little better balanced; the two people alone are a bit isolated. Yet I have to accept it as it is. The film has its life, even though I would like to see it better balanced.

GO: What's so astonishing about *Lessons of Darkness*, which the Pascal "quote" encapsulates, is that it's so beautiful and absolutely horrific at the same instant.

WH: Many others have done it before. [Stanley] Kubrick's *Doctor Strangelove*, for example, with its beautifully blossoming atomic explosions at the end, is the most painful film I've ever seen. I was furiously attacked in Germany over *Lessons of Darkness*. There was a howl of disgust and rage, and the press turned completely against me over it, blaming me for aestheticizing the horror. I stood there and said, "Idiots, Dante did the same thing in the *Inferno*, and Goya, and Hieronymus Bosch, and Kubrick. So what?"

GO: I was struck especially by the moment when you say on the soundtrack that "everything that looks like water is oil," and by the gorgeous fluidity of your images.

WH: The oil is treacherous because it reflects the clouds in the sky, trying to look like water. When you look at the surface of pitch-black oil, it looks like a serene lake reflecting the blue sky and the clouds. It's very, very strange.

GO: That brings us back to ancient poetry, which aestheticizes every-thing, including death and horror. Certainly the *Iliad* is nothing but a poem of blood and force. Are there other filmmakers with whom you feel some kind of kinship this regard?

WH: Thank God, there are many out there, and thank God there are many in film history. The greatest of all for me, the Shakespeare of cin-ema, is David Wark Griffith, and I mean all of his films—everything he did has a touch of greatness. Or Murnau, or Pudovkin—*Storm Over Asia*, what a great film that is! And *Freaks* by Tod Browning. The oddest thing about *Freaks* is that I suspect Browning didn't even realize what a mas-terpiece he had created; he thought it was some sort of a horror movie, and wrote an endless prologue apologizing for it. Or Kurosawa—my God, there are so many of them. . . . Or Abbas Kiarostami, a great Iranian poet in moviemaking. Of course, not even intelligent Americans look at Iran, because Venetian blinds have rattled down on it. Yet Iran is such a wonderful country, with five thousand years of high culture in poetry. When you take a taxi from the airport, a fifty-minute ride to downtown Teheran, the taxi driver will recite Omar Khayyam, Ferdowsi, and Hafiz to you, by heart. It's a complicated country, with a regime that barely tol-erates filmmakers, and yet it is, in my opinion, the most important film country in the world right now, together, of course, with China. Period.

GO: Watching the film today, I couldn't help thinking about Russian filmmakers like Tarkovsky and [Sergei] Paradjanov.

WH: I don't know much about Tarkovsky and have never seen a film by Paradjanov. Tarkovsky has made very beautiful films, but is too much the darling of French intellectuals; I suspect he worked a little bit towards that.

Let me make an addendum to my list of films: No one who makes films seriously can pass by Dreyer's *The Passion of Joan of Arc*, or any of his other films. It's not possible.

GO: Yes, I agree with you about Dreyer. Years ago I saw a traffic safety short he made for the Danish government in the 1940s, the most amaz-ing thing. It's called *They Caught the Ferry*, is five minutes long, and is about a couple in a car. They're speeding, going faster and faster to get

the ferry, and another car is keeping pace with them. Finally, they smash into the other car, and the driver turns out to be Death. The last shot is of the coffin being carried out to the ferry that they were racing to meet.
WH: Yes!

GO: That's it. It was only a traffic safety short, but it's one of the most beautiful short films I've ever seen.
WH: I would like to mention a few more German poets: Johann Christian Günther, one of the truly great ones, who died very young; and then some of the Baroque poets like [Andreas] Gryphius, [Friedrich] Spee, and Angelus Silesius. They were very deep-plowing men. I also love Osip Mandelstam and Robert Walser. The Chinese poet Li Ho I think is extraordinary. He goes boldly for the limits of our fantasies.

GO: His poems have an uncanny sense of the terror of unseen beings. One I remember was translated as "Don't Go out of the Door."
WH: There are demons out there. . . . In English, no writer can pass by Joseph Conrad—he is the poet's poet. If you seriously want to write in the English language, there's a poet in the landscape who cannot be avoided, and that's Conrad. How do you feel about Conrad?

GO: I prefer the early Conrad to the later, those early stories steeped in a Malayan setting, where he creates a jungle in the language.
WH: Or [Ernest] Hemingway's first forty-nine stories—who for heaven's sake can walk past them?

GO: What was the film that first excited you about movies?
WH: To answer that, I first have to step back a little bit into my childhood. I grew up in a very remote mountain valley in Bavaria. My mother fled with her boys to the mountains, because the house next to ours in Munich was hit directly by a bomb, and ours was half-destroyed; we just made it out alive. So until I was twelve I didn't even know movies existed. I had never seen a telephone, let alone TV. I had barely seen a car, and never an orange or banana. I didn't know what the word "banana" meant until I was twelve.

The first time I saw cinema was at the age of eleven or twelve in school: two documentaries which didn't impress me very much. One was about Eskimos building an igloo, and tried to suggest that Eskimos all lived in igloos; I could tell, as a country boy, that they weren't building it well, that they were struggling with it. The second was about pygmies building a liana bridge across a river in the Cameroons. Then, when I went to Munich and started to see films, it was mostly ones about Tarzan, Doctor Fu Manchu, and Zorro. For quite a while, I went along with my friend, who was absolutely convinced that everything he saw on film was real, that Zorro, surrounded by eight bad guys, flinging himself into the air, and swinging around with two pistols, could shoot them all. He demonstrated to me how Zorro did it. For a while it looked quite convincing.

But when I was thirteen or so I saw a film which was very decisive for me: one of those Doctor Fu Manchu films. In a gun battle between the bad guys (Doctor Fu Manchu and his henchmen) and the good ones, a bad guy got shot from a rock, somersaulted in mid-air, and fell to his death. It was something like a sixty-foot fall, and he did a strange kick in mid-air, which fascinated me. Three minutes later, there was another gun battle at a different place and with different people, and all of a sudden I realized I was seeing the same shot again—they had just recycled it and thought they would get away with it. None of my friends realized [that], but I did, because I saw this stuntman doing the same strange little kick in the air. All of a sudden, I knew how film was being narrated, how it was put together. This was the most decisive moment for me in cinema; I started to look at it with different eyes. I understood how and why a camera was being moved, how film was edited.

GO: That's very hard to understand; I think I saw a hundred movies as a child before I had the slightest idea about that.
WH: I can't learn from great films, because they mystify me and leave me in awe, having no idea how it was possible, for God's sake, to make such a great film. It's only from the bad films that I've learned, never the good ones. The sins are easy to name, and the ten commandments: "Thou shalt not. . . ." It's easy to find the negative definition. But what constitutes poetry, depth, vision, and illumination in a great film I cannot name, I do not know. It's like what William Butler Yeats called "a spume that plays upon the ghostly paradigm of things." In just one phrase, he tells us what it's all about.

Revolver Interview: Werner Herzog

Daniel Sponsel and Jan Sebenig / 1998

From *Revolver: Kino muss gefährlich sein*, ed. Marcus Seibert (Frankfurt am Main: Verlag der Autoren, 2006), 49–61. Reprinted by permission.

Question: What do images mean to you?

Werner Herzog: For me, they are a part of life. Without cinema images I would not be particularly fit for survival. Maybe that has to do with the fact that I don't dream. I belong to the very few who never dream. When I wake up in the morning, I experience it as a real vacuum, as something that's missing. Something is wrong with me.

Q: There seem to be two types of images in the cinema: images from an external reality and images that come from dreams, inner images. Are your images inner images?

WH: I think it's correct to say that much of what I have made—regardless of whether they are features or so-called documentaries—are inner views, visionary or dream images. Of course I have something like dreams, only day dreams, especially when I travel on foot. I've gone on foot very often—long stretches of two or three thousand kilometers—those are moments in which I suddenly find myself in entire novels and don't even notice that I'm thirty kilometers farther along. Or I find myself in a soccer game, where literally every play is an extraordinary one, when suddenly the referee whistles and I look around and I'm twenty-five kilometers farther—that happens. And maybe it is simply a need to make up for what's missing, a vacuum that has to be filled in some way.

Q: How did you come to make films?

WH: With me, it began very early, earlier than it normally does with other young people. And I have always avoided asking the question of why I actually do this work. I have always tried not to look so closely at myself. I don't even look at myself in the mirror, I don't want to. In the morning, of course, I have to shave and see that I don't cut myself, but to this day I do not know the color of my eyes.

Q: Should we tell you?
WH: It's indicated somewhere in my passport, but I find that rather suspicious.

Q: In Wenders's *Tokyo-Ga*, you say that we actually no longer have good images and that you have to climb an eight-thousander in order to get good images.
WH: I just vaguely remember. It's correct, though, to say that we are surrounded by used-up, worn-out images in magazines, on postcards, in advertisements, and on television. Those are images that are not really adequate to our state of civilization. In the last twenty, thirty years alone there have been enormous, dramatic changes and images are lagging behind. We have to find images and also a language that is commensurate to our situation. We need a new grammar of the cinema.

Q: What could that be?
WH: There are lots of people in cinema who are doing it right, I think—people who are really searching. Almost all the films that I have made are searching for images. I go relatively far, I invent landscapes and do things that are different from what you see on television.

Q: What do you mean, concretely, by worn-out images?
WH: When you go into a travel agency and see a poster of the Grand Canyon, or you see postcards of this city (Seville), those are images that were made fifty or sixty years ago and were actually already worn-out back then.

Q: How would a truly contemporary postcard of Seville look?
WH: I can't really answer that, because I am not a photographer, but it is obvious that not one in a thousand postcards shows anything other than a completely blue sky. There's not a single cloud to be seen. It rains here too, of course—today we had heavy rain—and I never see so much as a trace of a cloud in these images. Of course, these images have a certain charm, because we discover how the city would ideally look. I don't want to say that I'm fundamentally against this kind of image. It's just that when you make films, then you are in a better position to ask, What is your actual task with the camera? What is the camera doing

here? What does it impart to a spectator? What do you actually want to convey? What do you want to discover? And after there have been such dramatic changes, then, as a result, images would really have to change, along with the language. In the USA, for example, you see very clearly how the language changes. It happens very, very quickly. From one year to the next the kids can no longer communicate with those who are two, three years older, because they speak a new language.

Q: Why do you live in America?

WH: There are a number of reasons, private and above all reasons connected with work. I'm working on a larger, more extensive project, which can only be done with more money—in this case, San Francisco. Francis Ford Coppola has his production company (American Zoetrope) there and we're planning something ([an unrealized project named] Cortez). Aside from all that, I want to be and work in a country that has a very intensive work climate—something like we used to have here (which you have never experienced) at the end of the sixties, when all at once everyone had a camera and wanted to do something, and there was this whole atmosphere of innovation. And in San Francisco and Los Angeles, aside from the dominant industry, there's a permanent atmosphere of innovation. And that is something I really miss in Germany, where there doesn't seem to be a lot of energy and where you have the feeling everyone just wants to imitate Hollywood; somehow that's almost died. And I want to be where it's alive. At this point, I'd rather work in Algeria than I would in Germany.

Q: How do you come up with your themes?

WH: Somehow I always stumble over them. There's never been much planning involved. *Lessons of Darkness* came to me in less than twenty minutes and it was also quickly decided. Or *Land of Silence and Darkness* was a story, where I suddenly discovered a person while I was making a different film [namely, *Handicapped Future*], and only then did I learn that she was deaf and blind.

The only one that may have been planned for a while was *The Great Ecstasy of Woodcarver Steiner*, and that's because it had a lot to do with me personally. As a young boy, I had the crazy idea that I would one day become the world champion of ski flying. I mean, all the boys in the village went off the jump there and we all wanted to become ski fliers, and I was very serious about it, though of course I never became one.

A friend of mine was seriously injured [in a ski-jumping competition] when we were fifteen or sixteen years old. And from that moment on, it was over. Nevertheless, the whole idea that I would take part in such an event, that I wanted to be one of them, that remained. And for me, the greatest flyer of all was Walter Steiner, a Swiss, who in complete ecstasy actually almost sailed to death every time. If you fly too far, you land in the flat, and there you might as well have jumped from the Eiffel Tower.

Q: You once said that after your ski-jumping dreams had been dashed, film was inevitably all that remained. Why?

WH: I think wanting to become a ski jumper and world champion is an adolescent dream. Behind it lies a more profound dream: the dream of flying. We are bound too much by gravity, and I think it weighs on almost all human beings that we are unable to fly. *The Great Ecstasy of Woodcarver Steiner* is a film about the fear of dying and overcoming the fear of dying. It's a film about the moment when you're sliding down the ramp—a moment when nobody can stop you, not even God can slow you down or stop you. That means, it's always also a question, how do you overcome the question of death, how do such ski jumpers deal with their fear? In filmmaking, as in life, the question of fear emerges in the same way: All of a sudden your hands are trembling and you know that there's nothing you can actually do to overcome it, and yet you decide to risk it, to risk existence in spite of everything—because something lies behind it that is more significant than the individual. [...]

Q: What would you have done—bracketing off ski jumping for the moment—if you hadn't become a filmmaker?

WH: What are the alternatives? I've often thought this burden must be lifted from my shoulders. I really should also be making something other than things imaginary, ethereal, what is ultimately just a projection of light on a screen. I always thought being a cook would be a good alternative to filmmaking. In my case it would perhaps be different. I would have liked to become a mathematician, only I know that I started much too late for that. You already have to be at the forefront by the time you're fourteen or fifteen years old. All the great mathematicians, all the great discoveries came from people between the ages of fourteen and twenty-four. So I would've been too old for that. I would've liked to have played the cello. I would give ten years of my life, if I could really play the cello.

Q: You said these projects just come to you. That sounds like a chain of coincidences.

WH: No, of course there's never that sort of pure coincidence. I am always and very suddenly taken by things that have a deep fascination for me, otherwise I would never even begin a film. I have yet to make a film where there wasn't an extraordinary fascination, no matter how great the obstacles were or how difficult it was. In this respect, it's not like somebody said, "Now make this film." I stumble across these people or themes, and suddenly it's like an inner enlightenment: I must do that. I must do it, starting right now.

Q: Do you make films in order to cope with your own despair?

WH: You can't speak about that on camera. That doesn't belong in public. Nor can I speak with you about it, because you're not my friend—we just met. Perhaps one could talk about that with a life-long friend or with a woman, whom you can trust with everything. I once heard Ingmar Bergman in Cannes, at a press conference with fifteen hundred journalists, and Bergman began speaking about death. I shrank ever-deeper into my seat, in shame, and I thought, how can he do that—this can't be happening. I was completely embarrassed, even though I wasn't the one who was speaking.

Q: Do you think your films are understood in the sense that you intended when you made them?

WH: Yes and no. You never know how a film will come across, and frequently it is different from what you had imagined. I've shown the same film in a penitentiary, in Uzbekistan, in Algeria, and in Los Angeles. With each audience it was suddenly a different film, and you have to get used to the fact that, at a certain point, the work and everything you put into it is done, and the child begins to walk on its own legs. And you have to let the child find its own legs, so to speak, for now it finds its own way and becomes independent, and either it becomes something for the public or it just doesn't. But I think that what I've tried to show has generally been understood, for the most part, anyway—sometimes, oddly enough, after a long delay. Some of my films people didn't want to see until five, six, seven, eight years after they came out. Only then, for the very first time, did the films seem more or less alright.

Q: When you're shooting a film, or at the latest while you're editing, do you think of a potential viewer, someone you'd like to address?

WH: Not directly. I try to be a good storyteller. And when you have a good story, then it doesn't matter if the audience is a group of twelve-year-olds or people from the jungles of Brazil—there are universal laws. People recognize a good story relatively quickly and there's a pretty simple consensus on it worldwide. There's also relatively quick consensus on whether the music, for example, is good, whether the camerawork is good. There is never any consensus on the rhythm and the tempo of a film. That varies widely, and you somehow never hit it just right, no matter where you may be showing the film. In the U.S., everyone thinks the film is too long and boring. In Scandinavia, it needs to be twice as long in order for people to find it interesting. So it's very difficult to predict. But of course I think about who will see it, who could see it, whether they might be bored or not.

Q: You mentioned the word *storyteller*, that you see yourself as a story-teller. Does that apply more to the features or does it also apply to the documentaries?

WH: For me, there is no clear distinction between so-called documentaries and feature films. The boundary is always blurred. For example, a film like *Fitzcarraldo*, in which an enormous ship is hauled over a mountain, largely works with so-called documentary methods. Nobody knew in advance what would happen when we pulled the ship over the mountain—how it would look, how it would sound—nobody had ever done it before. So, all of a sudden, the feature film transforms into a very strange, stylized form of documentary—but it always seems as though it were a grand operatic spectacle in the jungle. At the same time, the documentary films are staged so that they actually look like documentaries, but some of them totally come from my imagination. For me, it has always mattered how truth is constituted in images or in the cinema. It's difficult to talk about, because not even the philosophers or the mathematicians can give you a precise answer. And yet, when you read a great poem, then you notice, beyond the language, which is fascinating and beautiful, that in it there lies a profound truth for us. The cinema can provide that as well. Only *cinéma vérité* cannot. That reaches a merely superficial layer of so-called truth. In order to reach a really deep inner truth, you have to invent. So I work with my imagination. I have made "documentaries," always with quotation marks, in which every single shot is invented, scripted, staged—in which almost every detail is fabricated. And yet, overall, it reveals a very deep truth about the person who's the subject of the film.

Q: We spoke yesterday about a film by Jean Rouch, *Les maîtres fous*. Jean Rouch claimed that his camera itself was drawn into a state of ecstasy. What do you think?

WH: In a certain sense, I believe him. That is, insofar as the camera and the person behind it become almost indistinguishable. The camera was so simple, a small wind-up Beaulieu with a single lens—and with that he made one of the ten greatest films of all time. He's probably right. But I've never thought about that question before, it's very interesting. *Lessons of Darkness* also has moments when there is a sort of ecstasy of the camera—when you go beyond it.

Q: Was it like that during the shoot?

WH: With *Lessons of Darkness* and with some other films I had that feeling during the production that something is there that is way beyond me—that just falls into my lap. Even when we were shooting I had the feeling that suddenly the laws of gravity no longer apply and everything suddenly disappears in a strange state of ecstasy.

Q: And yet sometimes in the course of work one experiences great moments, which later however are not recognized by others.

WH: Fortunately, that has never happened to me. The really great moments are always somehow recognized as something special by all audiences, even by the dismissive ones. Of course, you have to be prepared, if you write or if you make films or music, that people will find it terrible, bad, boring, or something else. That happens to me again and again, and you have to be able to live with it.

Q: To what extent are your films about the individual person, and to what extent are they about phenomena?

WH: It's always both, of course. Take my latest film, for example, *Little Dieter Needs to Fly*. There of course it's very much about the person, about his incredible story of captivity and escape—a Passion story. And yet, in order to be able to look as deep as possible into him, I invent stories. Right at the beginning of the film, for example, he is opening and closing doors, over and over, which he never does in his private life, it was invented for him.

And then he says to the camera: "You know, when I was a prisoner and I was in foot blocks and cross-handcuffed with six other people for six months, I could never even open a door. It's like a dream, it's freedom—to open and close a door is the most precious thing I can do," or something like that. Then he opens and closes the door two more times, and goes inside the house. It's totally invented, but it reveals a profound truth, which lies within him. And, curiously, right where you walk into the house, he has all these paintings of open doors, and I didn't fake those, he really has them there. So, working from an element that I observed in his house, I suddenly invent an inner life for him, which isn't really true and yet, in the most profound way, it's much truer than anything else. I'm constantly inventing.

Q: The conversation with Reinhold Messner, in *The Dark Glow of the Mountains*, about meeting his mother after his brother died—how did it come about?

WH: The scene with Messner has a backstory. At the very beginning of the shoot we passed by Nanga Parbat, a brilliant clear day, and the peak was visible for the first time in weeks. And I said: We're filming right now, quickly, Reinhold, let's go . . . and we set up the camera. All of a sudden he starts talking in front of the mountain as if he were a television host, explaining the mountain's history and how his brother died. After two or three minutes I said, I'm not making *that* film, I'll turn around and go back down the mountain right now. We always wanted to have a deeper insight, I'm not making a film with a television host, we have to go deeper and we also have to trust each other. Are you ready to do that? And he thought about it for a while and then he said: I think I understand you. And I also told him that, whatever happens, the camera knows no mercy. The point where he cries, where he's suddenly torn— he had told the story many times before—possibly came from the way of asking. If I would ask him, wasn't that terrible, how you came home and had to tell your mother that your brother died and that you've come home alone—he probably would've just kept talking. But all of a sudden I ask him, very biblically: And how did you then stand before your mother? Like a homecoming right out of the Old Testament, where the mountains teem with rage and anger and won't have anything to do with human beings, and simply kill them off. And his younger brother remains on the mountain, dead. All at once, because it was biblical, it tore him to pieces. And I just nodded to the cameraman: keep filming, keep filming, no matter what happens. There were actually long discussions about whether we should or not we should leave it in the film. I showed it to Messner, who wavered, and then I think we both said, it belongs in the film. It goes very far, but it should go in the film. Now, as then, I think it was right.

Q: I think so too, by all means. Was there any doubt about whether to continue during the "scene" itself?

WH: It was clear that in such a case you keep filming. The first cameraman I ever worked with, an Argentinian, Jaime Pacheco, told me something during my very first film. It was some situation that I don't quite remember any more, when I thought: stop filming. And then he said: Werner, the camera knows no mercy. The camera has its own law, the eye must be opened, no matter how terrible the thing is that's happening in front of it. But there are limits and for me the limits are very clear. In Nicaragua, for example, with the Miskito rebels (*Ballad of the Little Soldier*), there were ugly aspects on both sides—prisoners were shot and killed, for example—I would never let a camera go into such a situation, even if they were to haul me in and say: Film that! I wouldn't do it. So there's a pretty clear boundary and I recognize it.

Q: To treat war cinematically is almost an irresolvable problem. In *Lessons of Darkness*, you chose a form that wasn't interested in explaining when and where it happened, but a form that sought to get hold of the theme aesthetically.

WH: And war, by the way, practically doesn't even appear in *Lessons of Darkness*. Twenty seconds—and it's a completely abstract war. In the commentary it says, the war lasted only minutes—so it's a very strange science-fiction war, which is totally unimportant, which doesn't even play a role in the film. There are only traces that remain, and those are important.

Q: Is it, nevertheless, an anti-war film?

WH: I think it was seen that way. Curiously, it was also seen as an ecological film. In the U.S., I even won a prize for the best ecological film of the year, and all along I thought it really should have been the best science-fiction film. However the film is understood, seeing all this destruction almost automatically stirs anti-war feelings in the viewer. Seeing this film also stirs a desire to protect this poor Earth, that's for sure. But the center of things is the footage that we've never seen before. After seeing it hundreds of times every night in ten-second television spots, I knew of course there is an enormous event that has yet to be properly filmed. We had to film it for the memory of mankind alone. Nobody had done it right.

Q: The idea to over-aestheticize it, was that clear from the start?

WH: Never in my life have I thought about aesthetics. I swear. Strangely enough, it always just happens, and later of course I realize there's a certain aesthetic. It's like writing a love letter by hand. You write because you want to convey a feeling. But only later do you notice that your handwriting has a certain character. But if you just wanted to stylize this character of your handwriting, you would no longer be able to write the love letter. The feeling wouldn't come across any more. And I have to say, I'm like someone who writes—who writes by hand—and never gives a second thought as to how the letters are going to look on the page. I have never worried about aesthetics, but I obviously know it happens in one way or another. How, I'll never know—it's a riddle to me—but it happens. In Germany I was severely attacked. They called it "the aestheticization of horror." The answer was very simple: Dante did it, too. Goya and Hieronymus Bosch—and only at the high level of aesthetics and stylization has Goya remained such a vibrant figure, or Dante or Hieronymus Bosch or whomever.

Q: As part of this aesthetic, you also use quotations from the Bible. Does that have anything to do with a belief in God? Or are you just using them in the film?
WH: These quotations from the Bible—and they're slightly modified— create a certain atmosphere, an atmosphere of biblical catastrophe. [. . .]

Q: Do you believe in God?
WH: Perhaps in this film and in other films there is a distant echo of a very intensive religious phase that I had when I was fourteen or fifteen years old. I converted to Catholicism in a family of militant atheists, and it caused quite a stir back then. The word "God" also appears in a number of titles—*Aguirre, the Wrath of God* or [the German title for *Kaspar Hauser*] *Every Man for Himself and God against All*—which could almost be a motto for my life.

Q: Filmmaking could also be described as a form of adventure. Is that part of the appeal, the heroic process?
WH: For some reason I have the reputation of making films because I am searching for adventure. Of course that's nonsense, because I'm a very professional person and I just want come back with images and with a film. I'm also one of those who are vehemently opposed to every sort of pseudo-adventure that you have today. For me, ever since people tried to reach the north and south poles, adventure no longer exists.

Even there it degenerated into absolute ridiculousness, it's just embarrassing. All these pseudo-adventurers, who are doing it for the people at home watching television, and who are searching for ever-greater obstacles—climbing Mount Everest barefoot or walking backwards across the Sahara—it has degenerated into absurdity. I'm not one of them. I've always just been interested in the themes and in the people in my films, anything else would be absurd.

I should qualify that by saying, strangely enough, through the themes of my films, I am more frequently drawn into situations that are difficult, physically or otherwise, than many other filmmakers. Whenever it was clear that there were going to be problems, I never shied away from them. So, for example, when you take a 340-ton riverboat, a steamship, and try to drag it over a mountain, then you know—every idiot knows that he's going to have problems, that it won't be simple. And yet I did that, not to better understand myself or for the sake of adventure; rather, it was about the story, and the story called for it.

Q: But for you, the physical act is a part of filmmaking?
WH: No. But I think it's no coincidence that a very high percentage of the really good people in film history were very physical, athletic people—a much greater proportion than with painters or writers, for example. I believe there is a physical understanding of space and movement in the cinema, and those who are athletic have a relatively good understanding of that. So whenever it becomes physical, if I am wading through the swamp with an army of Spanish conquistadors somewhere in the jungle, I make better images than I would if I were in a studio. I don't belong in a studio, that's too artificial, that's too dead.

Q: When you think about the future of film, will there be a role for new possibilities, new technologies?
WH: Perhaps, yes, but we don't have to focus so much on whether there are new channels for delivering it. At this point, we don't know very much about that. We only know that the explosive development of new media and communication technologies simultaneously creates increased isolation. So it is our task to make films in which we create for spectators, wherever they are, moments in which they suddenly realize that they are no longer alone—no matter what the channels or technologies that make the films accessible. For me, that is the greatest thing I can experience. The film may be sixty years old and the man who made it may be long dead—but I come out of the cinema and I realize, I am not alone.

The Wrath of Klaus Kinski:
An Interview with Werner Herzog

A. G. Basoli / 1999

From *Cineaste* 24, no. 4 (September 22, 1999): 32–35. Reprinted by permission.

By the time Werner Herzog and Klaus Kinski teamed up for the filming of *Aguirre, the Wrath of God*, Kinski had appeared in scores of films and Herzog, with five features behind him at the age of twenty-eight, was one of the most promising directors of the New German Cinema. The role of Aguirre, the mad sixteenth-century conquistador leading a splinter group of rebels to self-destruction while searching the Amazon for the fabled El Dorado, had appealed to Kinski enough to brave the prospect of two grueling months of filming on location in the Peruvian jungle.

After weeks of drifting down the Amazon on a raft, wearing heavy period costumes in the sweltering heat, with little food or drinking water on account of Herzog's alleged hell-bent quest for authenticity, Kinski's already feisty disposition turned lethal and he threatened to quit the production. "You can't do it," replied Herzog, who was filming on a tight budget that allowed little room for mistakes, let alone starting over with a new leading man. "I told him I had a rifle," Herzog explained, "and he would only make it as far as the next bend in the river before he had eight bullets in his head—the ninth would be for me." "Whoever heard of a pistol or rifle with nine bullets," Kinski commented about the incident in his autobiography—but the pact was sealed. Kinski completed the film and *Aguirre* went on to become Herzog's first international hit.

The unlikely allegiance forged by the two men on the location of their first film together spawned a creative relationship which lasted over fifteen years and produced four more extraordinary films, regarded by many as Herzog's masterpieces, including *Nosferatu* (a remake of Murnau's classic), *Woyzeck*, and *Fitzcarraldo*. But the storm never abated: over the years their fights became legendary and in his outrageous autobiography, *Kinski Uncut* (1996), Kinski repeatedly lambasted Herzog with interminable, blistering tirades: "Herzog is a miserable, hateful, malevolent, avaricious, money-hungry, nasty, sadistic, treacherous, cowardly creep," he wrote. "He doesn't care about anyone or anything except his wretched career as a so-called filmmaker. Herzog doesn't have the foggiest inkling of how to make movies!"

Of course, Herzog's own version of the relationship (including an intriguing explanation for Kinski's vituperative comments) was bound to follow at some point, and *My Best Fiend*, his feature-length documentary on the late Klaus Kinski, who died in 1991, premiered at the Cannes Film Festival this spring.

Echoing the beginning of Kinski's autobiography, *My Best Fiend* opens with an incident that occurred during Kinski's tour of Germany with a one-man show in which he played Jesus. The location is the Deutschlandhalle in Berlin, capacity twenty thousand, in the early seventies. A tight close-up of a wild-eyed Kinski widens to reveal him alone on stage, glaring into the dark auditorium. Someone in the audience just heckled him and he's trying to locate the voice. Suddenly a man is next to him and reaches for the microphone. Kinski pushes him away and a fight ensues. Kinski thunders on: "I am not the Jesus of the official church tolerated by those in power. I am not your superstar." The heckler finally gains the microphone: "I doubt that Jesus was like Kinski. Jesus was a patient man; he didn't say 'shut up' to those who contradicted him!" Kinski wrangles the mic away from him and declares that he will not continue until this "miserable jerk" leaves. Then he walks away in great, angry strides, throwing microphone and tripod off the stage.

Using this footage out of context, *My Best Fiend* succeeds in creepily establishing the tone of Kinski's madness, and then proceeds to expose Herzog's peculiar brand of lunacy. Through a tightly woven tapestry of remarkable archival footage, excerpts from the feature films, interviews and personal recollections, Herzog chronicles the pivotal points of their collaboration—from a thirteen-year-old Herzog's first encounter with Kinski, to their early fights on the set of *Aguirre*, his plans to burn down Kinski's house with him in it, their reconciliation at the Telluride Film Festival, and the incidents during the making of *Fitzcarraldo*.

"Kinski seriously thought that I was crazy. Of course, I am not—not 'clinically,' at least—but he was right in that I was perhaps too choleric," concedes Herzog, although some might argue that hauling a ship over a mountain from one tributary to another—the central metaphor of *Fitzcarraldo* and an enterprise that delayed the completion of the film by four years—is a dead giveaway in matters of insanity. When everyone else deserted him, however, Kinski stood by Herzog. The film was eventually completed and won the Director's Prize at Cannes in 1982.

As if Herzog himself were addressing the jeers and accusations of an unseen spectator, *My Best Fiend* seems to waver between a harangue and a plea, often portraying Kinski as the culprit rather than the subject of the documentary. But when Herzog resists the urge to play the impoverished but visionary filmmaker victimized by a megalomaniac prima donna, an ineffable sense of loss seeps through. Kinski becomes the recipient of a rueful and formidable homage made all the more poignant by Herzog's reluctant appreciation of his belligerent muse and by his struggle to defer to a powerful bond that shaped both his filmmaking career and, as he puts it, his destiny.

A. G. Basoli: What motivated you to make a documentary about Klaus Kinski now?

Werner Herzog: The time was right. I couldn't have made it five, six, or seven years ago. I always had the feeling that I should round the films up, that something was missing—like the chain was missing a link. There's something mysterious about time. All the turbulence, all the turmoil, has somehow settled. My perspective has shifted and that's why the film has humor in it, and people laugh. Of course, some of it is very bizarre. I see it myself and I can face it, now, with calm humor and a certain serenity—but only because time has passed.

AGB: In the film you chose to ignore Kinski's background, personal life, psychological make-up—how he became Klaus Kinski. Why?

WH: It never interested me. I never wanted to make an encyclopedic film on Klaus Kinski. It was always evident to me that it should be my Klaus Kinski. That's why I have this extra, whom I met at the airport, carry a sign that says, "Herzog's Kinski." My intention at the beginning was to call the film "Herzog's Kinski," but I think *My Best Fiend* is a better title. The film is as much about me as it is about him, about our strange relationship. Which is the reason why, for example, Nastassja Kinski is not in the film and Pola Kinski isn't in it, either. I believe his character becomes somewhat evident as seen through my eyes and through his deeds.

AGB: How did you choose the footage and the people you interviewed? It seemed as if his female co-stars had only good things to say about him.

WH: I could easily have found hundreds of female partners who would have told the most atrocious stories of what a permanent pestilence he was on set. But that would have been a stupid and easy game. I didn't want it. I see him differently now. Not that I can claim he was a good man—he was not. He was demonic, evil, but he was wonderful at the same time. Gracious and full of humor and warmth. Not only through the choice of witnesses, but of the footage as well, I wanted to create an homage, an apotheosis of Klaus Kinski. I'm sure he would have liked the film.

AGB: What was your technique for dealing with his tantrums?

WH: There was no technique involved. Here is this man, Kinski, and you have to put him on the screen. You have to take all his rage, all his intensity, all his demonic qualities, and make them productive for the screen. That was the task and there was no time for learning. I had to master the situation from day one, from the first day of shooting *Aguirre*. On the set you have no choice. I had to be strong enough to shape him and force him to the utmost, beyond the limits of what is normally required for the shooting of a film. But he would push me equally—to the limit. It was not permissible to take even a little step back from his level of intensity and professionalism. And, of course, he literally would have been ready to die with me, if I had died on the ship in the rapids. He would have sunk in the ship with me, and vice versa. But I cannot deny that there were moments, which were dangerous, when we could have killed each other.

AGB: In the film you alluded to the fact that he "wasted" himself in your films—you used that word "wasted."

WH: Yes, he was empty and destroyed to a degree that he needed a long time to get back on his feet, and for me it was similar. I needed some time to lick my wounds. The only exception was *Nosferatu* and *Woyzeck*, when we had only a hiatus of five days in between shooting. We did it back to back and, of course, it was a great strain on him in particular, and on me as well, but so what.

AGB: How heavy a toll was it for you?

WH: Nobody should be interested in the price one has to pay to work with extraordinary people. The film is the only thing that matters.

AGB: There is a moment in the film—when you are both at Telluride—when the affection between you two is palpable.

WH: Thank God that moment exists on film, because the media do not believe me. He was always labeled as the *Bosewicht* of film—the villain! And I tried in interviews, say after *Fitzcarraldo* or *Aguirre,* to put across that [other] side of Klaus Kinski. Nobody would ever print a word of that. He was grandiose and very generous. One time I said to him, "Klaus, you look so elegant, what is it?" I looked at him and I said, "Ah, it's the jacket," and he said, "Oh, Yves Saint Laurent made this for me and I got it yesterday in Paris." I said, "This is a wonderful jacket," and he ripped it off his shoulder and threw it on me and said, "Now take it. It's yours." He would give away his car in a split second—because he felt like giving me his car. Of course, I gave it back to him later.

AGB: But you kept the jacket.

WH: I still have it and I still wear it once in a while. It's a little bit short, his arms were a little bit shorter than mine, but I like it the better because of that.

AGB: Would you both have been lesser human beings had your encounter not taken place?

WH: I cannot answer because he was part of my life and I was part of Kinski's life. Of course there was life before Kinski and in between Kinski—in between the films I made with him. I made *Kaspar Hauser, Stroszek* with Bruno S., and *Land of Silence and Darkness,* and of course there was life after Kinski. I met him for the first time when I was thirteen. The film explains the chain of events.

We lived in the same *Pension* [boarding house]. The owner of this place had picked him up from the street, literally, and given him a room and food for free and did his laundry. He entered this place like a tornado, a force of nature, and it didn't take him one minute to destroy and lay waste to all the furniture. It was strange because I remember that everybody was immediately scared of Kinski. I was the only one who was not scared. I was astonished. I looked at him as if an extraterrestrial had just landed, or a tornado had just struck—the way you watch a natural disaster, sometimes with strange amazement. That is the feeling I remember.

Of course, he didn't remember me, I was a child at the time, and the next time we met it was for *Aguirre.* As a private person and a filmmaker,

I think it was a necessary collaboration, that the two of us found each other. There was a certain inevitability about it—it was destiny, though the ancient Greeks would use this term with necessary caution.

AGB: Were there any similarities between Kinski and Bruno S.?
WH: Both of them had an enormous presence on screen, a presence and intensity that is almost unprecedented in cinema. Kinski was not an actor—I wouldn't call him an artist either, nor am I. Of course, he mastered the techniques of being an actor, the technique of speech, of understanding the presence of light and of the camera, the choreography of the camera and of bodily movements. Bruno S. didn't have that and so had to be taught. But at the core of Klaus Kinski was not his existence as an actor—he was something beyond that and apart from it.

AGB: Would you say, then, that your fiction films with him were documentaries about Kinski, as well?
WH: If you use the term "documentary" with very wide margins, yes. And of course *Fitzcarraldo*—moving a ship of that size over a mountain is a deed that bears a certain affinity with him, but only would take place in a documentary. The line between documentary and fiction film is obviously blurred for me. They bear such an affinity to each other that I can't really distinguish that easily.

AGB: What role does the German tradition play in your aesthetics?
WH: I grew up in Bavaria. My first language was Bavarian and my own father could not understand what I was saying when I spoke in Bavarian to him and he needed my mother to translate. I had to painfully learn to speak *Hochdeutsch* [High German] in high school later on, because I was ridiculed for my dialect. I have to say, with a rather primitive metaphor, that the only other person capable of making *Fitzcarraldo* would have been King Ludwig II. He was quintessentially Bavarian. It's not that easy to define it, but when I name him and you look at the castles, there's a kind of dreaminess and exuberance of fantasies that is specifically Bavarian and Austrian. There's an affinity, and it is certainly distinct from the Teutonic German culture and imagination.

AGB: Now you live in San Francisco?
WH: Yes, but that shouldn't worry you. I never left my Bavarian culture. Nor has *Aguirre* left its culture, it's a Bavarian film. And *Fitzcarraldo* is a

Bavarian film. Strangely enough I function very easily in the jungle, in the Amazons, or in the Sahara Desert.

AGB: Would you like to talk a little about your *Lessons of Darkness*, which is the title of one of your films and of your manifesto ["The Minnesota Declaration"]?

WH: *Lessons of Darkness* fits in very well with my manifesto, in what I define as ecstatic truth. We have seen fifteen-second film clips of fires in Kuwait hundreds of times on CNN and that is the accountants' truth. But in this film, more visibly than in others, I was searching for something different, for something beyond that, for an epic, ecstatic truth. *Lessons of Darkness* is a fine example for me to use in order to clarify what I mean by the terms in my manifesto—of what distinguishes the accountants' truth, what constitutes fact, and what constitutes the inherent truth of images in cinema and, of course, in poetry.

AGB: Why issue a formulation against *cinéma vérité* now?

WH: It's not something sudden. Since my earliest filmmaking days I have preached that I would like to be one of the gravediggers of *cinéma vérité*. But it was not so clearly articulated. Only after some intensive years of "documentary" filmmaking could I better articulate what I meant. I did so finally in the manifesto that I wrote in anger—after a sleepless night, because I was too jet-lagged to sleep. I had a feeling it should be written down.

It was very strange because it was a night when I had just traveled for thirty hours from Guatemala to Catania, in Sicily. I went straight from shooting a film in Guatemala to a rehearsal of *The Magic Flute*. I couldn't sleep and then, when it was finally time, after forty-five hours, to go to bed, I couldn't sleep. I turned on the TV and again found the same thing on Italian TV as on Austrian, Dutch, Canadian, and American TV. Documentaries are always the same sort of boring, uninspired stuff. So I tried to force myself to sleep, but I couldn't, and I turned the TV on again. There was a porno film on and I had the feeling, yes, even though it's just a physical performance, it comes closer to what I call truth. It was more truthful than those documentaries. I couldn't fall asleep, so I got up at three o'clock in the morning and, in this anger of not being able to sleep and seeing all these things on TV, I wrote down the manifesto, in fifteen minutes. Not to exaggerate, but the fact is it contains in a very condensed form everything that has angered and moved me over many years.

AGB: Last year two films, *Celebration* and *Idiots*, shown at Cannes were based on Dogme 95, a manifesto written by Lars von Trier. Are you familiar with Dogme?

WH: I've seen it very recently for the first time. For me it's a little uninspired because it's a technical cookbook on what to use and what not to use. But I think the basic aim of this manifesto is very necessary, seeing how much cinema has been overwhelmed by special effects and technicalities and a huge apparatus that has reduced the real life that is possible in movies. It's very strange because this year I acted in a film by a very young American filmmaker, Harmony Korine, who made his movie, *Julien Donkey-Boy*, according to the rules of Dogme. I played his crazed father in a dysfunctional, white-trash family. He wanted me very badly in this film as his father. For him it was important to have me in the film because he sees me as some sort of predecessor to Dogme, for the reduced technical apparatus—not as reduced as the Dogme postulates, but essential, physical, direct cinema, with all the possibilities of all the exuberance and vitality of life in it. It's very telling that you do not find this quality anymore in the big Hollywood action or special-effects movie.

AGB: Is your manifesto in opposition, or better, in response to Lars von Trier's Dogme?

WH: No, they're after something completely different.

AGB: Would you ever consider doing a Dogme film?

WH: No, it would reduce my possibilities and my subjects. I could not do *Aguirre*, for example, because a historical film in costume is not permitted. Music would not be permissible and I love to work with music. So, no, certainly not, but I have respect for what they postulate and I do believe, even though it reduces a lot of possibilities, that it is at least an answer. It doesn't make filmmaking more democratic as they say, but it brings down the apparatus to its essential size. I wish that Dogme had been a manifesto that had more substance as far as, let's say, storytelling. But I think as reduced and stark as it is, it's a step that is quite interesting.

AGB: Do you feel that the new millennium is urging filmmakers to define new ways of making movies with manifestos, declarations, and so on?

WH: No. Who cares about the millennium? It's an artificial date! Even the church doesn't know when Jesus was born. I think it's obvious that in the cinema new ways have to be found en route all the time.

A More Athletic Approach:
An Interview with Werner Herzog
on *Grizzly Man*

Cynthia Fuchs / 2005

From *PopMatters*, http://popmatters.com, August 11, 2005. Reprinted by permission.

Werner Herzog is perched on one of those not-so-comfy hotel settees, half-sofa, half-chair. He rises and smiles, weary and imposing. The sixty-three-year-old filmmaker doesn't count talking about his work among his favorite activities—as he puts it, "I have a more physical approach than a cerebral approach, a more athletic approach"—but he remains enthused about his new documentary, *Grizzly Man*. It traces the life and death of animal activist Timothy Treadwell, who spent some thirteen years camping in Alaskan bear sanctuaries and what he called "the grizzly maze." In October 2003, Treadwell and his girlfriend Amie Huguenard were killed by a grizzly in the Katmai National Park and Reserve.

Most of Herzog's movies explore indistinctions between truth and fiction, the ways we tell, comprehend, and need stories. Like his previous films (*Aguirre, the Wrath of God, Even Dwarfs Started Small, Fitzcarraldo, Nosferatu, Where the Green Ants Dream*), the new one considers processes of self-invention through competing drives to community and individuality. "I think Treadwell has affinities with Woyzeck and Kaspar Hauser, with a lot of the characters I've created," Herzog says, "I feel as though I was the girl in the fairy tale, and gold coins came raining down into my lap."

Cynthia Fuchs: How did you come upon the material?
Werner Herzog: It was a chain of lucky coincidences. I was at the office of Erik Nelson, who works a lot for Discovery Documentary and National Geographic. And he was completely selfless, connecting me with

network executives. I've done three films for them now, two more after *Grizzly Man*. At the end of our meeting, I tried to find my reading glasses, and I had my eyes downcast on his table, which was filled with papers, books, half-eaten lunch, and videos. He, thinking that I spotted something in particular, shoves me an article across the table. And he said, "Read this, it's a fantastic story we are doing." I read it and returned right away to his office and asked who was directing it, and he said he was "kind of" directing it. I just stared him in the eye, and I said, "No, I will direct it" [laughs].

CF: That was generous of him.
WH: He's the secret father of the whole project. But he understood there would be a different vision, something helpful to the project. And of course he had a lot of other work to do. So it's not pure bank robbery, not a hold-up [laughs]. But I did usurp the project, within five seconds.

CF: How did you construct the film, between Treadwell's footage and your own?
WH: It's about half Treadwell's footage and half mine. There was no construction, there was just very fast work. I started shooting Labor Day, the fourth of September, and on the third of October, twenty-nine days later, I delivered the film. So there was no thinking, no reflection.

CF: But you had to go through quite a bit of his footage?
WH: Sure, over one hundred hours. It would have taken me about a fortnight just to view it. So I had four intelligent people who sifted through, with very clear directives about what to look for. I kept looking over their shoulders. And I ended up seeing about fifteen or twenty hours of his footage. I make my choices very fast and they are irreversible [laughs].

CF: So much of Treadwell's film seems to be a process of self-invention, remaking his own choices, going back and . . .
WH: . . . and repeating, yes. Sometimes he was dissatisfied, and would erase it. He was like a professional filmmaker, and didn't want anyone to see his failure on camera. He would tape over it. Sometimes there were fifteen takes of a scene, as he would name them on the tape, but what we see is take number two and take number five, and take number fifteen. And all the rest he would erase. What he left was meant somehow to be part of a big movie, where he would be the star.

CF: As you were watching all this footage, what was your sense of how he understood an audience?

WH: I can only guess. But I think he tried to address an audience who was feeling like him, that there was harmony in nature, that the bears were good and fluffy. You see this all-pervading Disney-ization of wild nature on TV, and because of that, I have an ongoing argument with him throughout the film, I contradict him. And he saw himself as Prince Valiant, and stylizes himself (though I think the haircut was more because of his receding hairline), as his friend tells us about it in the film. [His self-stylization] has a certain charm and it touches me very deeply. I like him also for the times when he failed and wrestles some meaning from his existence. He says it verbatim, "I had no life, and now I have a life."

CF: And he also touched other people.

WH: Yes, in particular, children. He addressed tens of thousands of schoolchildren over the years, and none of these children will ever harm a bear. So he was a great educator.

CF: And yet, as you put it in the film, he crosses a kind of invisible boundary.

WH: It was immediately evident. You see his quest to be close to the bears, even morph into a bear. And I and other people argue against that in the film, including the museum curator in Kodiak.

CF: He talked about it as respecting difference.

WH: Yes. Don't love the bear, respect the bear. There's a fundamental difference between these two attitudes. For Treadwell, it was something almost religious to step outside of your humanness and into an ecstasy.

CF: Is there also a tension between his individual pathology and his representativeness, so he seems both specific and symptomatic?

WH: There were some moments of paranoia that are very conspicuous, but at the same time he made a lot of sense, he was a great educator. He brought the peril that is out there for the bears into our common consciousness. He shot footage that is unprecedented in its beauty and depth, and he allows us inside, into our innermost human condition. So it's not so much a film about wild nature as an insight into our nature.

CF: He created some remarkable images.

WH: The film shows these wonderful moments, and I want to give him the space and the credit as a fellow filmmaker that all of us can only envy. Even if I gave you $50 million of Hollywood money, you could never achieve what he did with a little video camera. And I believe the best of the best is in the film. In a case like this, you have to approach everything with a certain respect, because he cannot defend himself. And of course I had the eyes of Jewel Palovak [with whom Treadwell co-founded Grizzly People and co-wrote the book *Among Grizzlies*] upon me, and she is the guardian of his materials, not only the video, but also his diaries.

CF: What was your thinking behind the scene where you listen to the tape she has of Treadwell and Amie's deaths?

WH: The background to that scene is that I wanted to listen to the tape. But she would only let me do it in her presence. There were practical reasons; she wanted to make sure I didn't secretly copy it, even though there was a deep trust between her and me. But I filmed it so you hardly see me, but instead focus on the echo on her face, trying to read my face. The deep anxiety in her face, it's very moving for me. It wasn't planned, but as soon as I heard [the tape], I knew she should never listen to it, because she was so close to Treadwell. And out of the blue, I advised her to destroy it, which she did not do. What she did was more intelligent: she separated herself from the tape; she put it in a bank vault. It was the audio from the video camera. What happened was, there was commotion outside. Amie Huguenard is still inside the tent, switches on the camera, but doesn't have time to remove the lens cap, and drops the camera. So the last six and a half minutes that were left on the tape recorded only the audio. And the camera was found inside the tent.

CF: You make an observation late in the film about her absence from Treadwell's footage.

WH: I wanted to know more about her, because she's almost excluded from his film. Is he a misogynist? Does he not like her? Treadwell hid her presence. In one hundred hours of film, there's only something like forty seconds of her, trying to duck out of view. He tried to stylize himself as the Lone Ranger. The other side is that I would have liked to talk to her family. A sister apparently was prepared to speak to me on camera, but the family held a council and decided they did not want to appear in the film. So out of respect for the wishes of the family council, I did not pursue that, and she remains the great unknown of the film. She was at the point of leaving him for good, and one of the last entries in

Treadwell's diaries says that Amie confronted him and called him "hell-bent on destruction." She wanted to leave on the next plane and take a new job she had accepted. And at the moment of the attack, Treadwell screams at her, "Run, run!" and she doesn't. Instead, she takes up what I assume is a frying pan and starts banging on the head of the bear. Even though this petite woman was about to leave him for good, in the moment of this utmost challenge, she stands by him. There's something deeply heroic and deeply tragic about her. So of course, I'd like to do a separate film on Amie, but I can't because I don't have access to what I'd need to understand.

CF: It's unusual these days for survivors not to appear on camera, what with reality TV and cable news sensationalism.
WH: And not to play the tape, for it would have violated the intimacy of their deaths. It would have been a transgression of your own right to die. As I understand it, no one has ever heard it except for the coroner and a few park rangers, who discovered it.

CF: The medical examiner [Franc G. Fallico] plays a very interesting role in the film.
WH: Yes, I like him a lot. I told him, "I don't want you just to be the expert witness in a court of law," which is his daily routine. I said, "I want to see the human being." Because his routine is the most horrifying catastrophes, he sees murder victims and ugly deaths on a daily basis. And yet this case shook him to the marrow of his bones. I told him, "You can be the expert in court, but not in my film. You'd better take your pants down now" [laughs]. I was blunt, and I like him for his courage.

CF: So many of the characters seem isolated, even lonely. Certainly Treadwell, who has made something of a choice, though he agonizes about his romantic travails.
WH: [laughs] Very often, you don't get the chick you want. And what a wonderful man he was, as he advertises himself. It has a wonderful warmth about it, even his stupidities. There's something very beautiful about him. You see what he tries almost to ignore, the ferocity and vileness of bears.

"I've Never Stood Still":
A Conversation with Werner Herzog

Dietmar Kammerer / 2007

From "Ich bin nie stehen geblieben," *die taz* (Berlin), June 28, 2007. Reprinted by permission.

Dietmar Kammerer: Mr. Herzog, in 1998 you filmed the documentary *Little Dieter Needs to Fly*, about a young German who joined the U.S. Navy. When did you decide to make the feature film, *Rescue Dawn*, from this material?

Werner Herzog: During the production of the documentary—what I like to call "a feature film in disguise"—it was already clear to us that a big film had to be made out of this, with a great actor. At first, there just wasn't any money. *Rescue Dawn* only came about after the logistics, the financing, and the star [Christian Bale] had been secured.

DK: In *Little Dieter*, you say what's extraordinary about a figure like Dieter Dengler is that he's actually a very ordinary person. Isn't it then a contradiction to replace him with a star?

WH: When you make a film for the big screen, it's obvious that you need a star, somebody who's larger than life. The story of Dieter Dengler is itself an epic film.

DK: Some of the story's details aren't used in *Rescue Dawn*. For example, how Dieter gets his wedding ring back. One of his guards had taken it from him and a Vietcong officer chops this man's finger off and returns the ring to its owner.

WH: There are a number of scenes from the screenplay that didn't make it into the film for reasons of length. It's not like I slavishly transformed the documentary into a feature. The scene with the finger, by the way, was actually filmed. I left it out, because I can't stand violence on the screen, especially violence against the defenseless. As a spectator, I'm not okay with it, for reasons I can't quite explain. I don't want to see something like that.

DK: The [2007] retrospective at the Munich Film Festival carries the subtitle "Of Freaks, Titans, and Obsessions." To me, that sounds like a very typical, hopelessly distorting description of your work.
WH: You shouldn't assign much importance to titles in some festival program. Don't lose any sleep over it. I think my films speak for themselves. Of course, there are always difficulties in the perception of my work.

DK: Do these clichés bother you very much?
WH: Not particularly. When people speak of "freaks" or "curiosities" in my films, I always say it's not Kaspar Hauser who's actually deformed but rather the narrow-minded society in which he lives. Hauser is not an outsider; with his radical human dignity, he stands absolutely central to that which makes us human.

DK: You once described your characters as "unhinged," as people who've lost their center.
WH: Only when someone is under intense pressure—because he's fighting to survive, for example—does the character of a person reveal itself. It's like the materials that a physicist wants to examine. Only when you subject a metal alloy to extreme pressure or heat does the unknown material give you any information. There are people who are put to the test. Like the ore that the blacksmith forges and refines.

DK: And it's about the encounters between you and your characters. I've always wondered how you manage to find the subjects of your documentaries. It's often hard to avoid the impression that there are people who have just been waiting to meet Werner Herzog.
WH: It's strange, but I always run into these people. I don't know how it happens.

DK: Your research into human nature often takes place in a nature that is extremely hostile to human presence.
WH: Nature and landscapes in my films are not just pretty backgrounds as they are in commercial films. In a way, they are inner landscapes. The jungle as a place of fever dreams, for example, plays a role in many of my

films. During the production of *Grizzly Man*, everyone expected it to be a nature documentary. I always said to them: Have no illusions, this won't be a film about nature outside, but about inner nature.

DK: In *Grizzly Man* you also say that the common denominator of the universe is not harmony but rather chaos, hostility, and murder. Is nature always destructive?

WH: Not necessarily. But if you look at space then you very quickly recognize, even without a telescope, that it's very chaotic and absolutely life-threatening. The power of the sun alone—it's as if four million atom bombs were constantly exploding. Not too friendly.

DK: Under the right conditions, though, it can also be beautiful. That's what the footage of outer space demonstrates in *The Wild Blue Yonder*.

WH: That's right. You have to be able to wrest something good from all this.

DK: You voice the commentary on your documentaries, as a rule, even though you're not a trained speaker.

WH: It's important that I'm the one who speaks, and that to some extent I contradict my subjects, as I do in *Grizzly Man*. It makes the films more authentic. When the German DVD of *Grizzly Man* was set to appear, I found out that some actor was going to be hired for the commentary. There I objected. I may not have a documented right, but I do have a natural right, to speak the part. Or rather, it's not my natural-born right, but that of the film itself.

DK: The retrospective, because it brought together almost all your films, allowed one to search for entire chains of images and themes. Certain animals cropped up again and again—the bear and the jellyfish—and all kinds of flying machines. Are there many different films of Werner Herzog or is there just one big film divided into many different reels?

WH: At a retrospective of course you can very quickly find interconnections. You see a style and certain fascinations. Not that that was planned! They get into the films almost by themselves. I've developed over time, I've never stood still. But the impression, that it may be a single film that I've been working on all along, is not false. Sometimes I have that impression myself.

DK: Audiences have certain expectations of "a Werner Herzog film." Are they a burden or an incentive?

WH: No, they aren't a burden. But I'm not really under any pressure of expectation. I think audiences are happy when they can recognize my handwriting, but they wouldn't come if I always did the same thing, if I just sat there in the field like a cow chewing his cud.

DK: Many of your characters go abroad in search of happiness; they leave their homeland and emigrate. You left Germany, too, and for years you've been living in Los Angeles.

WH: I didn't "emigrate." It's not like I couldn't have realized my dreams here. In fact, that's exactly what I did. Some of my most important films were made here in Germany. But you're right that many of the characters move away geographically. Fitzcarraldo must go to the jungle in order to realize his dream of great opera. Stroszek goes to America because the conditions in Berlin are so oppressive for him. But it's no better in Wisconsin, either. It's not like I want to set out and live somewhere completely different, because only there could I possibly realize "my dreams" (in quotation marks, please). Essentially, I live on my locations and they are in many different countries, in many different landscapes.

Defiant Werner Herzog to Defamer: "Who Is Abel Ferrara?"

Gawker.com / 2008

From http://gawker.com, June 4, 2008. Reprinted by permission.

Question: So, yes or no: Is *Bad Lieutenant* a project you're working on with Nicolas Cage?
Werner Herzog: Yes, but it's not a remake. It's like, for example, you wouldn't call a new James Bond movie a remake of the previous one—although the name of *The Bad Lieutenant* is a different one, and the story is completely different. It's very interesting because Nicolas Cage really wants to work with me, and just anticipating working with an actor of his caliber is just wonderful.

Q: Why *this* project, though? You could have worked on anything.
WH: There's an interesting screenplay; it's a very, very dark story. It's great because it seems to reflect a side of the collective psyche—sometimes there are just good times for film noir. They don't come out of nowhere. There was some sort of a mysterious context with the understanding of people in that particular time. *And* it's going to be in New Orleans, which is a fascinating place. Part of it was the decision of the producers for tax incentives—which is totally legitimate. However, I thought to myself: "We have seen a lot of New York in movies; we have not seen New Orleans in feature films." Or very few feature films. After Katrina it's a particularly interesting set-up. The neglect and politics after the hurricane struck are something quite amazing. It has to do with public morality.

Q: Speaking of which, the original film's director, Abel Ferrara, has vowed to fight this project, and—
WH: Wonderful, yes! Let him fight! He thinks I'm doing a remake.

Q: Have you talked to him?

WH: No. I have no idea who Abel Ferrara is. But let him fight the windmills, like Don Quixote.

Q: Have you heard his comments at all? He says he hopes "these people die in Hell."

WH: That's beautiful!

Q: Do you relate to that passion?

WH: No, because it's like theater thunder. It's like being backstage in the nineteenth century, with the machines that make thunder. It has nothing to do with his film. But let him rave and rant; it's good music in the background.

Q: You did a remake before with *Nosferatu*, but—

WH: It was not so much a remake as an homage to Murnau. But I don't feel like doing an homage to Abel Ferrara because I don't know what he did—I've never seen a film by him. I have no idea who he is. Is he Italian? Is he French? Who is he?

Q: Oh, come on.

WH: Maybe I could invite him to act in a movie! Except I don't know what he looks like.

Q & A: Werner Herzog

Daniel Trilling / 2009

From *New Statesman* (London), April 24, 2009. Reprinted by permission.

Daniel Trilling: Your new film, *Encounters at the End of the World*, is a documentary about Antarctica. You say you were inspired by some footage that divers had shot of the world beneath the frozen Ross Sea. So what exactly attracted you to the place?

Werner Herzog: It's too obvious; it is a place so strange and so unusual it's as if you were not on this planet any more. It's pure science fiction without any technical trick. I just was curious and I wanted to go there and dive myself and film myself. Of course I was not allowed to dive.

DT: So you didn't dive, but did you at least make it to the top of Mount Erebus [Antarctica's active volcano]?

WH: Of course, you actually cannot film there unless you are up there yourself. I was the sound man as well. We were only a two-man crew.

DT: You mention science fiction, but there seemed to also be a religious element, carried by the soundtrack—all that choral music and chanting which soundtracks the underwater sequences.

WH: Yes, you saw it correctly.

DT: To me that contrasted with the contempt you express in the narration for "new age ideologues" and "tree huggers." Do you see wild nature as having a spiritual element?

WH: Well, it's a question of great complexity and the film of course has some sort of an answer, or parts of an answer. When you ask about how I see wild nature, you have to see for example *Grizzly Man*, which dealt with it in more depth, you have to see *Fitzcarraldo*, well, I could rattle down twenty others, let us [not] bear that problem now! Of course

I think it's a very unromantic, very stark view of nature. It's strange that sometimes I have been labeled a romantic, because nobody can be more unromantic than I am!

DT: Yes, I saw you described recently as "a great German Romantic imagination," which I thought was odd.
WH: It's very odd, but these categorizations are not my problem. They are yours, or the problem of the media. But let it be, I cannot change it.

DT: You seem ambivalent towards the impact humans have on the environment. The way you treat McMurdo, the U.S. scientific base on Antarctica, suggests you think it's a blot on the landscape.
WH: It's a very strange place, actually, and it's very ugly. When we think about Antarctica, we always think: ah, yes, Shackleton and Scott and Amundsen and all those heroic deeds and hardships. Whereas in fact you have a place full of Caterpillars, and it looks like an ugly mining town, and you have, as I say, such abominations as an aerobics studio and yoga classes.

DT: Other people might find those things comforting!
WH: Of course yoga classes *are* an abomination. The funny thing is that when you see the film with audiences, every single audience I have witnessed so far laughs out loud as if I was saying something that was obvious to everyone but nobody dares to say it.

DT: The scenes where you go looking for gay and insane penguins must also create laughter.
WH: Yeah, but it's a very tragic moment, when the penguin, who is certainly in some way deranged, walks into the interior of the continent. He has five thousand kilometers ahead of him and of course is walking to his death.

DT: At the start of the film you say you're not going to Antarctica to make a documentary about "cute penguins." Was that aimed at any other films in particular? The Disney film *Happy Feet*, or the documentary *March of the Penguins*, perhaps?
WH: That's an attitude against the Disneyfication of wild nature. Walt Disney is a bastard child of Romanticism, the only real surviving bastard child of Romantic attitudes. But I am not.

DT: Are you opposed to imposing any kind of human characteristics on animals?

WH: Well, I'm not into this business. But it's OK to be in this business for the four-year-olds.

DT: You say that, but the footage of the penguin walking to its death reminded me of nothing more than Klaus Kinski floating down the Amazon in *Aguirre* . . .

WH: Ah-ha, that's a very unusual parallel you are drawing. I like what you are saying, I never thought of it like that. But I think there's a common quality in it.

DT: So really, you're objecting to humans finding nature cute and cuddly, like in a Disney film.

WH: Yeah, well, it's more complicated because ultimately we are part of nature—though in a very specific role. Of course I do not see our role as the *Happy Feet* penguins film would see it.

DT: Antarctica also occupies a place in our minds because of climate change. Did you intend to alert viewers to that process?

WH: The film is not about climate change, it has other focal points of interest. I don't need to add to the films about that subject. Besides, that is probably only one of the many elements which show clearly that our presence on this planet is not sustainable. That doesn't make me nervous. It doesn't make me nervous that the dinosaurs died out. And it doesn't make me nervous that the trilobites died out, hundreds of millions of years before the dinosaurs. Life on this planet has been a constant chain of cataclysms and extinctions. But it is obvious that we are going to be next.

DT: There is a tension in many of your films between acceptance of that fact, while at the same time a great care for a more intimate aspect of humanity. You say humans dying out doesn't worry you, but then in *Encounters* . . . you talk about lost and dying languages as if that were a great tragedy.

WH: Of course, it does worry me. But it doesn't make me afraid. But everybody talks about extinction of whales or endangered whales, and we are not aware that at the same time, at a much more rapid rate, human languages and cultures are dying out. And the speed of it is staggering.

You see, within the next fifty years, 90 percent of all spoken languages on this planet will have disappeared without a trace.

DT: Would that be a catastrophic loss for you?

WH: It's a catastrophic loss for human culture. Language is always a way to understand the world, to draw perspectives, to view the world. And you just have to imagine what happens if tomorrow the last speaker of the Russian language dies out. There would be no more Tolstoy, no more Mandelstam, no more Akhmatova, no more Dostoevsky, no more Orthodox music, no more scientists from Russia, no more philosophers, no more Orthodox church. It is catastrophic. While we are talking there are, I think, sixteen known persons out there who are the last remaining speaker of their language. I just want to point to things like that. It's not just climate change.

And by the way I'm planning to do a long-term film project on dying languages.

DT: Any idea when that will be ready?

WH: It will be a project over many years because you have to go to New Guinea, you have to go to Amazonia, you cannot just do it over three weeks.

DT: In *Encounters . . .* , you suggest that once the North and South Poles had been reached by explorers, humanity lost something by reaching the physical limits of the planet we're on. Does art go some way towards filling the gap? Have you ever thought of your own films in that way?

WH: You have to be cautious, films do not have much function, poetry doesn't have much function, music doesn't have much function, but of course they are a very important part of our collective soul. I wouldn't like to answer it now by giving you a reasoning about the role of films and the responsibility of films.

DT: But in this film, at least, it seems that one of the things you were doing was making the Antarctic strange again—in the way that it would have been strange and unknowable to the first explorers who set foot there.

WH: That's an interesting aspect. I didn't see it that way, but I think you're right. There is a strangeness and beauty out there that really attracted my curiosity. And it's like always, the images that you have not seen before that are not worn out yet in commercials or on television or in advertisements in magazines, all this kind of imagery that is deeply somehow embedded in our collective soul and we haven't discovered it yet, we haven't articulated it yet. Like all the underwater footage, all the footage of the South Pole, how strange it is; under the ice of Mount Erebus, in these tunnels of ice, what a strange beautiful world this is. I'm just naming the glories, I'm just trying to name the glories of this continent.

DT: These images gain even more power combined with the soundtrack. The music seems absolutely crucial to this film.
WH: Yes it is, sure. It makes certain things more visible than they were without the music.

DT: Like when the Ross Sea, trapped under meters of ice, is described as a "cathedral" in your film?
WH: Yes, there's a sacrality to the place. And the music of course makes it also visible.

DT: This brings us back to the tension between human settlement and the "sacred" landscapes—those landscapes are inhuman in a way, very inhospitable to humans. Yet as the film progresses, you develop a kind of reverence for the settlers in McMurdo—something that is emphasized again by the soundtrack, in this case a very gentle blues guitar tune.
WH: You have to view the film also as something very spontaneous of course. You cannot plan things in advance in Antarctica. You have only one chance, you do not know what to expect. You cannot pre-arrange things. Much of what you see has an immediacy to it which brings a lot of life into the film. And it's not all completely pre-planned and organized and mentally structured. I follow from surprise to surprise, in a way.

DT: At the beginning of the film, you ask a strange question: "Why do humans put on masks or feathers to conceal their identity?" Are you any nearer the answer now?
WH: It's a question which is still open! Why is it that certain species of ants keep flocks of plant life as servants, as slaves, in order to milk them for droplets of sugar? But why is it a monkey does not saddle a goat and ride off into the sunset? It's that kind of question that fascinates me. And my fascinations are clearly in the film. I actually love the film. And you know what is also the beauty of it? Every single film student could make

the same film, because it was made with only one cinematographer and me the filmmaker as sound man. With only two men you can make a film that ends up on screens in theaters.

DT: Would you like to see more people making films in that way?
WH: No, I say it to the people who complain about the difficulty of making films and about financiers who do not understand their quest. My answer is that the cameras are very much advanced now, the cameras are inexpensive, there is no excuse any more. Go out, do the sound yourself, have one man doing cinematography and come back with a feature film in five weeks. That was exactly my task—go down to Antarctica and you'd better come back with a movie.

DT: To British viewers, at least, *Encounters . . .* will seem like a very warped take on the traditional TV nature documentary.
WH: Yeah, but I wouldn't put them down because in Great Britain you have some of the very finest nature documentaries worldwide.

DT: Are you a David Attenborough fan, then?
WH: I am. I like his excitement, I like the fervor and how he comes across to an audience is just wonderful. You see the excitement that you feel as a child when you discover for the first time that there are mountains on the moon when you look through a telescope. He transports this kind of excitement, this spirit of wonder, into what he sees and what he presents. So I would not like to put down what you see on television. Some of it is phenomenally beautiful.

DT: In a way, you and Attenborough are trying to get at the same thing, just approaching it in different styles.
WH: In different styles, but the wonder and excitement makes us brothers. I salute Attenborough.

DT: Let's hope he sees this interview!
WH: Whatever. He knows that he's good.

Out of the Darkness: Werner Herzog's *Cave of Forgotten Dreams*

Samuel Wigley / 2011

From *Sight & Sound* 21, no. 4 (April 2011): 28–30. Reprinted by permission.

With typical perversity on the part of Werner Herzog, his first (and likely only) foray into 3D forsakes the pulsing immensities of ocean and cosmos—the bread and butter of three-dimensional documentary-making—for the restrictive murk of a cave in the South of France. Discovered in 1994, the Chauvet-Pont-d'Arc Cave contains the oldest known artworks in the world—pictures of bears, cattle, lions, and bison painted on to the cavern walls by early man some 32,000 years ago. Sealed off by rockfall, this prehistoric gallery survived unseen and untarnished for millennia. Even now, its rarefied atmosphere is too fragile to allow public access; the cave hosts an ultra-exclusive private view to which only a select few scientists are invited. All of which sounds like a red rag to a bull for a director like Herzog, whose reputation for filming in far-flung and insurance-policy-voiding conditions needs no introduction—and who claims to have been so possessed by a book he saw at the age of twelve featuring a Lascaux cave painting on its cover that he got a job as a ball boy solely to save up for it. By unique arrangement with the French government, Herzog and a crew of three men were granted access to Chauvet—a privilege denied even Judith Thurman, the journalist whose article in the *New Yorker* first piqued the interest of Herzog's producer Erik Nelson.

Last spring, film critic Roger Ebert wrote a polemic in *Newsweek* entitled "Why I Hate 3D," in which he nonetheless conceded interest in what a filmmaker of Herzog's vision might do with the format, adding that Herzog had promised him that in *Cave of Forgotten Dreams* "nothing would 'approach' the audience." Herzog hasn't exactly kept to that pledge: one scene involving a spear sends up the tawdry tactics of 3D cinema even as it has us dodging in our seat.

But Ebert was right to be optimistic that Herzog would also light out for less banal territory. His third dimension gives a reach-out-and-touch physicality to the contours and cavities of the stony canvases, bringing us as close as we'll ever be allowed to get to works that—as Herzog reasons—evince the awakening of the soul of man.

Samuel Wigley: How did you go about persuading the French government to allow you access to the Chauvet Cave, where others had failed?
Werner Herzog: Let's say it was a quest of some complexity, because the French are usually territorial when it comes to their patrimony. I was very lucky because the French minister of culture, Frédéric Mitterand, turned out to be a great fan of my films. When I met him, I was just about to explain my project when he asked to have the first word and for ten minutes spoke about how deeply moved he had been by my films. So [I was] like the little girl in the fairytale who opens her apron and golden stars fall into her lap.

SW: Did he talk about any of your films in particular?
WH: He knew my films from very, very early on, and he said he even interviewed me once for French television! I said, "*Monsieur le ministre*, I do not remember." There was then a straightforward attitude that I would work as an employee of the Ministry of Culture. I would ask for one Euro as my fee, and the French government could use the film in forty thousand classrooms in France—everything non-commercial, everything in perpetuity, for no money, for nothing. So there was a proposal that apparently made sense to the French government. But of course there's more than just the Ministry of Culture, there's also the curator, the custodian of the cave delegated by the scientists. . . . So it took a while. I think my enthusiasm was kind of convincing, otherwise I wouldn't have made the film.

SW: They imposed a lot of restrictions on you while you were shooting inside the cave.
WH: Yes, sure, but understandably so. You see, from the first moment of this cave's discovery, the three discoverers did everything right. They sealed the cave instantly. They would only move [around in there] by rolling out and walking on a strip of plastic foil—every single step was done right.

You have to see it in the light of other caves, like the famous cave of Lascaux, which had to be locked down completely because too many tourists went in and left mold growing on the wall from their human exhalations. The same happened to a famous cave in Spain, Altamira. So these restrictions are completely understandable. You do not step off a metal walkway that is two feet wide, because when you step off there are human footprints 32,000 years old and charcoal and whatever other forms of evidence—the cave was completely hermetically sealed for tens of thousands of years.

SW: How did you find the atmosphere inside the cave? There were toxic gases.

WH: You do not see the CO_2 gas, but after an hour or so you feel woozy. There are guards with you and they keep measuring the level of toxic gas and make sure they move you out soon enough. There are safety precautions, gas masks and oxygen tanks, all sorts of things. In another part of the cave is a fairly high concentration of radon gas—this has a cumulative effect, so you don't stay too long.

SW: What was your reaction to seeing the paintings for the first time?

WH: Well, stunned! Completely and utterly stunned. I had seen photographs—there are two books of photos out. I had some idea what I was going to see. But seeing it in there, in this silence where you can hear your own heartbeat, is really, really something very special. And besides, two things caught me unawares: I had no idea how beautiful the cave was, with all its stalagmites and stalactites, nor how many bones there were—four thousand bones, mostly from cave bears.

SW: You describe these paintings as representing the awakening of the modern human soul.

WH: It seems to be evident, because at the same time [they were painted] you still had Neanderthal men roaming this area. And Neanderthal men never created culture: there were no burials; there was apparently no religious belief system. Here you clearly have hints of first religious belief systems. You have figurative representations of animals, of humans. There is evidence of musical instruments. There is evidence of body adornments. And, of course, technical inventions like the spear thrower, which was invented some 15,000 years before the bow and arrow—extraordinary inventions that Neanderthal man didn't have. So it's quite, quite evident that it is *us*. It is us 32,000 to 35,000 years ago.

Of course we have no idea what the paintings meant to them. We can only take some educated guess by looking into cultures that were in a

Stone Age existence until fairly recently, like Australian Aborigines or bushmen in the Kalahari Desert.

SW: I was particularly struck by how multi-dimensional the paintings are.

WH: I like that you saw it in 3D, because I keep saying this film is the only 3D film where I really know it was imperative to do it in 3D. I was and I still am a skeptic of 3D, but the moment I saw the cave it was absolutely clear it had to be done in 3D, no question, no discussion about it.

SW: It must have been difficult using the camera in that confined space.

WH: The steel door was hermetically sealed behind us—they didn't want to open and close the door all the time because the climate inside is so delicate. I was only allowed three people with me, and so on this two-foot-wide walkway we had to reconfigure our camera from scratch. We started out with literally a steel plate with holes and two parallel steel rods for the two eyes, or the two lenses. I had very, very excellent people: cinematographer Peter Zeitlinger and his assistant Erik Söllner, a very, very good craftsman. And we were blessed that we had Kaspar Callas, a man from Estonia, who not only developed some of our software but built our hardware as well! Just a phenomenal, phenomenal talent. He's also a filmmaker, so what was good [was that] I never talked to a technician—I spoke to a fellow filmmaker.

SW: Have other 3D movies inspired you?

WH: No, not really. There is not much inspiration [to be had] from 3D films, and I can tell you why. Number one, our eyes are not really comfortable with seeing 3D over lengthy periods of time. We see the world with one eye dominant and the other one peripherally seeing the third dimension. Of course, when you're a basketball player in the NBA you have to use full 3D throughout the game to understand the movement of people, the ball and the position of the target. But it's not very comfortable and the brain is very selective, so it somehow dims down our 3D vision in everyday life. So it's fine for when you do real "fireworks" like some of the 3D films [do], like *Avatar*. Yes, it's OK. But 3D is not going to take over everything, like from black-and-white television to color television. It's not going to happen like that . . .

I have developed a dictum, but I have to explain it first. When you see a firework, there's nothing beyond the firework effect. There's no depth to it, there's no deeper meaning to it. When you see a romantic comedy, for example, we as an audience live and develop through a parallel story—we hope and pray that our young lovers should, against all obstacles, find each other by the end. In 3D you only have what is in 3D and nothing beyond—it's a very strange effect. And hence, this is my dictum: you can shoot a porno film in 3D, but you cannot film a romantic comedy in 3D.

SW: The format is perfect for bringing out the contours of the cave, but you also seem to be having some fun with the format, notably with the scene in which a spear is thrust towards the camera.
WH: Yes, I'm making some fun of the 3D effect, sure.

SW: The other interesting thing is that you're bringing what is seen to be one of the most cutting-edge forms of cinema to what is the most primitive form of cinema, as you refer to cave painting in the film.
WH: There's something like proto-cinema in some of the paintings, like a running bison with eight legs, somehow hinting at movement, and a rhinoceros in seven or eight phases, like in an animated film, [seen] bit by bit by bit. It's quite astonishing.

SW: How did you find Maurice Maurin, the master perfumer who appears in the film?
WH: I was searching for him. I learned that there are plans to build a replica of the cave for tourists, about three miles away, and I was told that there are even plans to recreate the prehistoric scent of the cave. I got in touch with this perfumer lady who wanted to speak in front of the camera, [but] she was unreliable and not really good on film.

So I was searching for a perfumer and by coincidence, only twenty miles away, there lived this perfumer who used to be the president of the Master Perfumers of France. He was just wonderful and I loved his enthusiasm and his way of talking. But of course I asked him to sniff out cracks in the rock and describe the scent emanating from it.

SW: And how did you discover the albino crocodiles featured at the end of the film? These reptiles seem to link back not only to the iguanas in *Bad Lieutenant—Port of Call: New Orleans* but all the way back to the lizard specialist in *Fata Morgana*.
WH: They are wonderful. They happened to be not too far away, on the Rhône River, near a nuclear plant. I didn't even know they were albino

crocodiles—I went there because I was just curious to see the three hundred or more crocodiles. Right next to the entrance there's this separate enclosure and I saw these two albino crocodiles—I could not believe my eyes and I said, "They have to be in the movie."

It's pure science fiction, but of course related to the film. How do we see images that were made 32,000 years ago? How would an albino crocodile see images by human beings? Very, very strange, and for me a very deep question, of course. And, strangely enough, the film speaks about [the fact that] the site is widening and soon these crocodiles will reach Chauvet Cave and penetrate it—only four months ago a handful of crocodiles escaped from this compound. They were all recaptured with the exception of one, which is still at large somewhere in the French countryside. I really love that idea.

SW: At one point you describe the scientists' digital mapping of the cave as akin to drawing up the Manhattan telephone directory. Were you frustrated by the experts' more clinical, pragmatic approach?

WH: No, thank God there is a new generation of scientists who are very diligent in describing the status quo and who are not like the previous generations in immediately declaring this as a cult site. They are much more cautious. I think it's quite good that they are mapping, and then after that they try to understand the stories behind it. They are very cautious in their assessments.

A long time ago I made a film—one of my first films—*The Flying Doctors of East Africa* [1969]. Villagers in Uganda were taught about preventing trachoma and eye disease, and for two years they were teaching using posters. I had the feeling the villagers did not see [the posters] the way we saw them, and I asked: "What is this here?" (An eye.) They said, "This is the rising sun," though for two hours they had been taught about this eye and how to clean it. And I asked, "Can you show me a single eye?" Some people pointed at windows of a hut. I had the feeling I should dig deeper into this, and I hung four posters parallel to each other and, on purpose, I hung one upside down. On camera, I explained to the villagers: "I have four posters here. You have seen these posters all day long, and I have hung one upside down on purpose. If you were suspended by your feet by a rope and your head was dangling down, which of the four posters would be upside down?" Less than half could identify the poster that was upside down. They probably saw some abstract specks of color. They must have seen the image in a different way to the way we saw it.

Until today I have had no idea how they were seeing it. I have tried to explore the procedure of human vision: How would we know what these animals in the paintings on the walls meant for humans that were 32,000 years ago? It was a time when Neanderthal men were roaming around, a time when the Alps were covered by 9,000 feet of ice, when you could walk from Paris to London with dry feet because the ice absorbed so much humidity that the English Channel didn't exist. So, how do we understand, beyond such an abyss of time, what was going on in [their minds]?

We also have to speculate that there might have been cannibalism, because in all Palaeolithic and Neolithic cultures you have evidence of it. When for them did the human being start to exist? It's an interesting question, because you find skeleton remains of babies with the garbage, but children who were over three years old were buried. So, human toddlers, who did not speak yet, apparently for them didn't yet have human nature. So there are very deep questions about human beings who are, in a way, us, and yet separated by an abyss of time. In other words, I'm glad that there is a new generations of archaeologists out there.

SW: I know you usually work very closely with the musicians scoring your films. What sort of instructions did you give Ernst Reijseger for his music?

WH: I showed him materials as quickly as I could—long, long takes of images that I had filmed, uncut. He immediately understood and proposed that there should be a choir and an organ. We recorded in a church and I was always there during the recording. In a way I was also guiding the inner *ductus* of the music. There was one piece that was too *motorik* in its rhythm and I said, "No, this is not going to work, we have to have it slower. It has to flow, it has to float." We have an intense rapport when he's recording the music. I love Reijseger. In my opinion, he's of the caliber of a young, emerging Stravinsky. You will not easily find music of that caliber in a film in the next few decades.

SW: Assuming you're not tempted by the idea of making a narrative film in 3D, can I ask what you are working on at the moment?

WH: On Monday I will continue filming on death row, first in Florida and then in Texas, for a film project, *Death Row*. It will be a one-and-a-half-hour documentary, but I'm also planning to make four separate one-hour films on individual cases. And I'm working on a feature-film project, which is a sort of big epic in the Arabian desert. And I have some five or six other feature films pushing at me, lining up. And I will hold my Rogue Film School in London, in March. I'm viewing DVDs and applications at the moment. I like what I do.

Key Resources

Website
www.wernerherzog.com

Books
Ames, Eric. *Ferocious Reality: Documentary according to Werner Herzog.* Minneapolis: University of Minnesota Press, 2012.

Herzog, Werner. *Herzog on Herzog.* Ed. Paul Cronin. London: Faber and Faber, 2002.

Prager, Brad. *The Cinema of Werner Herzog: Aesthetic Ecstasy and Truth.* London: Wallflower, 2007.

Articles and Chapters
Chatwin, Bruce. "Werner Herzog in Ghana" (1988). *What Am I Doing Here.* London: Jonathan Cape, 1989. 136–49.

Ebert, Roger. "A Letter to Werner Herzog: In Praise of Rapturous Truth." *Chicago Sun Times.* November 18, 2007. http://rogerebert.suntimes. com.

Farber, Manny. "Werner Herzog" (1975). *Farber on Film: The Complete Film Writings of Manny Farber.* Ed. Robert Polito. New York: Library of America, 2009. 711–16.

Koepnick, Lutz. "Archetypes of Emotion: Werner Herzog and Opera." *A Companion to Werner Herzog.* Ed. Brad Prager. Oxford: Wiley-Blackwell, 2012. 149–67.

Vogel, Amos. "On Seeing a Mirage." *The Films of Werner Herzog: Between Mirage and History.* Ed. Timothy Corrigan. New York and London: Methuen, 1986. 45–49.

Interviews
"Film and Friendship: Werner and Errol" (2007). By Alice Arshalooys Kelikian. *Errol Morris: Interviews.* Ed. Livia Bloom. Jackson: University Press of Mississippi, 2010. 210–29.

"Jonathan Demme Interviews Werner Herzog." *Encounters at the End of the World*. Image Entertainment, 2008. DVD Disc 2.

"The Lion-Tamer of the Unexpected" (1996). By James Fry and Lloyd Chesley. *Moon City Review* 7, no. 1 (Fall 2005): 96–139.

"Signs of Life." By Jonathan Cott. *Rolling Stone*, November 18, 1976. 48–56.

"Werner Herzog." By Elvis Mitchell. *The Treatment, KCRW*, Podcast Audio, December 2, 2009. http://www.kcrw.com/etc/programs/tt/tt091202werner_herzog.

Documentaries

Burden of Dreams (Les Blank, 1982)
Werner Herzog Eats His Shoe (Les Blank, 1980)

DVD Audio Commentaries

Aguirre, the Wrath of God, Werner Herzog and Norman Hill
Fata Morgana, Werner Herzog, Norman Hill, and Crispin Glover
Signs of Life, Werner Herzog and Norman Hill
Stroszek, Werner Herzog and Norman Hill

Index

Lightning Source UK Ltd.
Milton Keynes UK
UKOW01f0154070416

271744UK00004B/197/P